THE CATHOLIC CHURCH
AND THE NORTHERN IRELAND
CRISIS 1968–86

GERALD McELROY

The Catholic Church and the Northern Ireland Crisis 1968–86

GILL AND MACMILLAN

Published in Ireland by
Gill and Macmillan Ltd
Goldenbridge
Dublin 8
with associated companies in
Auckland, Delhi, Gaborone, Hamburg, Harare,
Hong Kong, Johannesburg, Kuala Lumpur, Lagos, London,
Manzini, Melbourne, Mexico City, Nairobi,
New York, Singapore, Tokyo
© Gerald McElroy 1991
Print origination by Irish Typesetting & Publishing Co. Ltd, Galway
Printed by Billing & Sons Ltd, Worcester

British Library Cataloguing in Publication Data

McElroy, Gerald
  The Catholic Church and the Northern Ireland crisis 1968–86.
  1. Northern Ireland. Political events. Attitudes of Catholic Church, 1969–
  I. Title
  941.60824
  ISBN 0-7171-1761-8

Contents

Introduction

RELIGIOUS division is frequently associated with political conflict in Northern Ireland. Yet, during the present troubles there has been little analysis of the Churches' political stance,[1] especially that of the Roman Catholic Church.[2] This book therefore analyses the reaction of the Catholic Church* to the Northern Ireland crisis between 1968 and 1986.

The structure of this book is simple. Each chapter assesses the Church's position *vis-à-vis* an important aspect of the Northern Ireland situation. Thus, chapter 1 examines the Catholic Church's contribution to the search for political progress in Northern Ireland from 1968 to 1986. The next chapter provides a political profile of Catholic priests in Northern Ireland which is based on the results of a postal questionnaire conducted in 1986. Chapter 3 analyses the nature and effect of the Church's response to controversial aspects of the administration of justice in Northern Ireland, while the next chapter examines salient aspects of the relationship between clerics and republicans. Chapter 5 provides an analysis of the Catholic ethos in Ireland, with particular reference to how it impinges on the Northern Ireland situation. The concluding chapter considers some of the wider implications of this study.

In order to put such a study into perspective, however, it will first be useful to provide a synopsis of events in Northern Ireland during the period in question. Political life in Northern Ireland between 1968 and 1986 has been largely dominated by two distinct, though interacting characteristics: (i) a lack of political consensus; (ii) violence. These two themes will provide the framework for the brief outline of events that is to follow. It ought to be noted that such an account is written from what can be described as a Catholic perspective so that the events under

---

* For details of the bishops in each of these dioceses during the period of this study, see appendix A.

discussion are especially pertinent to the main body of this work. Perhaps the work that most systematically illustrates the different perceptions held on Northern Ireland is that of R. H. Hull, *The Irish Triangle: Conflict in Northern Ireland.*

I

No one could have foreseen the full effects of the civil rights campaign which proved to be such a pandora's box for Northern Ireland. Violence has never been far from the surface in the North, and this was underlined by the first civil rights march which was held at Dungannon in August 1968 (see *Dungannon News and Tyrone Courier,* 28 August), where only a police presence had helped to avert clashes between the marchers and a crowd of militant Unionists. More than any other single protest, however, it was the meeting in Derry on 5 October 1968 which shook Unionism to its roots. On that day civil rights activists were unceremoniously batoned off the streets by the police. Street violence, of course, was nothing new in Northern Ireland: what set the October meeting apart from all previous protests that had ended in bloodshed, however, was the presence of television camera crews. In a few vital minutes, television had done more to expose Unionist policies than the cumulative efforts of parliamentarians and paramilitaries alike over a period of nearly fifty years. The ramifications of these events were far-reaching. Significantly, the unofficial convention whereby British governments had not involved themselves in Northern Ireland affairs was brought to an end (see Longford, McHardy, *Ulster,* pp. 112–114). For the first time since the inception of the Northern State, a central reality *had* to be faced: although Belfast had its own devolved government and parliament,[3] the British Government and Parliament had *unlimited* power to alter the *status quo* in Northern Ireland if they wished to do so. In October 1968 many members of the British Government did not even try to conceal their contempt for the discriminatory practices of successive Unionist administrations. They demanded the implementation of reforms and although many members of the Northern Ireland Government accepted the inevitability of change, many more 'traditional' Unionists

were simply not prepared to consider the matter. The incongruous position of Ulster Unionists was suddenly highlighted: a
seemingly monolithic party had been split down the middle
over the question of reforms for Northern Ireland; loyal British
subjects were being *told* to adopt British standards of democracy
by a British Government, and in the process, were becoming
increasingly isolated from Westminster. For their part, the
position of Northern Catholics was equally incongruous: people
whose identity had never really been anything but Irish, and
many who had never fully accepted the legitimacy of the
Northern State, now looked to the British Government as the
guarantor of their rights. In the course of his questionnaire
during the late 1960s, Richard Rose, in *Governing Without Consensus: an Irish Perspective*, p. 485, question 18A, found that 76
per cent of Catholics saw themselves as Irish. Five per cent of
respondents described themselves as Ulster people (which is
not necessarily exclusive from being Irish). Fifteen per cent saw
themselves as British.

The situation was deteriorating rapidly, and when the Stormont Government introduced a five-point plan for political
reform the deep divisions within Northern Ireland became
increasingly manifest. In stark contrast to loyalist cries of 'not an
inch', Catholics rejected the package by calling it 'too little and
too late'.

By August 1969 the tragic consequences of this polarisation
were becoming only too clear. The rule of law had totally
collapsed in parts of Belfast, Derry and Armagh City.[4] In Belfast
alone, seven people were shot dead and destruction of property
occurred on a wide scale. Eventually British troops were deployed and an uneasy peace was established. An important
effect of all this on the Catholic community was, *inter alia*, a
realignment of republican forces. The most prominent con-
tenders for paramilitary leadership within the most affected
areas turned out to be the Provisional IRA. Whether through
accident or design, by the time of their clear emergence as a
serious guerrilla movement, relations between the Catholic
community and the British Army had soured. A major turning-
point in the deteriorating relationship was the military decision
to impose a curfew on Belfast's Lower Falls area in early July

1970 (see Sean Og O'Fearghail, *Law (?) and Orders*), when the other wing of the IRA, the Officials, had openly engaged British troops in combat. After the Provisional IRA had claimed its first military victim in February 1971, a virtual war was declared between republicans and the authorities.

Against a background of mounting death and destruction, the Government decided to introduce internment without trial. Far from improving the situation, internment led to the almost universal alienation of Northern Catholics and the widespread rebirth of republicanism. Many already troubled areas had now assumed the appearance of battlegrounds: prior to the introduction of internment, approximately fifty people had lost their lives during the previous two years; within sixteen hours of its implementation, a further fourteen people had been killed (see *Irish News*, 10 August 1971). While republicans attempted to establish no-go areas for the authorities in Northern Ireland, even the most moderate constitutional nationalists demonstrated their sense of alienation. This was exemplified by the unanimous call of local MPs for the minority to withdraw from public life.

If anything, 'Bloody Sunday' was a *coup de grâce* in the process of minority alienation from the *status quo*. When the British Government finally suspended the government and parliament of Northern Ireland in March 1972, the decision was, from the nationalist viewpoint at least, only a formal recognition of a long-standing reality: the failure of one-party rule in Northern Ireland. Indeed for many members of that community, it was evidence of Northern Ireland's failure as a state.

In the months that followed the suspension of Stormont, the British Government set itself the task of defining a framework for political development in Northern Ireland. The central element of the Government's blueprint was that any future administration would have to include members of the Catholic community at the highest level. In January 1974 the Northern Ireland Executive (which included SDLP members) was opposed by traditional Unionists. Anti-Executive Unionists were triumphant in the British general election of February 1974, winning eleven out of the twelve Northern Ireland seats and, in the process, securing 50.8 per cent of the total votes cast (see W. D.

Flackes, *Northern Ireland: A Political Directory, 1968–79*, p. 171). When the Executive collapsed because of the Ulster Workers' Council Strike three months later in May,[5] loyalists had clearly demonstrated that they too had the power of veto.

Much subsequent thinking in British Government circles appears to have recognised a dual veto in that Catholics can make one-party rule unworkable just as loyalists can destroy power-sharing between representatives of the two communities in Northern Ireland. As a result direct rule has been continuous from 1974 to the end of the period in question. During that time successive British governments have encouraged local politicians to reach agreement between themselves, but all such attempts have failed. Elections were held in 1975 to the Northern Ireland Convention with a view to encouraging agreement between local political parties. The Unionist coalition, the UUUC, secured 54.8 per cent of the total poll and a clear majority of seats (Flackes, *Northern Ireland*, p. 174). Totally opposed to the principle and practice of allowing nationalists into Cabinet, the Convention report which was drawn up by this majority, was rejected by the then British Government and the Convention was wound up. The next attempt to revive devolved government in Northern Ireland occurred in 1979–80, when the then Secretary of State, Humphrey Atkins, held a series of talks with the various political parties. Again, no agreement was forthcoming and the talks came to a halt. In 1982, elections were held for the Northern Ireland Assembly as a means of at least providing a forum for discussion. From the outset, the Assembly seemed doomed to fail as it contained no significant Catholic voice: both the SDLP and Sinn Fein members elected to the body adopted abstentionist policies. The British Government dissolved the Northern Ireland Assembly in June 1986 (see Anthony Kenny, *The Road to Hillsborough The Shaping of the Anglo–Irish Agreement*, p. 12).

It is only within the framework of Anglo–Irish relations that any visible progress on Northern Ireland has been made. Anglo–Irish relations have constantly fluctuated since the late 1970s when, although the official policy of the then Fianna Fail Government (see *Fianna Fail Policy on Northern Ireland*, 1975) was to seek a British 'commitment to implement an ordered withdrawal' from Northern Ireland, Taoiseach Jack Lynch abandoned this line. Even when Lynch's stated objective became one of pressing for a 'British initiative', London placed greatest emphasis on security matters. The first *appearance* of progress from the nationalist point of view occurred in the 1980–82 period when the new Taoiseach, Charles Haughey, and the Prime Minister, Mrs Thatcher, had talks. The relationship between the two premiers cooled, however, at the time of the Falklands War. In late 1982 a Fine Gael–Labour Government headed by Dr FitzGerald returned to office.* Anglo–Irish talks resumed during the same period when SDLP leader, John Hume, succeeded in bringing all shades of constitutional nationalist opinion together in the New Ireland Forum. In its report of May 1984, the New Ireland Forum recommended Irish unity and within this framework listed three possible options: (i) a unitary state; (ii) a federal/confederal state; (iii) joint authority. (See *New Ireland Forum Report* 2 May 1984, pp. 31–38.) Following the publication of the report, there was a summit between Dr FitzGerald and Mrs Thatcher. In her subsequent press conference, Thatcher dealt what seemed to be a crushing blow to nationalist hopes when she rejected the three main options of the Forum report out of hand. Despite this setback, London–Dublin talks continued until an Anglo–Irish accord was finally reached in November 1985. Under its terms, institutionalised involvement by Dublin in the administration of Northern Ireland is guaranteed for the first time since partition. What this might mean in practice, however, is not altogether clear—the Anglo–Irish Agreement is extremely amorphous in nature. In any event, while many nationalists see the agreement as a step forward, Unionist reaction to it has been almost universally negative. Despite a variety of protests by Unionists, the Anglo–Irish Agreement was still in place at the end of 1986.

Whatever can be said about British Government attempts at resolving the Northern Ireland crisis, or even mitigating its worst effects through either an internal Northern Ireland framework or an Anglo–Irish process, it must be stressed that all such

---

* There had been an earlier coalition government headed by FitzGerald between June 1981 and March 1982. This latter government was still in office at the end of 1986.

attempts have taken place against a background of continued violence.[6] In terms of fatalities alone, approximately 2,500 people died as a result of the troubles during the period of this study. Each year between 1974 and 1976, there were over 200 violent deaths in Northern Ireland. Since 1977, however, the level of violence has tended to be considerably lower, and as a result, fewer people have been killed: 112 in 1977 (see Murray, *Integration and Division*, p. 311, table 12.1); 81 in 1978; 113 in 1979; 76 in 1980; and 108 in 1981 (see White in *Northern Ireland The Background to the Conflict*, p. 192). Towards the end of this period, the figure had dropped further with 57 such deaths occurring in 1985 and 64 in 1986 (*Irish Times*, 1, 2 January 1987, p. 10). This overall improvement may be attributed to two factors: the strategy of the IRA since 1977 to wage what it calls a 'war of attrition', as well as the virtual cessation of the loyalist campaign, which had been overwhelmingly directed at Catholics.

This reduction in the level of violence, however, has not been parallelled by a softening of political attitudes in Northern Ireland. In fact the period has seen the emergence of the Provisional IRA's political wing, Sinn Fein, as a major electoral force within the Catholic community. Following the by-election success of the late hunger-striker, Bobby Sands, in Fermanagh and South Tyrone and the subsequent success of his election agent, Owen Carron, in the same constituency, Sinn Fein began to flex its political muscles. In the Republic's general election of June 1981, H-Block candidates won two seats in the Dail.[7] In its first ever large-scale attempt at contesting elections in Northern Ireland, Provisional Sinn Fein won 10 per cent of the vote to the Assembly in 1982. Moreover in the British general election of June 1983, this percentage of the vote was increased further when Sinn Fein gained 13.4 per cent of the total votes cast. The share of the SDLP vote in the same election was 17.9 per cent (White, *John Hume*, p. 248).

In short, despite past and present political agreements, there has been a lack of political consensus in Northern Ireland. In spite of the decline in violence, moreover, an end to violence was not in sight at the end of 1986.

1

In Search of Political Progress

ALL THE studies of the civil rights campaign in Northern Ireland, viz. Feeney (1974, 1976), Kane, Leon, Scott, Thompson and Morgan, overlook the subtle influence that the Church exercised on that campaign. This is partly due to the fact that all these authors, except Morgan, largely focus their analyses on the executive of the Northern Ireland Civil Rights Association. For any comprehensive assessment of the civil rights movement, however, the following points must be borne in mind. First, it is necessary to recall the central objective of the civil rights movement: expose the injustice of the *status quo* in Northern Ireland. At the centre of the campaign was public protest (marches, meetings, etc.), the effectiveness of which depended not only on the leadership of the civil rights movement but on the behaviour of large crowds. In any case, it is misleading to conceive of the Northern Ireland Civil Rights Association as a movement *per se*, for what in fact existed was a large number of local civil rights groups throughout Northern Ireland. It was not until April 1969, for instance, that there was an attempt to centralise these various bodies (see *Mid-Ulster Observer*, 17 April, p. 5), and even when this was done, the executive of NICRA was prone to internal ideological tensions.[1] In short, it was precisely because the civil rights movement involved mass mobilisation[2] without strongly centralised leadership that considerable influence was exercised over the civil rights campaign from *outside* the civil rights movement proper, and since grass-roots support for the civil rights campaign was overwhelmingly Catholic, the amorphous nature of the civil rights movement allowed the Catholic Church to use its influence during this period.

Before identifying and analysing clerical influence, however, it is necessary to point out the unique position of the Catholic Church within the Catholic community of Northern Ireland at the time. Certainly its unique position has been borne out by the results of three studies carried out in the late 1960s. Thus in a survey conducted among Protestants and Catholics in East Belfast in spring 1969, it was found that Catholics had warmer feelings for their church than for any other organisation, group, political party or political leader (see Malcolm Douglas Jr, *Conflict Regulation vs Mobilization: The Dilemma of Northern Ireland*, PhD Thesis, Columbia University, 1976, p. 352). In an earlier poll in 1968 conducted among young people between seventeen and twenty-four, Catholics chose priests as the most respected occupational group within the community, while Protestants chose medical doctors. Indeed 46 per cent of Catholic respondents indicated that they respected priests more than members of any other occupational group. At the other end of the scale, there was an apparent lack of anti-clericalism: no Catholic respondent chose priests as the *least* respected group in society.[3] The third, and most substantive survey was carried out by Richard Rose which clearly acknowledged the importance of the Catholic Church within the Catholic community:

> The role of the Catholic Church as the central institution in its community is demonstrated by the fact that only 19 per cent of Catholics belong to a voluntary association other than the church or a trade-union; among Protestants 41 per cent are members of such associations. The fact that many people do not belong to a voluntary association does not mean that they are socially isolated, but rather that *religion is sufficient* to provide them with a network of social relationships.[4]

The fact that the Catholic Church was more central to the Catholic community than the Protestant Churches to their respective communities was clearly indicated by the reply to another question from Rose's survey. So that while 30 per cent of Protestants felt it 'very important' to do whatever their ministers told them, the corresponding figure for Catholics was 62 per cent. However, when Rose asked, 'if you wanted some advice on a political question, who would you go to for help?', he found that only 16 per cent of Catholics would go to a priest. While this answer may *appear* to weaken my argument, this is hardly the case: in terms of the period under examination, such a question would not have arisen since the demand for civil rights in Northern Ireland was something that all non-Unionist groups could and did support.[5] In any event, as we shall see later in the chapter, neither the higher nor the lower clergy conceived of the civil rights movement in 'political' terms. Rather they spoke of it in terms of *social justice* thereby depoliticising their activities in the minds of many people.

Since Derry was most clearly affected by civil rights agitation,[6] the theme of the Catholic Church's influence on the civil rights movement in that city will be the focal point for a good deal of the analysis which follows. Two other areas which were noticeably influenced by civil rights activities, Armagh and Dungannon, will be considered primarily in relation to Derry in order to identify similar or dissimilar patterns of clerical influence in these regions.

To begin with, then, it might be effective to identify the most pertinent ways in which clerical influence entered the civil rights movement in Derry:

  (i) through the relationship which existed between the Catholic Church and the Derry Citizens' Action Committee;
 (ii) as part of a multidenominational group in the city called the Industrial Churches Council;
(iii) by co-operation between the Catholic and Protestant churches;
(iv) through the activities of Catholic priests at grass-roots level;
 (v) the endorsement of the civil rights campaign by Cardinal Conway and the then Bishop of Derry, Dr Farren.

From October 1968 to April 1969 the campaign for civil rights in Derry was organised by an *ad hoc* body calling itself the Derry Citizens' Action Committee (DCAC). The DCAC came into existence following a demonstration on 5 October 1968, which had a most devastating effect in exposing Unionist injustice to the outside world (especially Britain), as well as encouraging the growth in civil rights movements elsewhere in Northern Ireland.[7] Ironically, the DCAC emerged because the protest of 5 October had been organised by a left-wing group, the Derry

Housing Action Committee, which was not seen as representative by the major interest-groups in the city. Following the serious disturbances of April 1969, the Derry Citizens' Action Committee went into decline. While none of its elected officers came from the ranks of the clergy, it is clear from the time of its inception, that the DCAC enjoyed the support of the Church and other interested bodies. This was clear from the description of the new committee in the *Derry Journal*, 11 October 1968, p. 1: 'The committee was elected at a meeting attended by about one hundred people, representative of the business, professional, religious and trade union life of the city.' Such an informal alliance of interests worked well together within the DCAC. This was clearly exemplified by the response of Church, trade union and civil rights leaders in January 1969, to the news that an obscure group calling itself the Socialist Labour League had called for a one-day strike throughout the city. A statement was issued by representatives of these various groups which strongly condemned the strike call: among the signatories was the then Catholic Bishop of Derry, Dr Farren, and his Church of Ireland counterpart, Dr Tyndall.[8]

Clerical support for the Derry Citizens' Action Committee was exercised through yet another group called the Industrial Churches Council. Comprising representatives from the four main religious denominations in Derry (Roman Catholic, Church of Ireland, Presbyterian and Methodist), this group made three important interventions into the political life of Derry. The fact that each intervention involved some type of appeal or other to the Unionist Government was significant in itself. As a multidenominational body, moreover, it was likely that its activities would be taken more seriously than those of any exclusively Catholic organisation. First, at a meeting on 21 October 1968, the Industrial Churches Council, in its own words, called for the holding of 'an impartial examination of the allegations made in matters such as housing, employment and the electoral system'. The effect of such a call could only have added to the discomfit- ure of an already beleaguered government. Not only had what many Unionists dismissed as 'Catholic' demands been made by representatives of all the churches, but such a call went to the very heart of civil rights demands.

A few weeks later, the Council demonstrated its solidarity with DCAC once again, when the Minister for Home Affairs, William Craig, imposed a ban on a civil rights march that was due to be held in the city. The *Derry Journal*, 15 November 1968, described the move in the following terms: '. . . It is planned to present the petition to Captain O'Neill through the Industrial Churches Council which is representative of all the main denominations in the city. It will ask him to reconsider the ban on portion of the route for Satur- day's march and that the Citizens' Action Committee should be allowed to use the route they had origin- ally requested.' The situation was clearly explosive in the city and the march in question, described by the *Derry Journal*, 19 November 1968, p. 6, as 'Derry's greatest ever demonstration', attracted a crowd of some 15,000 people. The Government re- fused to lift its ban and violence was only averted by what amounted to a symbolic breach of police barriers by members of the DCAC executive.[9] It is a moot point whether the restraint shown by the police that day was in any way attributable to the appeal by the Industrial Churches Council. One thing was clear however: had there been violence, the Council's appeal could only have added to the embarrassment of the Government. The third, and arguably the most dramatic intervention on the part of the Industrial Churches Council, occurred when it played a key role in successfully negotiating the temporary and partial withdrawal of the police from the Bogside on 20 April 1969. The immediate background was one of mounting tension and viol- ence in Derry following the decision of civil rights organisers to call off a march that was scheduled to take place between Burntollet Bridge and Altnagelvin (a mainly Protestant area). As a result, a spontaneous protest took place in Shipquay Street in the city centre, and this was followed by Paisleyite counter- demonstrations and riots in the city. In the words of the Cameron report:

> The next morning there was an acute risk of very grave violence. That this was averted is due to the constructive actions of various responsible citizens, including church and political representatives . . . a smaller group of church and civic leaders was persuaded by Mr Hume to ask the

Minister for Home Affairs to withdraw the police from the Bogside, in an exchange for an undertaking that peace would be preserved. Mr. Porter, with what we could with respect call great courage and wisdom, accepted the proposal, to the extent of withdrawal of the reserve force . . . These actions were justified in the event and in the release of tension and of risk of grave disorder which might well have passed beyond control of the available police forces . . .'[10]

The Churches in Derry co-operated in other ways to lessen tension in the city though the effect of their activities is, in the final analysis, impossible to measure. Overall, however, co-operation between the Churches had its limitations.

In an interview several years after these events (see *Holy Cross*, September 1975, p. 5), Bishop Edward Daly recalled how as a priest, he and his fellow-clerics had attended various civil rights demonstrations in Derry. (The fact that priests tended to participate in such meetings is borne out by a report in the *Derry Journal*, 22 October 1968, p. 1, informing its readers that priests from both Derry City and parishes outside the city had been among the estimated 5,000 people taking part in a sit-down rally.) The mere presence of Catholic priests at such protest meetings was politically important for two main reasons. First, given the unique status of Catholic priests within the Catholic community indicated earlier, the attendance of priests at civil rights events could only have served to encourage *participation* in civil rights activities by Catholics — especially among the less politically aware or naturally timid members of that community. In effect, the most respected group within the Catholic community was ratifying the first effective non-Unionist body in the history of Northern Ireland.[11] Second, given the importance of international publicity for the civil rights movement, the position of priests in Derry could only have helped to add respectability to the campaign as a whole.

In their support of the civil rights campaign, moreover, many priests assumed a peace-keeping role. Even in the violence that followed the march of 5 October 1968, a protest which had been largely organised and attended by various socialist groups, at least one priest did his best to discourage violence on the streets. Moreover, during the lifetime of the Derry Citizens' Action Committee, priests assisted members of that organisation who tried to deal with violent or potentially violent situations. This is clearly underlined by the action of certain clerics on 20 April 1969. The pro-Unionist *Londonderry Sentinel*, 23 April 1969, p. 13, vividly describes how two local priests played a major role in calming a dangerous situation:

> . . . many young men in their ranks were carrying cudgels and hurley sticks and dustbin lids for use as shields.
>
> While the parade was on the way back, a small group of people gathered at the lower end of Fahan Street and the position was explained to them by Rev. A. Mulvey, C.C., St. Eugene's Cathedral, and Rev. H. B. O'Neill, Adm., St. Eugene's.
>
> Shortly after the police had withdrawn, two police patrol cars, each carrying four men, entered the area from the Butcher Gate direction and they were met and stopped by Rev. A. Mulvey half-way down the street. Meanwhile, the first of the residents of the area commenced arriving back and, when the police cars were seen, leading columns of the marchers broke away and attacked the vehicles with sticks and stones, and the cars had to reverse quickly up Fahan Street. The windscreen of one of the vehicles was shattered.
>
> The crowd continued towards Butcher Gate and there was a stone throwing exchange between them and a small group of counter demonstrators gathered on the city walls. On the advice of Rev. A. Mulvey and Mr. Hume the crowd eventually returned to the bottom of the street where a meeting was held . . .

Whatever the motives of priests who helped to keep order on the streets, the *political effect* of such activities should not be overlooked. More than anything else, civil rights activities were directed towards British public opinion so that reforms would be introduced by the Northern Ireland Government as a result of pressure emanating from Westminster. Under the circumstances of the time, therefore, violence on the streets could only have damaged the credibility of the movement, and *ipso facto,* strengthened the position of the Stormont regime. The fact, therefore, that local priests and local civil rights leaders were largely successful in averting trouble, or at least in minimising violence throughout much of the period, was of great importance for the image of the civil rights movement as a genuinely non-violent organisation.

As the crisis deepened, however, clerical influence began to wane. Certainly, by the time of the next serious confrontations in July 1969, the advice of clerics was ignored by many rioters. Although the cause of the mid-July violence was 'somewhat obscure' according to the *Derry Journal,* and did not occur at the time of civil rights protests, it did little to help the image of the campaign as a whole. In condemning the disturbances, local curates described (in their addresses at Mass the following day) how they had tried to dissuade a mob from engaging in violence. Fr Edward Daly (later to be Bishop of Derry) and Fr J. J. McCullagh both claimed that many of the young men involved were drunk. Fr Mulvey, who had played such an important role in defusing a potentially disastrous situation in April, described in the *Derry Journal,* 15 July 1969, pp. 5 and 9, how he was told to move out of the way when he attempted to persuade a gang of youths not to attack the premises of a Protestant businessman. There is no doubt that these events clearly reflected the 'failure' of local priests to successfully use their influence in averting communal violence. Still, it could be argued that it was a measure of clerical prestige in Derry that priests had been successful in discouraging violence on the streets for so long. It must be remembered, after all, that the situation in Derry and Northern Ireland as a whole was deteriorating. (Only four weeks after the above incidents occurred, British troops were to be deployed throughout Northern Ireland.)

For their part, Cardinal Conway and the local bishop, Dr Farren, had made their position quite clear on the civil rights movement in Derry. Within days of the first such march in the city on 5 October 1968, Cardinal Conway issued a statement on the matter:

The immediate causes of these events are social. They grow

out of the frustration of ordinary people who want houses and a fair chance of jobs and equitable representation.

I know the people who are suffering from these injustices well enough to realise that they will respond to any credible sign that their position is going to be remedied soon.

To put off tackling these injustices realistically until the extremists who support them fade away is, I believe, misguided and dangerous, and I believe that the broad spectrum of public opinion throughout the community would welcome concrete action now and that such concrete action would itself influence attitudes for good . . . (*Irish News*, 14 October 1968, p. 1)

Such a statement was important for five main reasons. First, not only did it represent unequivocal support for the objectives of the civil rights movement in Derry, but in so doing, *asserted* that their allegations were justified. Second, the Cardinal had explicitly highlighted the kernel of the movement's demands throughout Northern Ireland: the fair allocation of public housing, an end to discrimination in employment and the granting of universal franchise in local government elections. Third, at no point did the Cardinal condemn either the decision to hold the civil rights march or the marchers themselves which was significant since, technically speaking, the march had been declared illegal under an order from the then Minister for Home Affairs, William Craig. Fourth, by describing the possible efforts of the Northern Ireland Government to put off addressing these problems as 'misguided and dangerous' the Cardinal was, in effect, throwing down the gauntlet to the authorities. Indeed, implicit in what he said about the 'extremists' who were supporting such injustices was that the government would have to confront such people and defeat them politically. As events unfolded, such a confrontation did indeed take place, but in the process it was the so-called extremists who came to enjoy most support within the Protestant community.[12] Fifth, it was extremely prescient of the Cardinal to state that the immediate causes of these events were 'social'. By doing so, not only was he attempting to depoliticise his own statement, but in stressing the social nature of civil rights demands, his statement was, in effect, challenging the belief of many Unionists that the civil rights movement was little more than a republican attempt to destabilise Northern Ireland.[13] Equally supportive of the civil rights campaign were the statements by the Bishop of Derry, Dr Farren. Throughout the period in question, he made a whole series of statements whose dominant themes were calls for peace and justice in Derry. For example when speaking at Solemn Mass on Christmas Day 1968, at St Eugene's Cathedral, Dr Farren paid tribute to the peaceful and orderly fashion in which people had striven to achieve their rights. Conspicuous by its absence was any reference to the fact that the largest protest to have been held up to that time (November 1968), had been illegal. What this meant, in effect, was a full endorsement of the activities of the Derry Citizens' Action Committee. Other statements by Bishop Farren were presented in a similar vein. In January 1969 for instance, he appealed to the civil authorities to consider the validity of local protests, while a number of weeks later he made a plea for peace and justice in the city. However, from the summer of 1969 on, Bishop Farren, as reported in the *Derry Journal*, 18 July 1969, p. 6, and 12 August 1969, came to emphasise the restoration or maintenance of peace more than the attainment of justice. More than anything else, such statements tacitly acknowledged the fact that no one (and this included priests) could prevent violence on the streets of Derry.

Clerical involvement in the civil rights campaign in Armagh was comparable to that of Derry in certain respects: (i) the widespread attendance of local priests at civil rights meetings; (ii) the assumption of a peace-keeping role on the part of clerics in the area; (iii) support for civil rights activities from the higher clergy.

In his study, *Violence in Ulster*, pp. 78–79, which largely comprised interviews with a variety of people in Northern Ireland, Van Voris was told by a priest in Armagh that all his clerical colleagues had attended civil rights marches in their area. Certainly in the case of the well-known civil rights march of 30 November 1968, the *Armagh Observer*, 7 December 1968, p. 12, names four local priests who took part.

In addition, clerics used their influence in Armagh to avert or minimise street conflict. A notable example of this occurred in Armagh City on 14/15 August, after the 'B' Specials had opened fire and killed a local Catholic, Mr John Gallagher. Only shortly after Mr Gallagher had been taken to hospital, a local curate, Fr Malachy Coyle, addressed the Catholic crowd and successfully persuaded them to disperse and return to their homes. For his part, Cardinal Conway spent much of the following day, 15 August, visiting Catholic families throughout Armagh City, calling on them to stay off the streets and made the same appeal yet again at evening Mass. (See *Armagh Observer*, 23 August 1969, p. 3)

Just as he had supported the civil rights campaign in Derry, Cardinal Conway warmly endorsed the civil rights movement in Armagh at an early stage. In fact only days after the first civil rights march in Armagh, the Cardinal, in his dual capacity as Archbishop of Armagh and Primate of all-Ireland, paid tribute to all who took part in the march, including the organising committee and the stewards. 'By their conduct', he said, 'they had proved more clearly than mere words could have done, their essentially peaceful nature.'

While clerical influence on the civil rights campaigns of Derry and Armagh was considerable, it must be said, again, that such influence was exercised from *outside* the civil rights movement proper. This cannot be said of the civil rights campaign in the Dungannon area, where one priest in particular, Fr Austin Eustace CC, openly participated in the *organisation* of local civil rights activities. Only days before the first civil rights march in Northern Ireland on 24 August 1968,[14] Fr Eustace was one of the speakers at a meeting whose purpose, in the words of the *Mid-Ulster Observer*, 22 August 1968, p. 3, was 'to assist in the organisation of the civil rights march between Coalisland and Dungannon'. Paying tribute to the work of civil rights groups in the area, he encouraged the largest possible turnout for the protest: '. . . I have no doubt that many thousands of people in this area would wish to be associated with them [civil rights activists] in the work that they are doing, and that they have an excellent opportunity of doing just this by participating in the civil rights march next Saturday and the subsequent meeting in Dungannon.'

A year later, Fr Eustace was part of a civil rights deputation which travelled to Belfast to see the then Minister for

Development, Mr Brian Faulkner. Although the main purpose of the visit was to complain about the allocation of council houses in their area, Fr Eustace took advantage of the opportunity to express his concern about local unemployment and its effects. The *Irish News*, 5 August 1969, put it this way: '. . . Rev. Austin Eustace, CC, pointed out to the Minister that on average 43% of all children at Catholic schools in the area had to emigrate before 25 years of age; that in spite of this mass emigration the Catholic male unemployment rate in the area was 25% – a figure which was so high as to be unbelievable in the western world.' Only days before, Fr Eustace (and Fr Denis Faul) had attended an *ad hoc* meeting at which there had been a decision to press for a commission to replace the then urban council of Dungannon. The proposed method of achieving such a reform was a rent and rates strike.

Fr Eustace's speech at this meeting is extremely useful for putting such activities into some sort of perspective.[15] After all, he stressed that it was not the job of a priest to run either a civil rights campaign or a political meeting, but instead: '. . . it is his job to give the Civil Rights Movement his wholehearted support since its demands are just, and my purpose in being here is to give moral support to what your committee is doing.' The most crucial aspect of this statement is that it is not the cleric's role to *lead* a civil rights movement; certainly, such a statement contrasts with the situation in the United States, for example, where many Christian churchmen did lead civil rights groups.[16] Unlike Northern Ireland, however, the cleavages of ethnicity and religion[17] in the USA were to a limited extent crosscutting, i.e. some members of the Black community belonged to the major 'White' denominations, Episcopalian, Roman Catholic etc. In any event, even if priests had wanted to play a leading role in the Northern Ireland civil rights movement, such a course would have proven counter-productive. For in the context of a sectarian society like Northern Ireland, even the most liberal Protestants would have seen such activities as smacking of 'Rome Rule' politics. In any event, it is significant that Fr Eustace saw his motive for participating in these activities as advancing the cause of justice and *ipso facto*, saw himself (and by implication could be seen by others) as essentially 'non-political'.

Whatever about the role of the lower clergy in the civil rights movement, the Northern bishops were extremely supportive of civil rights in many ways, and in the process, showed themselves to be politically astute. This is underlined by the bishops' pastoral on education in Northern Ireland in January 1968 and by their lengthy policy statement on the civil rights movement one year later. Even when the Northern Ireland Civil Rights Association was, in its own words, 'nothing more than a pressure group',[18] the bishops had singled out local government for special criticism. In the course of a lengthy pastoral on Catholic education by the six Northern bishops, it had been stated that:

> . . . Without wishing to go into matters in any controversial way, we cannot avoid referring to the fact that in the arrangement for their election, in their composition, their nomination of committees, and their record on such matters as employment and housing, very many local authorities in Northern Ireland have manifested a bias against Catholics which is undeniable . . . (*Irish Catholic*, 25 January 1968, p. 1)

Without wider reference to the other hierarchical statement of the period, one could be tempted to see such a passage as justification for a hard-line policy on the education question, or quite simply, an intelligent ploy in the context of ongoing negotiations. Neither interpretation, however, appears justified in the light of the Northern bishops' statement of January 1969 which yet again emphasised local government discrimination: 'As recently as January last year we felt bound to draw attention in a public statement to serious abuses at local government levels in regard to jobs, housing, and the franchise.' (*Irish Catholic*, 23 January 1969, p. 1)

This assiduous attack on local government by the bishops reflected their considerable political insight. Allegations of anti-Catholic discrimination in Northern Ireland were widespread, of course, but local government discrimination differed from that practised by central government in one crucial respect: political patronage in Northern Ireland or anywhere else for that matter, was and is most easily exercised at a local level.[19] Moreover, Unionists attached great importance to controlling these bodies. Following the establishment of Northern Ireland, a situation had arisen whereby nationalist and Sinn Fein representatives enjoyed a majority in several councils of the new state. In effect, a deadlock occurred between these bodies and central government in Belfast with many councils refusing to recognise the existence of the border, and instead, pledging their allegiances to Dublin. The Unionists responded quickly by redrawing constituencies, abolishing proportional representation and limiting the franchise.[20] As a result central government had succeeded in many cases in transferring local powers from members of the Catholic community to fellow-Unionists. Indeed if one accepts the theory that the Unionist Party only maintained a high degree of pan-Protestant support through a system of patronage, the significance of local government went far deeper than that: it ultimately involved the survival of the state itself. Thus the emphasis placed on local government discrimination by the hierarchy during this period reflected an awareness of what political changes were really possible in Northern Ireland. As electoral defeat for a Unionist government was inconceivable, an attack upon the activities of central government could yield no effective results. As well as that, why make allegations of private sector discrimination if no positive response would be forthcoming? It must be remembered that the existence of a body such as the Fair Employment Agency* would have been unthinkable in the late 1960s.[21] So, in effect, by placing the emphasis on local government activities, the bishops had chosen to attack the most vulnerable, and, arguably, the most important aspect of Unionist policy in Northern Ireland.

In order to acquire a comprehensive view of the hierarchy's policy at this time, it is necessary to return to their statement of January 1969. The full text of that statement contained in the *Irish Catholic,* 23 January, reads as follows:

> The situation which has developed in Northern Ireland in recent months has given grounds for serious thought to everyone within the community and to many outside it.

---

* A body established in 1976 to deal with complaints of sectarian discrimination in the employment market.

That serious grievance existed here in the field of civil rights and the call for speedy remedies is now generally recognised by responsible people of different faiths and different political affiliations.

These injustices have existed for many decades and have been protested against, mainly by Catholics, all during that time. As recently as January of last year we felt bound to draw attention in a public statement to serious abuses at local government levels in regard to jobs, housing and the franchise. That the existence of these grievances is now so generally recognised is due in considerable measure to the civil rights movement. The sad fact is that virtually nothing was done until the people took to the streets.

We record these facts now because it is necessary to identify the root cause of whatever threat to public order exists in the community at the present time.

The civil rights movement has been essentially non-violent and non-sectarian in character and its fidelity to these principles has been clearly and movingly demonstrated on many occasions.

We believe that the most serious threat to public order in recent months has come from the activities of people who despite their almost cynical disregard for community peace were allowed to impede lawful and peaceful demonstrations with the threat to use force.

To this must be added the harrying of innocent persons — and also some measure of responsibility on the part of small groups of subversive militants who have associated themselves with the Civil Rights Movement for their own end.

We are confident that our people will keep alive to this last danger which should not be underestimated.

The recent decision to call off the march in Strabane is further evidence of the essential peacefulness of the great majority of those engaged in the civil rights movement. They have shown clearly that they have realised the harm which could be done to community relations — and to industrial and economic progress — if turmoil were to continue to escalate.

In recording our appreciation of this we once again urge

our people to shun all violence and we ask parents to instil this into our young people, some of whom may be carried away by excitement or provocation. In this connection we have some anxiety that a series of court hearings arising out of recent events may actually have the effect of prolonging tension.

We also wish to pay tribute to the service in the cause of social justice which has been rendered in recent months by many Protestant members of the community including leading churchmen. Their voice has given consolation and encouragement to those who have suffered from injustice for a very long time.

We profoundly hope that the government will demonstrate its good faith during the next few months by concrete action to remove the grievances with which the civil rights movement is concerned.

We welcome the decision to appoint an independent and impartial commission of enquiry and we trust that this commission will not be precluded from examining in depth the basic causes of the present unrest which have existed for many years.

It would be tragic if this opportunity to go to the root of the marches, and so lay the foundation of lasting peace were to be lost.

This statement not only represented complete support for civil rights, but clearly defended the Civil Rights Association as an *organisation*. First, in stating that the recognition of grievances in the area of local government policy was 'due in considerable measure to the civil rights movement' was obvious praise for a group that had done more in a few months than any other body had managed to do over several decades. Second, in claiming that the NICRA was 'essentially non-violent and non-sectarian', the hierarchy defended the image of NICRA at a time when disturbances were not unknown at civil rights meetings,[22] and when many Unionists interpreted such incidents as a sign that civil rights activities were mere fronts to destabilise the state. In a sense then, the bishops' defence of NICRA was an oblique rejection of this criticism.

Indeed it is interesting to note the adroit reference to this fact in the bishops' statement: 'These injustices have existed for many decades and have been protested against, mainly by Catholics, all during that time.' It is clear in the term 'many decades' that the hierarchy had only *implicitly* associated the existence of the Northern State with anti-Catholic discrimination. If this had been asserted in a more *explicit* fashion, the effect would have been to undermine the success of the civil rights campaign by provoking a debate on the 'constitutional' issue. To a large extent this was the true strength of the civil rights movement: by carefully avoiding the border issue and limiting its demands to reforms *within* Northern Ireland, NICRA had succeeded in gaining overwhelming support from Westminster.

Moreover, it is significant that the hierarchy refrained from acknowledging the illegal nature of some of the civil rights protests which had taken place. Instead, when attributing blame for the violence that had occurred, the bishops criticised 'militants' who had infiltrated the Civil Rights Association, and loyalist extremists. It was this latter group, in fact, which was most strongly criticised by the hierarchy: '. . . We believe that the most serious threat to public order in recent months has come from the activities of people who despite their almost cynical disregard for community peace, were allowed to impede lawful and peaceful demonstrations with the threat to use force . . .'

The hierarchy had, in effect, emphasised the need for quick governmental reform. In its opening paragraph, the statement called for 'speedy remedies' and expressed the hope 'that the government will demonstrate its good faith during the next few months by concrete action'. (In doing this, the bishops tacitly dismissed the government's five-point plan of November 1968 as all but irrelevant.) The urgency of the situation as the bishops saw it, was reflected by their remark that it was 'necessary to identify the root cause of whatever threat exists in the community at the present time'. Even more ominous, however, was the following plea to the Catholic community which clearly implied that the hierarchy could only use *moral* authority when appealing for peaceful protest: '. . . we once again urge our people to shun all violence, and we ask parents to instil this into our young people, some of whom may be carried away by excitement or provocation . . .'

Finally, this statement clearly reflected the bishops' attitude towards their non-nationalist neighbours. Apart from criticising the activities of extreme loyalist groups who had disrupted civil rights marches and rallies, the church found itself in a delicate position *vis-à-vis* the Unionist Government. A partial solution for this was found by making vague references to the past and present without appearing too negative. For example, when the bishops referred to loyalists who had been 'allowed to impede lawful and peaceful demonstrations with the threat to use force', it was implied but not stated that the police had failed to keep peace at these meetings.

Whatever about the failure of the police to maintain order in early 1969, by mid-August 1969 the rule of law had virtually collapsed in parts of Belfast,[23] Derry[24] and Armagh City. In Belfast alone, seven people were shot dead and destruction of property occurred on a wide scale. Eventually British troops were deployed and an uneasy peace was established. The same civil rights movement which had succeeded in giving Catholic politics some semblance of coherence for the best part of a year, now found itself marginalised by the large-scale violence. In the words of Scott in *Persuasion in the Northern Ireland Civil Rights Movement, 1964–1970*, pp. 144–145: '. . . Beyond the violence and destruction, the events in Derry and Belfast signalled the wane of the civil rights movement per se . . . In this environment, civil rights leaders found themselves increasingly without a constituency. Civil rights rhetoric bordered on irrelevance.'

What had clearly emerged was a greater political vacuum in the Catholic community than during the previous year, and it was in such a context that the Catholic Church found itself trying to promote a policy of political reform for Northern Ireland within the framework of Unionist majority rule. It will be argued here that the effectiveness of such a clerical policy was at its apex in the latter part of 1969 and quickly diminished in 1970, before totally collapsing in mid-1971.

Broadly speaking, this policy operated in two distinctive though interrelated ways: (i) through Church–State relations (especially through the activities of Cardinal Conway and the then Home Secretary, James Callaghan); (ii) through the defence committees which existed in Belfast at the time.

Alongside this, an early indication of the broad objectives of the British Government emerged on 19 August 1969 when a meeting was held between representatives of the Northern Ireland and British Cabinets. Afterwards, a communiqué and declaration were released in which it was acknowledged that the GOC in Northern Ireland had 'overall responsibility for security operations', and 'that in all legislation and executive decisions of government every citizen of Northern Ireland is entitled to the same equality of treatment and freedom from discrimination as obtains in the rest of the United Kingdom, irrespective of political views or religion'.[25] The response of both Bishop Philbin and Cardinal Conway to these announcements was one of guarded optimism, Bishop Philbin saying that 'it is very difficult to assess the full significance of what has been announced but there are grounds at least for hoping that it may mark the beginning of better days', and Cardinal Conway commenting that it marked an important step forward and should be recognised as such.

Some time after this, it became clear what the British Government meant by 'equality' of citizenship. Indeed at the end of a visit to Northern Ireland by James Callaghan, the British Government issued a communiqué in which specific objectives were cited. Significantly, paragraph 8 of that document identified five areas where effective action was 'fundamental to the creation of confidence':

(i) equality of opportunity for all in public employment;
(ii) protection against incitement of hatred against any citizen on the grounds of religious belief;
(iii) the allocation of public housing to be assessed by objective criteria;
(iv) effective means for the investigation of grievances against public bodies and ultimate redress against such grievances if necessary;
(v) proper representation of minorities 'by completely fair electoral laws, practices and boundaries, and at

nominated or appointed levels by a recognition that such minorities have a right to an effective voice in affairs'.[26]

Ironically, then, at a time when the civil rights movement was seen by many as having outlived its usefulness, the British Government had conceded its major demands (albeit on paper). Moreover, ecclesiastical endorsement of these governmental commitments was full-hearted. Cardinal Conway, for instance, described the programme of reform announced by the Home Secretary as an enormous step forward and something that would have been inconceivable a year earlier: 'If these reforms are carried out — and I feel confident that they will be — then they will really amount to a "new deal" for the minority in Northern Ireland.' (*Irish News*, 30 August 1969, p. 1) Mr Callaghan, for his part, recounts a telephone conversation he had with Cardinal Conway *just* after he completed the communiqué:

> I was holding on to an extension as they put the call through and I could hear the flutter at the Cardinal's end too. I told the Cardinal the principal points in the communiqué and that, apart from the GOC, he was the first man to know because it was his community which was in trouble. I said I had a request to make of him. I wanted him to give his blessing to the communiqué as soon as it was announced on television. The Cardinal said that from what I had told him it sounded a very good agreement and certainly went further than he had expected. He was willing to say something that would be helpful. I thanked him very much and said I was now going to get on to the press and the radio and television and ask them to go down to Armagh and see him forthwith. So within an hour of the communiqué coming out the Cardinal had given the Catholic community a lead. Whether they agreed with him was another matter but at least they knew his opinion and I was very grateful . . .[27]

Implicit in this passage is Callaghan's belief that Cardinal Conway was the most important *political* voice in the Catholic community. In *realpolitik* terms, however, the Cardinal's pre-eminence was mainly a symptom of the fragmentation of

'Catholic' politics at the time.[28] Indeed, fear among opposition MPs of being completely overlooked by the British Government in discussions was clearly reflected in a statement by John Hume in which he urged the British to consult the opposition, insisting that their viewpoint had to be heard. The Catholic viewpoint in Westminster was equally diffuse. Thus, for instance, Bernadette Devlin owed her electoral success in mid-Ulster to the fact that she had been a 'compromise candidate': her nomination prevented a split in the 'Catholic vote' and thereby thwarted the election of her Unionist rival.[29] All these public representatives had at least one thing in common, then: none of them could claim to speak for the Catholic community as a whole. In short, Mr Callaghan chose the head of the Catholic Church to sell his reform package to the Catholic community. As the above passage suggests, however, Callaghan had doubts about the effectiveness of this strategy.

In any event this particular declaration did not prove especially divisive inside the Catholic community. Indeed, the *Irish News* reported no explicit criticism of the declaration by any political figure within the Catholic community. Even the fact that paragraph 2 of the declaration guaranteed Northern Ireland's position within the United Kingdom seems to have had little or no impact on Catholic opinion in Northern Ireland since most anti-Unionists at the time did not perceive the border as an *immediate* issue.[30]

Later still, when the Hunt Report which was issued in October 1969 recommended the disarmament of the RUC and the disbandment of the exclusively Protestant 'B' Specials,[31] Cardinal Conway's response was as swift as it was positive. Describing the contents of the report as 'important and far-reaching', he went on to remark: 'What is proposed is really a new kind of police force and one which should prove much more attractive as a career to all citizens. I imagine many policemen themselves will welcome these changes and I anticipate Catholics will be willing and anxious to join the new force in considerable numbers.' (*Irish News*, 11 October 1969)

The Cardinal's anticipation that many Catholics would join the newly disarmed RUC was in itself a remarkable statement given the bitterness and deep mistrust of that community towards the police, especially since the events of August 1969, in Belfast and Derry. But the Cardinal went further than this, a fact which Callaghan disclosed in opening a House of Commons debate on Northern Ireland:

> I was glad to note Cardinal Conway, Primate of all-Ireland, expressing his view publicly that Catholics should be encouraged to join the new unarmed civilian Royal Ulster Constabulary, and saying to me privately that he would discuss the matter with his priests so that they might give it encouragement too. I am absolutely satisfied that it was his firm desire that this civilian unarmed police force should be fully representative of all the community. (*Parliamentary Debates, (Hansard), House of Commons*, vol. 788, col. 53, 13 October 1969)

Underlying this statement, of course, was Callaghan's belief that clerical encouragement for the reform of the RUC would help to make the police more acceptable to members of the Catholic population. However, such a policy never seemed likely to succeed: while the unarmed police force returned to the Falls Road, Belfast, and Derry's Bogside in mid-October 1969, the escalating violence of 1970 left an unarmed police force in an impossible position. (In August 1970, the RUC made arms available at selected stations for issue as the occasion demanded.)[32] Even before that, however, the other major initiative on security from the Hunt Report, i.e. the creation of a reservist force to replace the 'B' Specials, had run into serious difficulties.

Within days of being founded, the Ulster Defence Regiment was seen by many anti-Unionist politicians as encouraging ex-'B' Specials to join its ranks. At Westminster, for example, Gerry Fitt met a large number of Labour backbenchers to express his anxiety over the new force, while two Stormont MPs, John Hume and Austin Currie (who had initially welcomed the creation of the UDR) found themselves expressing grave reservations. John Hume, for one, claimed that some 'B' Specials had received recruiting forms without the knowledge of the force's leader, the GOC for Northern Ireland, General Sir Ian Freeland.[33]

Despite this inauspicious beginning, however, the UDR did succeed in recruiting a significant number of Catholics and, at one point, had a Catholic membership of about 16 per cent.[34] Within a short period, though, this figure dropped because of wider events in Northern Ireland[35] and not least because an early IRA campaign was directed against Catholic members of the regiment in question.

In evaluating the political influence of the Church during this period, two broad points must be emphasised. First, as a result of a leadership crisis within the Catholic community, the hierarchy, especially Cardinal Conway, found himself in an almost unprecedented position of political importance. Thus, as we have seen, James Callaghan *perceived* the Catholic Church as the most influential single group within the Catholic community and sought its support. At the same time, though, there were many factors which militated against the Church retaining its pre-eminent political position. Among these, the following must be highlighted: (a) while James Callaghan sought the assistance of the Catholic Church in selling the reform package, the Church was ill-equipped to deal with the situation in a conventional party political way; (b) the Catholic community did not *perceive* any real political change in the months that were to follow; (c) the positive relationship between the British Army and the Catholic community[36] soured during the course of 1970.

In analysing this period, however, it is necessary to identify and assess clerical influence within the Central Citizens' Defence Committees during the period August 1969–1970 and pose the question which confronted these committees: if the barricades[37] were removed could people's safety be guaranteed? For the Church, the answer to this question was yes. Indeed, it could hardly be otherwise as no 'new deal' for Northern Catholics could conceivably take place for as long as the barricades remained. After all, barricades represented the *de facto* secession of many Catholics from the Northern State, a scenario which was clearly recognised by the editorial column of the pro-Unionist *Newsletter* on 16 September 1969, p. 4, which said that the barriers struck 'a blow at the very structure of the state'.

What is important here is that these last comments were made against the background of a meeting between a five-man deputation from Belfast (including Fr Padraig Murphy)* and the then Home Secretary, Mr James Callaghan, where a basic formula for taking down the barricades was agreed. Back in Belfast, however, a heated debate went on within the committees and, despite two meetings in as many days, the defence committees still failed to reach agreement on the Belfast barricades. As the *Sunday Times* Insight Team put it in *Ulster*, p. 157: 'On Monday, when the Army was getting desperate, Fr. Murphy had to involve the power of the church to get the deal through: he called in his bishop, Dr. Philbin, Bishop of Down and Connor, to work over the CCDC leadership.' As a result, Bishop Philbin took the unprecedented step of addressing members of the defence committees on the subject of the barricades. To quote the *Irish News*, 16 September 1969, p. 1:

> Two meetings in barricaded areas of Belfast decided last night to start immediate protection plan talks with senior British Army officers . . . Both of last night's meetings, which were attended by men who have been on duty at the barricades in Andersonstown and the Falls, were addressed by the Bishop of Down and Connor, Most Rev. Dr. Philbin. He urged the meetings to accept the terms of last week's British Home Office communiqué on protection and the removal of the barricades.

The fact that such ecclesiastical intervention succeeded was striking and marked the zenith of the Church's influence over the course of street politics. In *realpolitik* terms, moreover, it must be recognised that the removal of barricades was conducive to the implementation of the reform programme. None of this, however, could conceal the fact that there had been considerable opposition to dismantling the barricades which was not only based on fear but was also a reflection of a major political cleavage within the ghettos. As the *Sunday Times* Insight Team explained in *Ulster*, pp. 157–158:

* The deputation also included Gerry Fitt MP, Mr Tom Conaty, Mr Paddy Devlin MP, Mr J. P. McSparran QC.
Source: *Irish News*, 12 September 1969

Just before midnight on Monday 15 September, Major-General Dyball rang Murphy, and the priest said it looked all right for Tuesday morning, but not too early, for God's sake. Murphy still needed time to explain things, to get some sleep and get back on the streets for the demolition. They agreed on 11 a.m. Then Dyball called back to suggest 9 a.m. Murphy said it was too early—even when the Bishop then called, at Freeland's instigation, also to ask for 9 a.m. Murphy fell into bed at 5.30, to be awakened at 8.30 with the news that the Army had arrived.

When Murphy refused to come out, the Army waited until 11 a.m., when Murphy and his Bishop, Dr. Philbin, turned up and the demolition began. In front of the t.v. cameras, the Bishop received a denunciation from one of the future Provisionals. But all the barricades were down by Wednesday morning. When three Catholic houses were then promptly burnt out by Protestants, the barricades went up again. This time Murphy negotiated direct with Freeland. Once more they were removed.

As this passage suggests, if one regards such clerical influence on the defence committees as a victory, it was a victory that had been hard-earned. For not only had Bishop Philbin been rebuked by a future Provisional* but at earlier meetings of the CCDC attended by Fr Murphy, opposition to the idea of dismantling the barricades had been led by three men who were later to emerge as reputed leaders of the Provisional IRA: Francis Card, Billy McKee and Leo Martin. An even greater constraint on church influence within the CCDC was the fact

---

* Bishop Philbin took this opposition seriously enough to issue a statement on the matter, part of which read as follows:

> I wish to repudiate some press reports and many rumours which are current about discussions between a number of people and myself in the Falls district of Belfast on September 16 . . . I took no offence at anything that was said to me, nor indeed, did I hear anything that could be reasonably called offensive.
>
> People expressed opinions which differed from mine. I gave my views and insisted that certain other people should also be heard.
>
> I have no reason to be aggrieved. The whole incident has been absurdly distorted.

Source: *Irish News,* 22 September 1969, p. 3

that its then chairman, Jim Sullivan (later purported to be a leading member of the Official IRA), openly criticised clerical intervention: 'The clergy are deliberately trying to get the people to take the barricades down. We say that this is a decision which has got to be taken by a democratic vote of all the people.' (*Irish News*, 17 September 1969)

But the single most important factor in this regard was the mobilisation of republican groups in late 1969 and throughout 1970. Indeed the effect of republican mobilisation marginalised both the CCDC in its formal capacity as a *defensive* organisation, and the Church as an *effective* force in street politics. And this, coupled with the dramatic deterioration in relations between the Army and the Catholic community during this crucial period led to a shift (by early to mid-1970) in the balance of power which was clearly coming to reside more and more with local republicans.

In fact differences between the CCDC and the Provisional IRA manifested themselves as early as April 1970 following the riots that occurred in Ballymurphy. The significance of these riots lay not only in the fact that this was the first serious confrontation between Catholic youths and the British Army, but in the arguments that broke out among anti-Unionist groups as to *why* it occurred in the first place. Thus, certain MPs and members of the Central Citizens' Defence Committees claimed that the Provisional IRA provoked the riots in Ballymurphy, a claim that was quickly denied by the Provisionals.

Whether the Provisional IRA was actually involved in orchestrating these Ballymurphy riots is a moot point. What was not a moot point, however, was the diminishing influence of non-violent groups and individuals in the nationalist community (the Church included). Indeed, the rioting which occurred in Ardoyne six weeks after the Ballymurphy disturbances served to demonstrate how clerical influence over street politics was being eroded. Certainly the then Rector of Ardoyne parish, Fr O'Donnell, spent two successive evenings trying to dissuade youths from engaging in violent activities without success.[38]

Clearly sensing this shift within the Catholic community towards republicanism, the Northern Bishops issued a statement on the political situation only days after the Ardoyne riots in May 1970, whose most important passages were the following:

The overwhelming majority of our people do not want violence. They realise that it is morally wrong and that it is doubly so in Northern Ireland at the present time because of what it might lead to. It could lead to great suffering and death. It could lead to a repetition of the horrors we endured last autumn and even worse . . . Since this is the case it would be a betrayal of the Catholic community—a stab in the back—for any individual, or group, to take it upon themselves to deliberately provoke violent incidents. So far as our people are concerned this would be quite a turn of events, but there is some evidence that it may have happened in recent days. If this is so, then in the name of God and the whole Catholic community, we condemn it . . . Moreover, if such acts can be pointed to as the beginning of serious trouble, it is not the handful of self-appointed activists who will be blamed, but the whole Catholic community. Already people are not above suggesting that what has happened in recent days convicts the Catholic community for what happened last August . . . We therefore ask our people to make their voices heard in repudiation of individuals or groups who may appear to be interested in a continuation of violence. We ask them to cooperate with those groups who genuinely reflect the peaceful intentions of the people as a whole and who are working hard to restrain militant elements. We appeal in a particular way to the women—who are often the people who suffer most—and to parents . . . There are many deep-seated wrongs to be undone in our society. Violence will only delay the day when they can be removed . . . We regard it as essential that the programme of reform be adhered to, without any deviation, and pursued to its logical conclusion of fair treatment for all, in fact as well as in law . . . To anyone who thinks rationally about the future of the people concerned—and it is people, human beings that matter, not causes or ideologies—there can be no question of where the choice must lie between the violent way and the peaceful way. We warn those few individuals who would opt for the violent way that they have absolutely no mandate from the people . . . (*Irish News*, 22 May 1970, p. 1)

The central importance of the statement was that it was the
first time during the period of this study that the hierarchy had
felt it necessary to call on republicans, (however obliquely), not
to embark on a campaign of violence. The bishops' argument
consisted of three major tenets: (i) that violence was morally
wrong; (ii) that the effects of violence were devastating; (iii) that
no group had a mandate from the Catholic people for a
campaign of violence. Implicit in all this, of course, was their
obvious fear of the future, but above all, the fact that peaceful
groups were losing ground to republicans within the Catholic
community. Thus in a veiled reference to the CCDC, they asked
Catholics 'to co-operate with those groups who genuinely reflect
the peaceful intentions of the people as a whole and who are
working hard to restrain militant elements'.* The timing of the
bishops' statement was, to say the least, apposite. For not only
did it come at a time when there was 'some evidence' that there
were 'individuals or groups' who appeared 'to be interested in a
continuation of violence', but wider political events were conducive to the rise of republican violence.

Among these, the violence of August 1969 not only led to a
republican split between the Official and Provisional wings of
the IRA[39] but provided militarists with a *raison d'être*. Other
considerations in this regard were the electoral results secured
by extreme Protestant Unionists in Bannside and South Antrim:[40]
these results were hardly conducive to the implementation of
reforms in Northern Ireland, and in general, were perceived by
Catholics as irrefutable evidence of an increase in anti-Catholic
feeling among the Protestant community. An even greater boost
to the credibility of the emergent IRA, however, was the arms
crisis in the Republic at the beginning of May 1970,[41] which was
interpreted by a number of Northern Catholics as meaning that
Dublin had, in formal terms, abandoned them. In short, it
underscored how imperative it was for the Catholic community
in Northern Ireland to look after itself, without looking to the
Irish Government for any meaningful assistance.

The need for self-reliance among Northern nationalists was
forcibly brought home by events in July 1970 when relations

* Not surprisingly, the CCDC endorsed the hierarchy's statement.
Source: *Irish News*, 25 May 1970, p. 4

between the Army and the Catholic community were irreversibly damaged by the imposition of a curfew on the Falls Road, Belfast.[42] For their part, local priests had done everything in their power to prevent the violence which preceded the imposition of the curfew. Fathers Murphy, Teggart, O'Donnell and McCabe had spent several hours on the streets trying to calm their parishioners. According to these priests and local MPs like Paddy Devlin and Paddy Kennedy, however, each time they did succeed in pacifying local people the Army fired more CS gas into the streets. Such a claim is supported in a book subsequently published by the CCDC entitled *Law (?) and Orders*, whose author, Sean Og O'Fearghail, quotes a telephone conversation between Fr Murphy and General Sir Ian Freeland GOC Northern Ireland, about an hour before the curfew was imposed. (It is significant, perhaps, that the Army has never denied that this conversation took place):

Freeland: You will get on those streets and tell those people of yours to get in or they will be shot.
Murphy: This is the point I am ringing about. How can I do this without vigilantes?
Freeland: I don't recognise your vigilantes.
Murphy: I am only one man and there are about thirty-thousand people in this whole area. How can I go around and contact them all individually? I need men to help me.
Freeland: Very good then. Use your men.
Murphy: Can I tell my men that they will not be gassed?
Freeland: No. They are better gassed than shot.[43]

In the words of O'Fearghail, 'the fruits of a whole year of patient negotiation had been thrown away'. In reality, however, something much more fundamental had occurred than that since the curfew had succeeded in damaging the CCDC as an organisation. In fact this purported dialogue indicates just how dependent the defence committees had been on the Army and how, without military recognition, the CCDC simply could not perform its role as a defensive organisation. Even more serious than that, however, was a sudden change in the way Catholics perceived the Army, which far from being a means of protection from loyalist attack, had become something *from* which people needed protection. This was implicit in the response of the CCDC to the Falls curfew which called for statements by people who wanted to complain about the behaviour of troops. (Within a couple of days, 150 such statements had been filed and more were still pouring in.)

Other members of the community, however, saw more direct means of defending themselves: they joined the IRA. This is not to say, of course, that self-defence of the nationalist community was the only motive people had in joining republican organisations or that the Falls curfew* was the sole factor in their decision. Nonetheless I would still argue that this curfew profoundly affected the political consciousness of anti-Unionists in Northern Ireland, not least in the sense that it legitimised future violence against the British Army in the eyes of many people. Most significant in this regard was the finding of the Sunday Times Insight Team (see *Ulster*, p. 221) concerning the extent of Provisional IRA membership during 1970: in May–June of that year there were fewer than a hundred activists, while by December that figure had risen to nearly 800.

By mid-1970 then, Church strategy had come unstuck and, as we have seen earlier in the chapter, the nationalist community not only failed to envisage any reform of the Northern State, but clerical influence over street politics (both within and without the CCDC) had been marginalised by the growing strength of republican organisations. Indeed, a symptom of all this was the lack of coherence which characterised the Church's position from this period until the British Government decided to suspend the Northern Ireland Government and Parliament in March 1972. Among the major signs of this incoherence perhaps two might be mentioned: (i) the decision of the Catholic Church to appoint a chaplain to the Northern Ireland Parliament in February 1971; (ii) statements on the political situation by the Northern bishops in August/September 1971.

The decision of the hierarchy to appoint a chaplain to the Northern Ireland Parliament in February 1971 was more a sign

---

* In retrospect, it may be seen as ironic that it was the Official IRA and not the Provisionals who had engaged the British Army in this bloody confrontation.

of diminishing political options than of confidence in the institutions of the state. And while, as we have seen, the hierarchy had had an important working relationship with James Callaghan, no such rapport existed between the Catholic Church and the Northern Ireland Government. Indeed, when the Cardinal and the then Prime Minister, Chichester-Clark, met in February 1971, it was not only the first time the two men had *officially* met each other but the first meeting of its kind in fifty years (see *Belfast Telegraph*, 26 February 1971, p. 5). The appointment of a Catholic chaplain to the Northern Ireland Parliament was seen as a low priority (except in symbolic terms) by Cardinal Conway, a fact which is underwritten by the reality that this idea had been floated earlier but no decision had been taken by the Church. This was made clear by Cardinal Conway in an interview with the editor-in-chief of the *Belfast Telegraph* which was reported on 27 March 1969, p. 14: 'There is no difficulty in principle about this, and it may well come in due course when certain practical difficulties have been resolved. Last year was the first time I had any official request about it.'

Regardless of whatever practical difficulties may have existed regarding the appointment of a chaplain to Stormont, then, it would be unrealistic to believe that it would take three years to resolve such difficulties. Indeed, I would argue that the decision was only finally made after the influence of the Church in the period 1969–1970 was seen to wane. Moreover, the timing of the decision was significant in that it followed a statement made by Chichester-Clark in the House of Commons in which he hinted at giving Catholics a greater role in Northern Ireland life, both inside and outside parliament: 'It means a chance to participate at every level of society and in every aspect of our institutions ... We accept that the health of this society depends on the creation of new opportunities for participation by all.'[44] Clearly, the Prime Minister's statement was heartening news for the Catholic community and this was reflected by the response of the newly-formed SDLP, who were said to be 'encouraged' by the Premier's comments. Thus it is difficult to imagine how the timing of the Church's decision to appoint a chaplain to Stormont could have been unconnected to these wider events. Where it was all leading to, however, was a different matter: the political reality of the period was that the balance of power within the Catholic community had shifted towards more militant elements and that the Church, like the SDLP, was finding a position of peaceful reform more and more difficult to sustain.* In fact, the fear of being eclipsed by street violence soon became a reality and compelled the SDLP to withdraw from Stormont in July 1971.[45]

If this kind of parliamentary withdrawal symbolised the failure of the opposition to reform the Unionist system of government by peaceful means, their problems were only compounded when the Government introduced internment without trial in August 1971: internment added a further boost to the prestige of the IRA in areas which now assumed the appearance of battlegrounds. It is against this grave background, therefore, that the position of the Catholic Church in late 1971 must be assessed. At the end of August 1971, Cardinal Conway made a discursive statement on the political situation whose most salient features were the following: (i) a strong condemnation of violence; (ii) a placing of the blame for the crisis on the shoulders of Unionists, the British Government and republicans; (iii) a call for a political initiative. For our immediate purpose, though, the most relevant section in Cardinal Conway's statement dealt with political change when he said that 'the current of opinion which sees the need for a new political framework in this country is very strong, even in Britain. Is this not the time to give this opinion an opportunity to bear fruit'. In a pastoral issued by the Northern bishops some days later, this vague prescription was clarified still further: 'The problems of this divided community will never be solved until a radical reform of the institutions of democracy here is introduced. Mathematical "majority rule" simply does not work in a community of this kind . . .'[46]

While both these statements underline just how difficult the

---

* The disquiet among Northern Catholics was reflected by the formation of a small pressure-group in early 1971 calling itself The Catholic Minority Rights Group. Though an obscure and shortlived group, its significance lies in the fact that nine of its members, including its vice-chairman, were priests.
Sources: *Irish News*, 2 April 1971; *Belfast Telegraph*, 23 March 1971

position of the Church had become, the hierarchy still advocated reform of the Northern State.* Such a stance, however, could only regain credibility if and when some fundamental change occurred in Northern Ireland. As it turned out, such a change took place within months. When the suspension of Stormont was announced by the British Government on 24 March 1972, there was widespread jubilation throughout the Catholic community of Northern Ireland. Eamonn McCann, in *War and an Irish Town*, p. 104, describes the mood at the time as follows: 'The instinctive reaction of the people was unrestrained joy. Stormont had for decades been the focus of all our resentment. Now it was gone.'

It was at this point, then, that pressure came to bear on local republicans to cease military operations. In the process, the differences within the nationalist community, which had been somewhat obscured by events during the previous years, now began to manifest themselves. The most visible groups calling for an end to IRA violence consisted of the SDLP, the Catholic Church and grassroots peace movements. Indeed the momentum of this broad peace movement was at its strongest between late March 1972 and July 1972, when both wings of the IRA called ceasefires (although the Provisional ceasefire broke down within a matter of days).[47]

For its part, the Church's contribution to the overall movement can be considered under four broad categories: first, the support given to calls for peace by Cardinal Conway, Bishop Philbin of Down and Connor, and Bishop Farren of Derry; second, joint statements of priests in the most troubled areas of Belfast, and all the priests of Derry, which called for an end to violence; third, clerical support for peace petitions of local

* It ought to be noted that such a policy was opposed by a relatively small number of priests who belonged to a radical (though shortlived) group called the Association of Irish Priests. In late 1971, the AIP issued a lengthy statement calling for a united Ireland. Source: *Belfast Telegraph*, 3 December 1971. At no point, however, did the hierarchy respond to any of the AIP's initiatives. In September 1971, for instance, the Ulster branch of the AIP passed a motion calling on Cardinal Conway to suspend the accreditation of a chaplain to Stormont 'pending the establishment of a democratic and representative legislature in Northern Ireland'. For a copy of this motion, see appendix B.

people; and finally, the support of local priests for peace protests.

Thus, only days after the implementation of direct rule, Cardinal Conway observed that 'there is no doubt whatever that there is a deep yearning in the hearts of the people for an end to this campaign of violence'. Moreover, in a television interview on *Panorama*, the Cardinal expressed the same opinion. Alongside Cardinal Conway, it must be stressed that the widespread calls for peace within the Catholic community were endorsed by both Bishop Philbin and Bishop Farren in their Easter sermons of that year. In fact both churchmen's calls for peace acknowledged that the suspension of Stormont had altered the political landscape in Northern Ireland. For his part, Bishop Philbin said that 'no one can deny that new opportunities, new signs of life and hope are appearing', while Bishop Farren expressed similar sentiments at greater length:

> I know that all the people here desire peace . . . I know that you do pray that we may have a proper society set up; a society in which there will be justice, harmony and peace. I know you will pray that that will come about; but if there is disorder and a continuation of the state of affairs existing over the past months there may indeed be a stumbling block to proper ending of the trouble that has been ours in the past. (*Derry Journal*, 4 April 1972, p. 1)

At around the same time that these Easter sermons were delivered, the movement for peace in Belfast was given added stimulus when Mrs Martha Crawford was shot dead in crossfire during the course of a gunbattle between the Provisional IRA and the British Army. While local women expressed their anger about the shooting, Cardinal Conway said he had taken 'soundings' within the Catholic community and indicated that the people wanted the IRA to end its military campaign. When questioned about whether he was asking Catholics to put their trust in William Whitelaw, the then Secretary of State for Northern Ireland, the Cardinal said he was not but went on in this manner: 'In a sense there is no need for me to ask the Catholic people to have these views. I am quite certain that they have them already. I am simply articulating the *vox populi* which is already there.' (*Irish Times*, 3 April 1972, pp. 1 and 7) Whatever else can be said about the Andersonstown Peace Committee, it was largely a local and pro-nationalist movement. During the course of a statement which it issued on the political situation it clearly accepted the views of the Cardinal and the SDLP: 'We fully support the stand taken by our elected representatives in the SDLP and that of Cardinal Conway in calling for an immediate end to violence.' (*Irish Times*, 3 April 1972)

The problem of mobilising such a peace group in Andersonstown, however, was clearly underlined only the following day when a peace meeting was broken up by women supporters of the Provisional IRA. Such *apparent* republican strength in the ghettos, however, did not allay the fear felt by many Provisionals that the peace initiatives could affect their campaign. Certainly, the then President of Sinn Fein, Ruairi O'Bradaigh, felt it necessary to launch a blistering attack on Cardinal Conway's peace initiatives: 'In his excursion into politics, all the influence he can command is being thrown behind direct rule, just as his predecessors had urged successfully the acceptance of the disastrous treaty of surrender in 1921.' (*Irish Times*, 3 April 1972) Underlying O'Bradaigh's statement, of course, was his fear that like the Anglo–Irish Treaty of 1921, direct rule could come to be regarded by many people as an end in itself, and that the hierarchy could contribute to the acceptance of such a notion.

Only days later, the views of the lower clergy in areas of Belfast most affected by the troubles were presented to republicans. No fewer than thirty priests released a statement about the political situation which was read at all Masses in their parishes. An interesting passage from their statement read as follows:

> There are two possibilities—a continuation of armed conflict, or a cessation of it followed by political action, discussion, negotiation. The choice has to be made by the whole people and it has to be made without delay. We feel that the choice must be for a cessation of armed conflict on all sides and the use of peaceful methods. To ask for this is not to ask people to give up their political ideas; it is to say there is

a way to achieve them which does not involve continuing bloodshed and to invite them to examine it. (*Irish Times*, 10 April 1972)

By asking the IRA to pursue its objectives in a non-violent way these clerics demonstrated considerable political insight. Certainly, by stating that the choice between continued conflict or peace had 'to be made by the whole people', the priests were demanding (at least implicitly) a democratic form of decision-making within the ghettos, a feature of life that had been absent since August 1969, and arguably since the establishment of Northern Ireland itself. More than anything else, however, this statement was a clear attempt to speak on behalf of the Catholic community and, in its timing, to present a challenge to the Provisional IRA.[48]

Despite the continuation of republican violence in Belfast, then, the impact of these peace initiatives should not be dismissed. After months of virtual paramilitary control, especially in parts of the west of the city, the violent tactics of the IRA were being challenged by members of the community and the Church was in the forefront of that challenge.[49] In Derry, too, local priests issued a statement calling for an end to violence. This statement, however, differed from that of the Belfast priests in two ways. First, unlike the signatories to the Belfast statement who worked in the most troubled parts of their city, the Derry statement was issued by all the priests ministering in the five Derry City parishes and those on the teaching staff of St Columb's College. Second, but more importantly, the brief statement of the Derry priests was not really addressed to local republicans at all, but was instead, addressed to the community in general: 'we commend to our people for their support those in the community working for an immediate cessation of hostilities, in order that negotiations for a just peace be begun'. Indeed, implicit in this sentence was the desire of clergy in Derry to by-pass local republicans in the proposed negotiations for a 'just peace'.

When Catholics circulated peace petitions in Derry and Belfast, local clergy demonstrated their support, albeit in different ways. In Derry, a group calling itself the Creggan Men's

Committee claimed that 70 per cent of the adult population of Derry's 'west bank' signed the petition for peace. Significantly, various Catholic schools in the area had been used for this purpose. At around the same time in West Belfast, a peace pledge was circulated by a group of local Catholics. Parish Priests in the area stressed that while the campaign was not organised by them, it did receive their support. Significantly, not only were signatures to the peace pledge gathered outside Catholic churches, but among those who appeared at a subsequent press-conference to discuss these activities was Fr Padraig Murphy, Parish Priest of St John's. (*Irish Times*, 2 June 1972)

In contrast to west Belfast where, as we have already seen, it was extremely difficult to stage any peace protest, Derry was the scene of large peace-meetings. The immediate stimulus for these meetings was the killing of a local man, William Best, a member of the British Army, who had come home to visit his parents, was kidnapped, interrogated and killed by the Official IRA. Quite spontaneously, local women marched to IRA premises to protest about the killing and then proceeded to hurl abuse at republicans. The next night, as reported in the *Irish Times*, 24 May 1972, a hastily-arranged peace rally attended by over 2,000 people broke up in disorder after a senior officer in the Official IRA was refused the right to speak through the microphone. (Among those who were allowed to address the crowd were two local priests, Fr Hugh O'Neill and Fr Martin Rooney.)

Republicans in Derry had been put on the defensive for the first time since the beginning of the troubles. So much so, in fact, that when the 'peace women' decided to hold a rally in the city, a republican meeting was held at the same time in another part of town. According to estimates at the time, both meetings attracted similar crowds: the republican rally, which had for its slogan, 'peace with justice', attracted over 4,000 people, while the 'assembly of intercession for peace' drew a crowd of around 5,000. Clerics were prominent at the non-republican rally where one local priest, Fr Anthony Mulvey, delivered a lengthy address on the subject of a just peace.[50] On the same day, the leaders of the four main Churches in Ireland issued a joint statement in which they urged an end to violence. The timing of the inter-Church message was propitious—the following day, the Official IRA declared a ceasefire and admitted (in a subsequent statement issued by Sinn Fein in Gardiner Place) that 'the overwhelming desire of the great majority of all the people of the North is an end to military actions by all sides'. According to Barry White, at least, it was this Catholic reaction to the killing of William Best which led the Official IRA to lay down its arms. For Eamonn McCann, on the other hand, the Church had used the political conditions of this period to attack the IRA from the pulpit in a 'co-ordinated series of speeches'. One way or another, events in Derry more than anywhere else in the North, demonstrated the great desire for an end to military action. Equally, there can be no doubt about the significant part played by the clergy in the overall movement for peace in that city.

Naturally enough, after the decision of the Official IRA to declare a ceasefire, the Provisionals came under intense pressure to follow the same course. And, despite continued rejections of such a suggestion, the Provisional IRA did call a ceasefire a few weeks later.[51] As events unfolded, however, the ceasefire was to break down within fourteen days after a major confrontation occurred between loyalists, nationalists and the British Army in the Lenadoon area of West Belfast.[52]

Of course, in order to put these peace efforts into perspective, it is necessary to consider the perceptions and motivations of the groups involved in the Northern Ireland conflict. When this is done it can be argued that there were four main factors, distinct though closely related, which were inimical to a cessation of the Provisionals' military campaign. First, neither the imposition of direct rule nor the widespread yearning for peace among a war-weary people could obscure the profound ideological and tactical differences which existed between the two wings of the IRA. While many people took the decision of the Official IRA to call a ceasefire as a good omen, it must be stressed that because of their Marxist ideology, the Officials did not see the conflict in the more narrow nationalist terms of the Provisionals. Moreover, as a consequence of being more politically sophisticated, the Officials had been more uneasy about their military campaign than the Provisionals had been about theirs. Second, the long-term demands of the Provisional IRA were seen by the British Government as impossible to grant: a declaration by the

British that they would recognise the right to self-determination for Irish people, North and South; a declaration of intention on the part of the British to withdraw all troops from Northern Ireland within three years; and an amnesty for all political prisoners.[53] (Significantly, the short-lived ceasefire involved none of these issues directly but was called because of agreement over several short-term demands, including the granting of special category status to Provisional IRA prisoners.)[54] Third, when it was learned that the Provisionals had talked with representatives of the British Government, loyalists viewed this development as the ultimate act of betrayal by the British. So, while there had been a few instances of Catholics being assassinated by loyalist militants in earlier months, it was from July 1972 that a dramatic escalation of the campaign took place. Dillon and Lehane, in *Political Murder in Northern Ireland*, pp. 37–38, describe loyalist thinking as follows:

> The militant Protestants were ready to hit back. They had, as they saw it, been extremely patient under the most extreme provocation, but the suspension of Stormont in March, 1972, followed by the truce negotiated by the British government with the IRA in June were the last straws. The backlash emerged.

In the light of this loyalist campaign, it became even more difficult to promote the idea of a Provisional IRA ceasefire. After all, the Provisionals had largely emerged as a result of loyalist violence in 1969, and regardless of how much distaste there was for their methods, there was an underlying belief that the Provisionals could become the last line of defence in a deteriorating situation. Finally, in spite of widespread opposition to the Provisionals' campaign during this period, it soon became obvious that they had a sufficient level of support for a continuation of their campaign; certainly, apart from the period of the 14-day ceasefire the Provisional campaign lost no momentum.[55]

Moreover, beyond the immediate period of March–July 1972, prospects for a cessation of the Provisional IRA campaign became increasingly remote. In purely military terms, for instance, the Provisionals had never been stronger than during the period of the no-go areas, and when these areas in Derry were eventually regained on 31 July 1972,[56] the situation was even less conducive to the cessation of the IRA campaign than before. Certainly, if the Provisionals and the British Government could not negotiate a sustained ceasefire at a time of optimal Provisional strength, the Provisionals could hardly hope to get *better* terms at a time when they found themselves in a weaker negotiating position. This, coupled with the fact that the peace-movements which had arisen between March and July 1972 had disappeared into oblivion, underlined how difficult it was to sustain the momentum and morale of these groups against an unfavourable background of continued conflict. Moreover, following the breakdown of the Provisional IRA ceasefire, the British Government embarked on a policy of encouraging agreement between constitutional nationalists and Unionists in Northern Ireland. The fact that such an approach *excluded* the Provisionals from the negotiating table rendered it even more unlikely that the Provos would end their campaign.

Continued violence apart, the Catholic Church was not part of the political reconstruction that was attempted by holding negotiations between the British Government, constitutional nationalists and Unionists. For the moment, therefore, it was left with only one obvious approach: the moral authority to denounce violence in Northern Ireland. In the absence of a political solution, however, such denunciations seemed to ring hollow.

Nevertheless when the British Government's White Paper on Northern Ireland was released in March 1973 (see *Irish News*, 26 March), the Catholic Church gave the document its tentative approval. Cardinal Conway commented:

> Proposals have been put forward during the past week which could open a path to reconciliation and peace and a better life.
>
> The alternative is illustrated by the ghastly murders of three young soldiers and a civilian during the past 36 hours.
>
> There are two paths but unless there is an enormous groundswell of determination in favour of peace from the people themselves we will inevitably drift down the second path.

Implicit in this statement was not only the inability of the Church to prevent the continuation of violence, but the need for people to change their political ways if peace were to be achieved. Indeed, the Cardinal saw acceptance of the White Paper as something of a Hobson's choice: it was not so much that the document was a model of perfection but the consequences of its rejection were horrifying. A statement by the Irish bishops a few days later (see *Irish Independent*, 29 March 1973) re-echoed the Primate's position: 'Just now the course of events has entered on a new significant phase. We profoundly hope that recent proposals will be implemented in a way that will bring about true reconciliation in justice and peace and we ask the people of Ireland to pray to this end.'*

In primarily political terms, the principles outlined in the White Paper were translated into reality through the formation of the Northern Ireland Executive in November 1973. From the non-Unionist point of view the agreement's major strengths were not only the existence of a power-sharing Executive between members of the SDLP, Faulkner Unionists and the Alliance Party, but proposals for a Council of Ireland which was designed (in the jargon of the White Paper) to satisfy the so-called 'Irish dimension'. For its part, the hierarchy was not slow to give the accord strong support and Cardinal Conway spoke of the Executive in these terms:

> This is only the beginning, but it is a good beginning, and one prays that it may grow firm and strong and so help to bring peace and justice to this long suffering community.
>
> Those who are taking part in what is an historic initiative are deserving of every encouragement. (*Irish News*, 24 November 1973)

Several hierarchical statements of support for the Northern Ireland Executive followed: in one twenty-four hour period alone, Cardinal Conway, Bishop Philbin of Down and Connor, and Bishop Cahal Daly of Ardagh and Clonmacnoise, all voiced their support for the new body.

* Support for the principles contained in the White Paper came from the Vatican in the form of the Pope's Easter message a month later.
Source: *Irish News*, 23 April 1973, p. 1

It was in this context that several bishops renewed their call for an end to IRA violence. In Easter sermons of that year, for instance, Bishop Edward Daly called for a ceasefire, Bishop Philbin bitterly condemned 'violent men', while Cardinal Conway called on people to choose the path of peace. Shortly afterwards, one member of the hierarchy even went further — Dr Daly of Derry formulated a local peace plan which involved the following proposals: the call for an indefinite IRA ceasefire; the phased release of all Derry internees and the gradual withdrawal of British troops to their barracks. Beyond such immediate preconditions for peace, Bishop Daly also believed that vandalism in the community and the question of policing would, quite naturally, remain difficult but 'could be much more satisfactorily worked out in an atmosphere of peace and tranquillity'. The political importance of this peace plan was considerable. For one thing, it came close to the thinking of Provisional Sinn Fein and this was admitted by its then Vice-President, Máire Drumm.[57] The crucial weakness of this plan, as the IRA would have seen it, however, lay in its failure to address the most important of the republican demands: an acknowledgment by the British Government concerning the right of the Irish people to control their own destiny. In any event, the failure of such a peace plan should not be attributed to any of its intrinsic weaknesses, but rather to the policies adopted by the protagonists.

In fact, within a matter of weeks, the collapse of the Northern Ireland Executive[58] undermined whatever possible basis there had been for optimism among advocates of non-violent political change in Northern Ireland. While the continued campaign of the Provisionals had posed a constant threat to the viability of the Executive, the loyalist strike of May 1974 served as the *coup de grâce* for the power-sharing government. In effect, then, the loyalist community had vetoed the whole experiment and handed (ironically) the political initiative back to the IRA within the Catholic community.

Despite or perhaps because of the lack of favourable conditions for peace in Northern Ireland, the Churches increased their activities during the period 1974–1975. Several inter-religious peace rallies were organised in which clergymen of all denominations attended. This growing co-operation between the Churches was given expression in the Derry area when every available priest and minister met to discuss the whole question of Christian leadership in the community. With the obvious support of the Churches, moreover, a group calling itself People Together launched a peace petition towards the end of October 1974. The *Irish News*, 12 September 1974, described these activities in the following terms:

> Petition forms were passed along the seats at some churches for signature during Mass. They are to be made available in secondary schools throughout Northern Ireland during the coming week. The lower age group for signing is 14 . . . The aim of the organisers is to get 1,000,000 signatures of Northern Ireland citizens* . . . it looked as if the target could be met.

Sometime after this, it was announced by the leaders of the four main Churches that they had decided to launch a peace campaign. The Churches not only inserted a page-long advertisement in the local newspapers of 12 December 1974, but later that evening the church leaders prayed together on the Ulster Television programme *What's It All About*. More unexpected and potentially more effective, however, was the revelation that a number of Protestant clergymen had travelled to Feakle, County Clare, where they had met members of Provisional Sinn Fein for peace talks.[59] In the light of all these activities, it is hardly surprising that the movement for peace gained momentum once again. Prayers were said by hundreds of thousands in an estimated 4,000 churches and meeting halls throughout Ireland. (In Northern Ireland alone, it was estimated that one third of the entire population had participated in this exercise.)

After the Provisional IRA called a truce for the Christmas period, the Church leaders made repeated calls for an extension. The status of the Churches' peace campaign, moreover, was clearly enhanced when their leaders flew to London to meet the

* The petition eventually gained 130,000 signatures.
Source: *Irish News*, 22 April 1975

then Prime Minister, Harold Wilson, Secretary of State for Northern Ireland, Merlyn Rees, and his Minister of State, Stan Orme. In their meeting, which lasted two and a half hours, the churchmen claimed that there were now more grounds for hope of peace in Northern Ireland than there had been for some time. Unfortunately, though, the British Government was still uncertain as to the overall direction of its policy. As Merlyn Rees admitted in the House of Commons on 11 February 1975, 'there is no ready-made or well defined path ahead'.[60] In any case when the Provisionals renewed their truce at the beginning of 1975, the escalation in the loyalist campaign of violence which was overwhelmingly directed at Catholics had the effect yet again of endangering the IRA ceasefire.

Despite the best efforts of the Churches, therefore, their peace campaign and related activities had had no lasting, *tangible* effect. Although the Church leaders described themselves as 'more hopeful' at the end of 1975 than they had been at the beginning of the year, such a view seemed wildly optimistic. Certainly, Pope Paul VI did not share this feeling, but instead, spoke of his 'anguish' over the violence in Ireland (see *Irish News*, 2 January 1976). In truth, then, the attainment of a peaceful solution was as far away as ever: in the absence of any political agreement between the nationalist and Unionist blocs, together with an IRA truce that disintegrated against the background of a large-scale loyalist campaign, it was difficult to be hopeful about the future.

Yet the campaign of the peace people which started in August 1976 became the most famous of all the Northern Ireland peace movements. And in one crucial respect it differed from many other similar groups by distancing itself from the Churches. Thus in a pamphlet entitled *The Price of Peace*, Ciaran McKeown, on p. 10, pointed to what he saw as the failure of the Churches to provide a real Christian lead in Northern Ireland: 'The urgings, condemnings, sympathisings and non-condonings with which leading churchmen responded to the deteriorating situation were frustratingly redolent of a general establishment response.' Ironically, despite such criticism of the main Churches the peace movement had had authentic Catholic origins. In demonstrating their disgust at the deaths of the Maguire children,* for instance, the movement's first members had walked through parts of Andersonstown reciting prayers and singing hymns. Some of the women also asked a local priest, Fr Malachy Murphy, to recite the rosary at the spot where the children had died and Murphy agreed to do so.

The quintessentially Catholic origins of the peace group were quickly obscured, however, as it almost immediately became a mass-movement throughout Northern Ireland. If anything, this change in identity was facilitated by the way in which the Catholic hierarchy distanced itself from the peace people. Although the peace campaign had begun on 11 August, only hours after the deaths of the children, it was not until the beginning of September that the bishops publicly commented on the subject. The significance of such silence is pointed up by the almost blanket media coverage enjoyed by the peace people at this time. For example, in seventeen printing days between 12 August and the end of that month, the *Irish News* devoted twelve editorial pieces, seven of which dealt *exclusively* with the peace people. By contrast, the bishops' silence was only broken with a low-key statement from the Republic of Ireland based Bishop Cahal Daly† which appeared in the Australian *Morning Herald*. The following day in Derry, Bishop Edward Daly and his Church of Ireland counterpart, Dr Robin Eames, said they would be supporting the peace rally that was due to take place in their city. At other venues throughout Northern Ireland, large peace rallies were soon to be held at which members of the hierarchy were in attendance.[61] This hierarchical aloofness was also reflected by a statement of the Irish bishops on the peace people. For apart from praising the 'courage' of the peace women and pointing to 'the horrible crimes of ruthless men and women', the statement failed to offer support of a more tangible kind. The reason for such aloofness was that the hierarchy believed any greater involvement would have proven counter-productive. In speaking about peace movements in 1977, the Irish Catholic Bishops' Conference, as reported in the *Irish*

---

* The incident which gave rise to the movement. The children were killed by a car being driven by members of the IRA that had gone out of control after it had come under fire by the British Army.

† In 1982 Cahal Daly was appointed Bishop to the diocese of Down and Connor.

Times, 13 May, p. 8, said that a movement which sprang from the people and had noble and Christian objectives should be unequivocally supported by the Churches while keeping in mind the political facts of life: 'Such support should never be seen as a takeover bid. The presence of church leaders at rallies could be misconstrued by people with less than noble intentions.'

Of course the major problem for the peace people was *how* peace in Northern Ireland could be achieved: it was impossible for the peace people to sustain themselves as a mass-movement for the simple reason that any stand on public life in Northern Ireland tended to alienate some section of their support. Moreover, the peace people owed their existence more to emotionalism than anything else, and in a short time, the movement shrank. So much so, in fact, that in *Christians in Ulster*, p. 179, according to Gallagher and Worrall 'long before the two leaders received their Nobel award,* the movement had lost its impetus'.

If these activities tended to obscure the thinking of the Catholic hierarchy on the political future of Northern Ireland, their position was clarified by a statement in May 1977. The statement, which was issued under the auspices of the Irish Catholic Bishops' Conference, and reported in the *Irish News*, 13 May, p. 1, strongly supported the principle of 'shared responsibility' for government in the North. Recommending that all leaders and members of the Churches should publicly encourage such a course, at least for a specified period, the bishops asserted that 'no individual likes to be considered unfit to share in government. When this is extended to a whole community, it causes widespread resentment'.

After three years of a political vacuum in Northern Ireland, the Catholic hierarchy was prescribing a way forward that involved the most important element of the Sunningdale Agreement, that of power-sharing. While the emotive term 'power-sharing' was dropped from their political vocabulary, the bishops had, moreover, moved away from the 1974 agreement in two crucial respects. First, by not mentioning the 'Irish

* The two leaders of the peace people, Mairead Corrigan and Betty Williams, were awarded the Nobel Peace Prize in 1977.

dimension' in any form, the statement had avoided what was and is the greatest fear of Unionists: involvement of Dublin in any aspect of government for Northern Ireland. Second, by calling for shared responsibility in government *at least for a specified limited period*, the hierarchy was emphasising that such a government would not have the appearance of a permanent structure unlike the Northern Ireland Executive which had existed under the terms of the Sunningdale accord.

While such a call may be criticised in theory for weakening the position of constitutional nationalists in the North, it was designed (in practice) to strengthen their position. After all, not only had the loyalists applied a veto to the power-sharing Executive of 1974 but their position had been reinforced by the fact that the emphasis in British policy had shifted from implementing the Sunningdale accord to encouraging local politicians to reach agreement among themselves. When seen in this context, therefore, the bishops' position was at least clear — one which was in sharp contrast to that of the SDLP which was unsure of the best way forward.[62] Thus, one commentator described the SDLP's 1977 policy document, *Facing Reality*, as follows: 'It is amorphous to the point of caricature but has been cleverly prepared so that it satisfies the somewhat differing aspirations of the party factions.' (*Hibernia*, 4 November 1977, p. 5)

Within a year, the direction of the SDLP was to be more clearly defined when a majority of delegates at its annual party conference of 1978 accepted a motion calling for British with-drawal from Northern Ireland. In the words of Ian McAllister: 'The party mainstay, institutionalised power-sharing died on 28 May 1974, when the Executive resigned. Only recently have many in the party grasped the fact that power-sharing will not be resurrected.' What is more, McAllister identified three de-cisive factors regarding this change in policy: (i) internal party pressures; (ii) the formation of the Irish Independence Party in 1977 (formed by four members of the SDLP who wanted more nationalist policies and which posed a certain electoral threat to the SDLP); (iii) the fact that opinion poll evidence from Britain showed that a majority of people there had consistently favoured British withdrawal since June 1974.

While all of these factors were important, I would contend that such an interpretation is inadequate since it overlooks three other significant developments. First, there was a statement by the Taoiseach, Jack Lynch, who had spoken of encouraging British withdrawal from Northern Ireland. Second, an interview was given by the Archbishop of Armagh, Tomas O'Fiaich, in which he said he believed that the British ought to declare their intent to withdraw from the North. Finally, a discernible shift occurred in the editorial policy of the sole nationalist daily newspaper in the North, the *Irish News*, which involved an effective repudiation of power-sharing as a viable political option.

For our purpose, of course, the effect of Archbishop O'Fiaich's interview on nationalist thinking is of primary interest. In putting the importance of his contribution into perspective, however, it is necessary to discuss this in terms of the other two influences listed above. Within the first two weeks of January 1978, the statements of first Jack Lynch, and then Tomas O'Fiaich, had been taken on board by the editorial column of the *Irish News*. Remarkably enough, the last *Irish News* editorial of 1977 had, in the course of a discussion on political progress in Northern Ireland, dwelt entirely on the notion of devolution. By supporting the statements of Lynch and O'Fiaich only a few weeks later, the *Irish News* had, in effect, helped to jettison the notion of power-sharing as a realistic option for the future. So much so, that the editorial of 7 April 1978 had effectively thrown down the gauntlet to the SDLP: 'It is becoming painfully obvious that the belief that the only hope for a devolved government in the North is an agreement to share power is due for demolition . . . Now evidently is the time for everybody in the party [SDLP] to take a hard look at the uncomfortably cold facts.'

With regard to the essence of the O'Fiaich interview, its most controversial part was the Archbishop's response to the question about whether he favoured British withdrawal from Northern Ireland. O'Fiaich said:

I think the British should withdraw from Ireland. I believe in a declaration of intent. I know it's a coloured phrase but I think it's the only thing which will get things moving. I regret that it didn't happen after the collapse of Stormont. There were Protestants looking around in frustration for a friendly hand to grasp and a declaration, coupled with sincere gestures from the South, would have done good. I don't see any long-term solution for the Northern Ireland problem save in an all-Ireland context. We are only putting off the day.[63]

However difficult to quantify, these words must have had a considerable impact on the political consciousness of constitutional nationalists. Certainly, the timing of such an interview was extremely important as it came when constitutional nationalism was clearly looking for a positive direction. Ironically, however, I would argue that loyalist criticism of the Archbishop increased the acceptability of his ideas among many Catholics insofar as *any* loyalist criticism of a Catholic Archbishop was bound to reinforce a kind of communal solidarity among many ordinary Catholics. Even more important, however, was the fact that Unionist criticism was often so cumbersome that it only made a counter-productive exercise worse. A fine example of this was the statement by a spokesman of the Official Unionists in which he said the Archbishop's statement had shown that 'the Roman Catholic Church and the Eire Government were carefully in step regarding policy and statements on the tiresome claims of a foreign state'. What this statement overlooked, of course, was that Tomas O'Fiaich had said that he would not dream of using his ecclesiastical position to promote nationalism, though he would not abandon his personal views. Whether one accepts the Archbishop's reasoning or not, the Unionist statement with its conspiratorial overtones, only served to concentrate attention on the Archbishop's views on British withdrawal. Moreover, by equating the position of the Archbishop of Armagh with that of the Roman Catholic Church *in toto*, the Unionist statement only created more confusion in people's minds as to the *status* of O'Fiaich's statement due to the fact that each Roman Catholic bishop has a considerable degree of ecclesiastical autonomy,[64] something not widely grasped by many nationalists let alone unionists. For many nationalists, then, the fact that it was the Archbishop of Armagh (later a Cardinal) who had said these things implied that this was the 'position' of the Catholic Church.

In party political terms throughout Ireland, nationalism was beginning to define itself in stronger terms during the late 1970s. Not only had the SDLP changed its policy from one of seeking power-sharing to the call for British withdrawal from Northern Ireland but Fine Gael also jettisoned power-sharing as its official policy in favour of a condominium form of government for Northern Ireland.[65] Moreover, Tim Pat Coogan, in *On the Blanket*, p. 186, has even claimed that the resignation of Jack Lynch as Taoiseach and leader of Fianna Fail in late 1979 occurred 'largely because of opposition that centred around his Northern policies'. (Certainly, Lynch's successor, Charles Haughey, proceeded to espouse a more nationalist line.) (See, for example, *Irish Times*, 8 December 1979, pp. 1 and 5.)

For the Church itself, the position of Tomas O'Fiaich represented a watershed: since 1968 the Catholic hierarchy had merely advocated *reform* of the Northern State. By contrast, Archbishop O'Fiaich now called for a declaration of intent to withdraw from Northern Ireland. Moreover, a lasting consequence of Archbishop O'Fiaich's *Irish Press* interview was to render it impossible during the remainder of the period under examination for the hierarchy to *collectively* prescribe a way ahead for the political life of Northern Ireland. Indeed, far from prescribing a way forward for Northern Ireland, collective statements by the Catholic hierarchy in the future would be politically vague. A fine illustration of this was the pastoral issued shortly after the visit to Ireland of Pope John Paul II in 1979, which included, *inter alia*, the following: 'May all those to whom the Pope spoke, listen, reflect and act. May the paramilitary leaders, the politicians, the governments, those responsible for law and order, the people of the Catholic community, the people of the Protestant community, may they seize this opportunity, which the Pope's visit has given us, to work for peace with consent, with honour and with justice.'

If anything, the position of those advocating peaceful political change in Northern Ireland was rendered even more difficult by the events of the early 1980s. Certainly, the hunger-strikes of

1981 and the emergence of Sinn Fein as a major electoral force shortly thereafter* were hardly conducive to agreement within Northern Ireland. It was against such an unfavourable political background that the leader of the SDLP, John Hume, emerged as the prime mover in an attempt to organise an all-Ireland body which would attempt to produce a blueprint for a 'new Ireland'.[66] Thus, when the New Ireland Forum Report was eventually completed in May 1984, it described its purpose in the following terms: 'The New Ireland Forum was established for consultations on the manner in which lasting peace and stability could be achieved in a New Ireland through the democratic process and to report on possible new structures and processes through which this objective might be achieved.[67]

Before finalising its report, of course, the New Ireland Forum received written and oral submissions from a variety of interested groups and individuals. Among the most significant contributions to the Forum were those of the Catholic Church: a written submission from the Irish Episcopal Conference in January 1984,[68] and an oral presentation of the Irish Episcopal Conference Delegation a month later.[69] Perhaps it is sufficient to outline the nature of these two submissions† and consider how these contributions were perceived at the time.

To begin with, then, it should be explained that the written submission to the Forum from the Irish Episcopal Conference was a 32-page document containing five papers which addressed the questions of ecumenism, family, pluralism, alienation of Northern Catholics and the Catholic school system in Northern Ireland. The oral submission was made by the Irish Episcopal Conference Delegation which consisted of seven members, including three bishops and an auxiliary bishop.††

It was widely perceived on both sides of the border that the oral submission was more constructive than the written one. Thus, *The Church of Ireland Gazette* referred to the bishops'

---

* The Church's response to these developments will be considered at length in chapter 4.
† Key aspects of these Church submissions to the New Ireland Forum are analysed in chapter 5.
†† Members of this delegation were: Bishop Cahal Daly; Bishop Edward Daly; Bishop Joseph Cassidy; Auxiliary Bishop Dermot O'Mahony; Rev Dr Michael Ledwith; Mr Matthew Salter; Professor Mary McAleese.

written submission as being 'bound to harden the attitude of people reared to believe in the validity of private judgment'. According to the *Irish Times*, moreover, the written submission was seen 'by members of the Forum as damaging the prospects of reaching a broad accommodation with Unionists'. A *Fortnight* editorial (February 1984, no. 201, p. 3) went so far as to ask whether the bishops' submission would be the death-knell of the Forum. For his part, Barry White wrote that 'liberal commentators were disappointed or outraged by the submission's defensive, divisive tone, and Protestant politicians gladly seized on it as proof of the unchanging nature of the Irish Catholic Church with its clear commitment to majority rule'. By contrast, the same author considered the oral submission 'an impressive performance' which had put 'the Forum back on course'.[70] Similarly, the *Irish Times*, 10 February 1984, p. 1, claimed that the oral submission had helped to undo the bad feelings surrounding the written submission of the hierarchy and had opened up a new dialogue. Even an editorial in the *Belfast Telegraph** felt that the oral submission reflected a change in Church attitudes. (While the *Belfast Telegraph*, 10 February 1984, p. 1, still expressed reservations about the oral submission, it believed that this submission implied that the Episcopal Conference's written submission had been too strict on its interpretation of current Church doctrine.)

It is precisely because of these conflicting perceptions that it is impossible to objectively conclude whether or not the submissions of the Catholic hierarchy helped to promote or damage the broad objectives of the Forum as outlined in the New Ireland Forum Report. Ultimately, of course, the answer rests on a whole range of presuppositions concerning the *effect* of Catholic Church policy, and especially on two broad considerations: (i) whether the continued policy of the Catholic Church in the relevant areas is necessarily dysfunctional to the stated aims of the New Ireland Forum; (ii) how, if at all, any substantial changes in Church law and/or in the Republic's civil law might alter the attitudes of people in Ireland as a whole, not least those held by Ulster Unionists.

* While the *Belfast Telegraph* supports the union with Great Britain, it does not explicitly align itself with any political party.

When the Report of the New Ireland Forum was eventually completed in May 1984, it stated in chapter 5.7, p. 29 that while 'the particular structure of political unity which the Forum would wish to see is a unitary state', it went on to discuss a federal/confederal state or joint authority (chapters 7–8, pp. 34–38). Significantly enough, however, the report did not rule out other political possibilities: 'the parties in the Forum also remain open to discuss other views which may contribute to political development'.[71]

When the British response to the New Ireland Forum Report became known, it angered and outraged Irish nationalists. At a press-conference following her summit meeting with the Taoiseach, Garret FitzGerald, the Prime Minister, Margaret Thatcher, ruled out the possibility of her government adopting any of the three possible models outlined in the Forum Report. Not surprisingly, such comments created a great strain on Anglo–Irish relations, with FitzGerald later describing Thatcher's comments as 'insulting'.

It was in this context that the Northern bishops clearly indicated their concern by condemning the British response and calling for a new political initiative in Northern Ireland. Speaking in London only days after the Anglo–Irish summit, Bishop Cahal Daly said that constitutional nationalism had received a humiliating setback in the wake of the summit and that alienation among nationalists was now turning to anger and despair. A measure of the hierarchy's deep anxiety about the political situation in Northern Ireland was their decision to meet the then Secretary of State for Northern Ireland, Douglas Hurd. The bishops' delegation, which included the Cardinal, the bishops of Down and Connor, Derry, Dromore and three auxiliary bishops, spent one and a half hours with Mr Hurd, and although the churchmen decided not to make any comment on their meeting, it was believed that it had a far-ranging nature and involved discussion of the Anglo–Irish summit.

In analysing the Church's calls for a political initiative during 1985 a discernible pattern emerges: most of the bishops' statements were issued early in the year. It is a moot point whether this is attributable to speculation at the end of March that Mrs Thatcher was giving consideration to a settlement with the Irish

Government, or to the scathing criticism made by some Unionists and Protestant churchmen on the Catholic bishops' statements,[72] or indeed to the combined effect of all these developments. Whatever the reason, the Irish bishops did become less
vocal on the subject after March, but none of this is to suggest
that there was a change in their overall position. This was
implicitly underlined by the direct appeal made by Pope John
Paul II in June when he called on the British Government to
reach a fresh political solution in Northern Ireland.[73] It is surely
inconceivable that such a direct move by the Vatican would have
been made without the approval of the Irish hierarchy. Moreover, its intended effect could have only been to strengthen the
position of the Irish Government in the Anglo–Irish talks that
were then taking place (*Irish Independent*, 11 June 1985, pp. 1 and
2).

An important consequence of the various statements of
Catholic bishops in early 1985, was that they proved to be the
clearest indicator of hierarchical thinking on the Northern
Ireland situation since 1977 when the Irish bishops had, for the
last time during the period of this study, *collectively* prescribed a
political way forward for Northern Ireland. On the basis of
statements made in the first half of March 1985, the 'political'
positions of four of the six Northern bishops are clearly discernible. Only the positions of two bishops remained unclear: the
bishop of Dromore, Dr Brooks, and Dr McKiernan of Kilmore
(whose diocese only has three priests resident within Northern
Ireland).*

Indeed it is possible to identify two broad schools of thought
among the other four bishops of the Northern dioceses. For his
part, the Cardinal was well known for his anti-partitionist
views, especially since his interview with the *Irish Press* in 1978.
It was hardly surprising, therefore, when Cardinal O'Fiaich said
that he saw unity as inevitable, and a week later that he expressed the belief that British withdrawal could be carried out
successfully. What was surprising, however, was the similarly
anti-partitionist statement by Bishop Duffy of Clogher. What
made his statement so surprising was the apparent lack of

* See Irish Catholic Directory, 1985, Dublin: Associated Catholic Newspapers
Ltd, 1985, pp. 82–84.

continuity between what he had said about the future of Northern Ireland in 1982 and 1985. Thus, in a talk which he gave in spring 1982, Bishop Duffy had said that: 'What we need is a change of attitudes which will in time produce the structures or at least allow them to emerge. Attitudes rather than structures are the primary business of the churches.'[74] Yet, in 1985, Bishop Duffy called partition unjust and said that its injustice was not so much that it was imposed against the wishes of the Irish people, as that it simply did not work. He went on to comment that 'we are trapped in a political system which is crying out for radical reform—the matter is one of extreme urgency' (*Irish Times*, 11 March 1985, p. 7).

While these statements of Cardinal O'Fiaich and Bishop Duffy in March 1985 prescribed Irish reunification of some kind as the best way ahead, Bishop Cahal Daly of Down and Connor and Bishop Edward Daly of Derry did not prescribe a specific political model at all. Instead, both men spoke in different ways about creating structures acceptable to both communities in Northern Ireland. Re-echoing what he had said for more than ten years about the political future of Northern Ireland,[75] Bishop Cahal Daly claimed that:

> There can be no imposed unity within Northern Ireland, within Northern Ireland as it now stands . . . In both cases we have the need for consent. Consent requires persuasion. It requires dialogue. It requires assent; assent to structures which command the respect of both traditions and which give rightful expression to the two identities. That is our basic problem.

Inherent in the above passage is the necessary equality of citizenship for both communities in Northern Ireland, a theme which was more explicit in a statement by Bishop Edward Daly. Although the Bishop of Derry did not specifically speak of political structures *per se*, his emphasis on equality clearly implied what types of political structures he had in mind. Referring to a lasting solution of the Northern Ireland problem as 'the greatest and most important single challenge facing the people of these islands', Bishop Edward Daly went on to say:

It can only come when all the people in the North are regarded and treated as genuinely equal in that society, whatever their religious affiliation, whatever their political views or aspirations, whatever their social class—when all people living in that society can be treated as equal and gain access to every position in that society (*Irish Times*, 4 March 1985, p. 1).

These, then, were the two broad schools of thought which existed among the hierarchy during the final stages of the inter-governmental talks which eventually led to the signing of the Anglo–Irish Agreement in November 1985.[76] While it is a moot point what effect, if any, the Church activities of early 1985 actually had on British thinking, it must be said that in their statements, the bishops clearly aligned themselves with constitutional nationalists in their desire for some type of new political initiative for Northern Ireland. Indeed, a few days after the signing of the Anglo–Irish Agreement, the Catholic Press Office issued the following statement on behalf of the standing committee of the Episcopal Conference:

Sixteen years of violence have brought much tribulation and heartbreak to both Protestant and Catholic communities in Northern Ireland. There is in both communities in Northern Ireland a great and widespread longing for an end to the troubles. It is our sincere hope that the Anglo–Irish agreement will make a genuine contribution toward reconciliation. We ask our people to continue their prayers for peace (*Irish Times*, 19 November 1985, p. 8).

According to various sources at the time, the bishops had not wanted to issue a statement in favour of the specific proposals because their appeal might be interpreted by Unionists as 'Rome's blessing'. By the same token, they were aware that they should not be seen to ignore the signing of the Anglo–Irish accord. Whatever the bishops' reasoning, one thing was clear from the above statement—they avoided adopting a clear position on the new accord.

Throughout the remainder of the period in question there was little elaboration of the position of individual bishops *vis-à-vis* the accord. In fact, Cardinal O'Fiaich was most forthcoming in this regard when he said in March 1986 that his view of the agreement was the same as that expressed by the bishops' statement quoted above. At the same time, however, he asserted that while the Anglo–Irish accord had a lot of potential for the well-being of Northern Ireland, he accepted that polarisation had probably increased in the community as a result of the agreement. While the Cardinal believed that the accord had served to ease Catholics' sense of alienation, he expressed disappointment at some of the comments made by the Secretary of State, Tom King, who had described the agreement as a bulwark against a united Ireland (*Irish Times*, 31 March 1986, p. 9).

Before bringing this chapter to a close, it is interesting to note that such paradoxical views of the agreement were far from unique within the Church; indeed, not dissimilar perceptions and feelings existed among the ranks of the lower clergy. In my postal questionnaire of April/May 1986, I found that 86.6 per cent of my respondents said that on balance, they approved of the Anglo–Irish Agreement. Despite such an apparently overwhelming endorsement, many priests still had serious reservations about the accord. The respondents had been given a list of five reservations concerning the agreement and were told if they had any such reservations, they could choose more than one possibility if they wished. Thirty-two per cent of priests thought the agreement was 'deficient in satisfying nationalist aspirations', while 16.7 per cent of respondents felt the accord was unfair to Unionists 'as they were not consulted during the course of the negotiations'. Consistent with the nationalistic views of Catholic priests in general was the finding that only 1.8 per cent of respondents objected to the agreement on the basis that it 'undermines the position of Northern Ireland as part of the United Kingdom'. 32.5 per cent of priests felt that the accord would be 'destroyed by loyalists and/or republicans and in the process the Northern Ireland situation will get even worse'. Even this list of specific reservations failed to identify all the reservations which were held by the lower clergy of Northern Ireland towards the Anglo–Irish Agreement: another 19.3 per cent of respondents indicated that their reservations were based on 'none of the above reasons'.

2

A Political Profile of Catholic Priests in Northern Ireland, 1986: a multivariate analysis

THIS CHAPTER provides a political profile of Catholic priests in Northern Ireland which is based on the results of a postal questionnaire conducted in 1986. Except for members of the hierarchy and full-time diocesan administrators, the sample for this questionnaire is all-inclusive. 628 priests have been contacted, of whom 505 are diocesan priests, while the remaining 123 are members of religious orders. 232 valid responses were returned, giving an overall response rate of 36.9 per cent.*

That an overwhelming majority of Roman Catholic priests in Northern Ireland favour Irish unity has been suggested by the results of earlier studies of Northern Ireland clergymen. Fahy found that all the Roman Catholic priests in his sample of ten favoured Irish unity,[1] while Roche, Birrell, Greer found that 85 per cent of their Catholic respondents favoured Irish unity.[2] Birrell and Roche described 89 per cent of their Roman Catholic respondents as 'anti-Unionist' in their political outlook.[3] Not surprisingly, then, 91.4 per cent of respondents to my questionnaire indicate their support for 'the ideal of a united Ireland'. Moreover, this widespread aspiration to Irish unity appears to be shared by the Catholic laity in Northern Ireland. Moxon-Browne, for one, discovered, *inter alia*, that 82.9 per cent of Roman Catholic respondents agreed with the statement that 'a united Ireland is a worthwhile objective, provided it can be achieved by peaceful means'.[4]

Despite the widespread *aspiration* towards Irish unity, table 1 shows how pessimistic most respondents are in this regard.

---

* For a comprehensive treatment of the background to and the methodological details of this questionnaire, see appendix C.

Table 1 (question 10)

Leaving aside your own political viewpoint, do you believe that a united Ireland will come about

within 10 years	9.5%
within 25 years	24.6%
within 50 years	31.5%
within a century	18.1%
a united Ireland is unlikely to ever come about	9.1%
No answer	7.3%

Certainly, the above findings contrast somewhat with those of Moxon-Browne, who found, for instance, that 19.8 per cent of his Roman Catholic respondents believed that the border would disappear* in less than ten years, while 39.9 per cent of Catholics in his study believed that the border would be gone in less than twenty-five years.[5] In other words, while only approximately 34 per cent of my respondents believe there will be Irish unity in less than twenty-five years, Moxon-Browne found that 59.7 per cent of his Catholic respondents felt the border would disappear during the same period.

There are striking differences between the perceptions of respondents in the dioceses of Derry and Dromore. To cite just one example, while 15 per cent of Dromore respondents believe that Irish unity will come about within ten years, *no* Derry respondent expects such a scenario to emerge. The most plausible explanation for these differences is year of ordination. While the average year of ordination among respondents is mid-1960, the corresponding figure for those from the diocese of Derry is the most recent at mid-1963. By contrast, the average year of

---

* Such a comparison is based on the assumption that the overwhelming majority of Catholic respondents would see the disappearance of the border as synonymous with Irish unity.

ordination among respondents in Dromore is the earliest of all the dioceses at mid-1957. Hardly surprisingly, this trend is more broadly reflected by the tendency of priests ordained at an earlier date to be more likely than their colleagues to expect Irish unity to come about within a shorter time-span. Thus, the average date of ordination of those priests who believe Irish unity will come about in less than ten years is approximately mid-1953. The mean average year of ordination for the other categories is as follows: 10–25 years, mid-1956; 25–50 years, early 1962; 50–100 years, mid-1963; a united Ireland is unlikely to ever come about, early 1966. Significantly, this pattern is *completely* consistent with regard to the largest single group of respondents i.e. Catholic curates. Among parish priest respondents, the above pattern emerges for those in the first three categories, while among religious orders this tendency is evident *in all but* the last category i.e. that the most recently ordained group believes that a united Ireland is unlikely to ever come about. Finally, when the overall class backgrounds of respondents* are collapsed into four broad categories, it becomes clear that those of a farming background are most optimistic with regard to when they expect Irish unity to come about. While 47.3 per cent of this group expects Irish unity to occur within twenty-five years, the corresponding figures for the other three groups are as follows: self-employed, 30.8 per cent; middle-class, 31.8 per cent; working class, 36.1 per cent.

Question 11 points out that the new Ireland Forum Report recommends three possible models of government and provides a brief description of each model for the respondent. The question then asks the respondent which, if any, of these three models of government he prefers *in principle*. Question 12 then asks which of these three models is *the most likely to be realised*. Again, one is struck by the respondents' political uncertainty which is reflected by the gulf between their political aspirations and expectations. As table 2 shows, this is particularly

* For the purpose of this questionnaire, social class is defined by the 'social grade classification' in M. Fogarty, L. Ryan, J. Lee, *Irish Values and Attitudes: The Irish Report of the European Value Systems Study*, Dublin: Dominican Publications, 1984, pp. 296–298. This system has had to be adapted for 'farmers' in my study as many of my respondents failed to differentiate between 'large' and 'small' agricultural holdings.

Table 2

		Federal/ confederal state	Joint authority	None of the above	No answer
		Unitary state				
Q.11	preferred model	44.8%	39.7%	10.8%	2.2%	2.6%
Q.12	most likely model	7.8%	44.8%	39.7%	–	7.8%

noticeable in relation to the models of the unitary state and joint authority.

When put into wider perspective, this clear flexibility on the part of clerical respondents towards the institutional form that Irish unity might take is not totally surprising. Half of Fahy's sample indicated a willingness to consider federalism or other less specified forms of unity.[6] Moreover, the priests' attitudes reflect those of 'constitutional nationalist' parties in Ireland which (with the exception of Fianna Fail),[7] clearly accepted at the time of the New Ireland Forum Report that while a unitary state is the *preferred option*, it cannot be regarded as the *only* option.

A major cause of this flexibility on the part of my respondents in this regard is the widely-held perception that the unitary state is the *least attainable* of the three models in question. This trend is apparent even among those who prefer the unitary state in principle, with only 17.5 per cent of this group also believing a unitary state to be the most likely model of unity to be realised. By contrast, of those respondents who favour federalism/ confederalism in principle, 64 per cent believe this same model is the most likely to be realised, while the corresponding figure for those who favour joint authority in principle is 91.3 per cent. Put another way, for the comparatively small number of respondents, 7.8 per cent, who believe that a unitary state is the most likely model for Irish unity, optimism among this group about *when* Irish unity is likely to come about is highest. Thus, while 44.4 per cent of such respondents believe that Irish unity will take place within ten years, the corresponding figures for those who feel federalism/confederalism to be the most likely model of government for a future Ireland is 9 per cent, while this feeling is shared by only 5.9 per cent of those respondents who see joint authority as the most feasible model of the three outlined in the New Ireland Forum Report.

Two background variables are important with regard to respondents' *preferred* model of government in the New Ireland Forum Report, viz. diocese and place of birth. First, diocese is particularly interesting with regard to data from Derry and Clogher/Kilmore.* Only 27.8 per cent of Derry respondents indicate their preference for a unitary state as against an overall average of 44.8 per cent. Moreover, an above-average percentage of Derry respondents opt for federalism/confederalism, (55.6 per cent *vis-à-vis* 39.7 per cent), while similarly, 16.7 per cent of Derry respondents favour joint authority as against an overall average of 10.8 per cent. When it is borne in mind that Derry respondents are the most recently ordained group of participants in this questionnaire (see p. 68), such a finding suggests a general tendency on the part of younger clerics to be less nationalist-orientated than their older colleagues. By contrast, respondents in Clogher favour the unitary state more than their colleagues in other dioceses, with 64.5 per cent of these respondents indicating their preference for this option, a figure which is 19.7 per cent higher than the overall average. Moreover, *none* of the Clogher respondents prefers joint authority, (in contrast to the 10.8 per cent of all respondents who prefer such a model). This relatively nationalist tendency on the part of respondents from Clogher may be attributable to demography. With approximately 75 per cent of the diocesan area Roman Catholic, Clogher has a higher proportion of Catholics than any of the other dioceses in question.† Arguably, then, respondents in Clogher are, in general, less conscious than their colleagues of having to accommodate Protestants in a new Ireland, and consequently, tend to gravitate towards the 'purest' model of

* As there is only a negligible number of Kilmore respondents, the Clogher/ Kilmore group is treated here as Clogher priests.
† This is calculated through reference to the *Irish Catholic Directory 1985*, Dublin Association Catholic Newspapers, pp. 41, 54, 61, 72, 77.

unity, i.e. the unitary state. Second, there is a significant divergence between the preferred models of government of clerical respondents born in Northern Ireland and those born in the Republic of Ireland. Most notably, while 41.1 per cent of Northern-born priests prefer a unitary state, the corresponding figure among Southern-born respondents is 56.6 per cent. Again, a higher percentage of Northern-born respondents prefer the federal/confederal model (49.6 per cent) than do those born in the Republic of Ireland (30.1 per cent). From this evidence, it is plausible to argue that the greater commitment of Southern-born respondents to a unitary state reflects the effect-iveness of traditional anti-partitionist rhetoric which has been a dominant feature of Dublin's response to the 'national question'.

Table 3: (question 13) In the event of a united Ireland coming about

the State ought to legalise divorce	22.8%
the Irish bishops ought to liberalise their position on mixed marriages	9.9%
both changes ought to occur	17.7%
neither change should occur	36.6%
no opinion	6.0%
no answer	6.9%

Whatever about models of government for a new Ireland, an overwhelming majority of respondents (91.4 per cent) support the ideal of a united Ireland. In anticipation of a response of this kind, question 13 asks respondents what changes they would be prepared to accept in both Church and State if a united Ireland were to come about. The proposed changes mentioned are in the area of the Roman Catholic Church's present position on mixed marriages and whether an all-Ireland State ought to legalise divorce. Respondents are given the opportunity to *choose more than one answer* to this question if they wish. Data from table 3 shows how deeply divided respondents are over these issues. Indeed, 50.4 per cent feel that *either one or both* of the proposed changes ought to take place.

Interestingly enough, the overall figure of 40.5 per cent of respondents who believe that divorce ought to be legalised in a united Ireland *would appear* to be consistent with the views of the Northern laity on this issue. While Moxon-Browne has put a question on divorce in a different form, i.e. 'the Irish Government should take the steps necessary to make divorce legal in the Republic', 47.6 per cent of Northern Catholic respondents agreed with this statement.[8]

Those respondents who feel divorce ought to be legalised in a united Ireland, appear however, to be isolated within the Irish Catholic Church as a whole. Certainly, their view is clearly incompatible with the official policy of the Catholic Church adopted in the referendum campaign on divorce which took place in the Republic of Ireland a few months after this questionnaire had been circulated. It must be acknowledged, of course, that the referendum did not involve any of my respondents who live in Northern Ireland where divorce has been available for many years. Nonetheless, while the official position of the Irish Catholic bishops on the divorce issue in the Republic was that members of the laity were allowed to follow their own conscience on the matter, clerical opposition to the proposed constitutional change was overwhelming (see chapter 5 for further details). So much so, that those few priests in the South who lent their approval to the introduction of divorce gained considerable publicity for adopting such a position.[9]

The teaching of the Roman Catholic Church on the upbringing of children of a religiously mixed marriage has been a highly contentious issue. As recently as 1983 the Irish Catholic bishops' *Catholic Directory on Mixed Marriages* was described by the Church of Ireland as 'profoundly disappointing'.[10] It is against such a background that 9.9 per cent of respondents feel 'that the Irish bishops ought to liberalise their position on mixed marriages from that outlined by the Catholic Directory on Mixed

Marriages (1983)', and an additional 17.7 per cent feel that *both* this change and the legalisation of civil divorce ought to take place in the event of a united Ireland coming about. In effect, therefore, just over a quarter of the respondents (27.6 per cent) feel that the Church ought to liberalise its position on mixed marriages in Ireland. Despite the vagueness of the term to 'liberalise', it is clear that a substantial minority of respondents would welcome some change in this area if a united Ireland were to come about.

Parish priests, who on average are more likely to be ordained at an earlier date than either Catholic curates or members of religious orders, are more likely to support *neither* of the suggested changes in Church and State than other categories of respondents. While 58.5 per cent of parish priest respondents believe that neither civil divorce nor a liberalisation of the Church's position on mixed marriages should occur in a united Ireland, only 35.3 per cent of curate respondents and 37.5 per cent of religous orders respondents accept this view. Similarly, an interesting set of statistics emerges in relation to the average year of ordination for respondents who take various positions on changes in Church and State in the context of a united Ireland. On the one hand, the average year of ordination among respondents who want neither of the above changes is early 1956, while on the other hand the average year of ordination for respondents who advocate both changes is early 1965. The average year of ordination of those who believe that the Church ought to liberalise its mixed marriage policy is late 1959, while the corresponding figure for those who believe the State should legalise divorce in a united Ireland is mid-1963. It is hardly surprising, therefore, that younger priests are generally more in favour of such changes. To cite just one example of this: while 30.6 per cent of respondents aged between 20 and 39 want neither change in Church nor state referred to above, the corresponding figure for respondents aged 50–59 is 43.8 per cent.

The attitudes and perceptions of respondents towards the Anglo–Irish Agreement are interesting in two respects. First, a large majority of respondents support the agreement. When asked 'on balance, do you approve of the Anglo–Irish

Agreement?', 86.6 per cent indicate their approval of the accord. This figure would suggest that Roman Catholic priests in Northern Ireland are more supportive of the accord than members of the laity there. In a survey which was conducted a few months before my questionnaire, it was found that approximately 50 per cent of Northern Ireland Catholics approved of the Anglo–Irish Agreement.[11]

Table 4 (question 15) If you have any reservations about the Anglo–Irish Agreement, it is because you believe that it

is deficient in satisfying nationalist aspirations	32.0%
undermines the position of Northern Ireland as part of the United Kingdom	1.8%
will be destroyed by loyalists and/or republicans, and in the process the Northern Ireland situation will get even worse	32.5%
is unfair to Unionists as they were not consulted during the course of the negotiations	16.7%
is none of the above reasons	19.3%

Yet, results in table 4 underline the tentative nature of clerical approval of the agreement. As can be seen in question 15 respondents are given five possible reservations about the Anglo–Irish accord and are told that they may choose more than one answer for the question if they wish to do so. It is worth noting that pessimism and nationalism underpin the most common reservations about the agreement among respondents.

In turn, the variables most strongly affecting such pessimism and nationalism are respondents' year of ordination and present status within the Church. For instance, while 28.1 per cent of those respondents who feel that the Anglo–Irish Agreement will be destroyed were ordained prior to 1955, and 18.4 per cent were ordained between 1955 and 1964, this figure rises to 42.9

per cent of respondents who were ordained between 1965 and 1974 and to 44.4 per cent of those respondents ordained between 1975 and 1986. Priests ordained at an earlier date tend to be more nationalist in their outlook than more recently ordained clerics. For example, the average year of ordination of respondents who perceive the Anglo–Irish accord as deficient in satisfying nationalist aspirations is mid-1957, while the corresponding figure for respondents who do not share this perception is late 1961. Similarly there is a consistent trend among respondents ordained in more recent periods to perceive the Anglo–Irish Agreement as unfair to Unionists as that bloc was not consulted during the course of negotiations. Thus, while only 9 per cent of respondents ordained prior to 1955 see the agreement as unfair to Unionists, this figure rises to 26.7 per cent among participants ordained since 1975. Closely related to period of ordination is clerical status and as parish priest respondents are, on average, ordained at an earlier date (mid-1948), than either members of religious orders (mid-1958), or Catholic curates (early 1968), it is hardly surprising that there are many examples of parish priests being relatively nationalist in their outlook. For instance, while only 5.3 per cent of parish priest respondents believe the Anglo–Irish Agreement to be unfair to Unionists, the corresponding figures for curates and religious orders are 17.5 per cent and 23.6 per cent respectively.

The only previous examination of party political identification among clergymen in Northern Ireland by Birrell and Roche showed a 63 per cent level of support among Roman Catholic priests for the SDLP.[12] By contrast, 87.9 per cent of my respondents indicate that they would be most likely to vote for the SDLP 'if a general election were to be held in the near future' (question 16). One plausible explanation as to why respondents to the study of Birrell and Roche indicated a relatively low level of support for the SDLP was that their research was conducted in 1972/73, which was a time when the SDLP had not yet contested an election as a party. Thirteen per cent of Birrell and Roche's Roman Catholic respondents indicated support for 'other' party.

In any event, the emergence of Sinn Fein as a major electoral force in Northern Ireland politics since 1982 has, *inter alia*, helped to crystallise political cleavages within the Catholic community. Among respondents to this questionnaire, however, support for Sinn Fein is rare: only 3.9 per cent of respondents indicate that they would be most likely to vote Sinn Fein in a general election. It must be emphasised, moreover, that the scope for statistical distortion in question 16 is extremely low insofar as the rate of non-response to this question, 5.2 per cent, is among the lowest rates of non-response to any of the questions in this study. In fact, approximately 93.9 per cent of all respondents indicate the likelihood of their voting for a specific political party in a forthcoming general election. Moreover, as an additional 0.9 per cent of respondents feel that they would abstain in a forthcoming general election, there is no evidence to suggest that there is some significant level of 'hidden support' for Provisional Sinn Fein. Given the hierarchy's constant condemnation of republican violence since May 1970, and the Sinn Fein strategy of the 'armalite and the ballot paper', it is hardly surprising that only a small number of respondents identify with that party. In wider terms, however, the position of the Church on this issue presents an anomaly: how an almost exclusively anti-Sinn Fein clergy can retain credibility among a large section of the Catholic community. It must be remembered, after all, that in the 1983 general election, Sinn Fein obtained 13.4 per cent of the overall vote in Northern Ireland,[13] a figure which represents as much as 40 per cent of the 'Catholic' vote.

The other political parties have an even lower level of support among respondents. For instance, only 1.3 per cent identify with the Alliance Party, while a further 0.9 per cent say they would be most likely to vote for the Workers' Party if a general election were to be held in the near future. No respondent supports the Official Unionist Party.

Question 20 measures the effect of the 1981 hunger-strikes on the attitudes and perceptions of respondents. Given the widespread view that the hunger-strikes have had a profound effect on the hardening of political attitudes among the Catholic community in general, it is significant that the vast majority of my respondents believe that they have not become more nationalist as a result of the hunger-strikes. Indeed, only 12.1

per cent of respondents feel that the hunger-strikes made them 'more nationalist'. Over half of all respondents (58.6 per cent), describe the hunger-strikes as having had 'no real effect' on their political views. An additional 18.5 per cent feel that the hunger-strikes have made them 'more disillusioned' with politics, while 5.6 per cent feel they have become less nationalist as a result of the hunger-strikes.

A significant pattern of nationalist feeling emerges among respondents when the effect of the hunger-strikes on them is cross-tabulated with their approval or disapproval of the Anglo–Irish Agreement, and their view of how satisfactory or otherwise the response of the hierarchy has been towards the troubles in Northern Ireland. Certainly, an important cleavage exists between respondents who support or oppose the Anglo–Irish Agreement over the effects of the hunger-strikes on their political attitudes. Of those who support the agreement, only 10.4 per cent feel that the hunger-strikes made them feel more nationalist, whereas 38.9 per cent of those opposed to the accord feel that the hunger-strikes have affected them in the same way. Finally, it is also worth noting that there is a significant relationship between the effects of the hunger-strike on the political consciousness of the respondents and how satisfied or otherwise they are with the response of the Catholic hierarchy to the troubles. While only 12.1 per cent of all respondents feel more nationalist as a result of the hunger-strikes, 26.2 per cent of those dissatisfied with the response of the hierarchy to the troubles feel affected in this way by the hunger-strikes.

While no controversy has occurred during the period of this study over priests having advised Catholics as to *how* they should vote in an election, it is interesting to note that some clerics were part of a group who advocated a boycott of the Northern Ireland Convention elections in 1975.[14] Cardinal Conway and four Northern bishops emphasised in a statement that the Church was not recommending an electoral boycott.[15] It is conceivable, of course, that priests can influence the electoral behaviour of at least some Catholics in a number of subtle and not necessarily conscious ways. Still, such an influence is impossible to quantify, so it has been necessary to put the question in a form which is empirically verifiable. In reply to question 17, only nine respondents or 3.9 per cent indicated that they have ever given advice to their congregations as to which way they should vote in an election. In practice, therefore, it is rare for priests in Northern Ireland to consciously promote party politics of one kind or another.

Given the small percentage of respondents who indicate that they have advised their congregations as to which way they should vote in an election, any conclusions about this group must be tentative. Nonetheless, there is evidence to suggest that a large percentage of such respondents hold relatively strong nationalist views. When question 17 is cross-tabulated with question 10, for instance, it is found that among priests who have given advice to their congregations as to how they should vote in an election, 42.9 per cent of this group believe Irish unity will come about in less than ten years (as against an overall average of 9.5 per cent). Another 42.9 per cent believe it will come about between 25 and 50 years, while a remaining 14.3 per cent believe it is unlikely to ever come about. Similarly, of those who believe a unitary state to be the most probable model of Irish unity, a disproportionately large percentage of respondents (22.2 per cent) indicate that they have advised their congregations as to which way they should vote in an election.

Certainly, one definite conclusion can be drawn concerning those clerics who have advised their congregations as to which way they should vote in an election, and that is that their year of ordination tends to be relatively early, regardless of their status within the Roman Catholic Church. Thus, while the average year of ordination for respondents who have given advice to their congregations in this way is early 1953, the corresponding figure for those who have not done so is late 1960. This pattern also emerges among parish priests and Catholic curates. While the average year of ordination among parish priest respondents who have advised their congregations in this way is mid-1944, the corresponding figure for his colleague who has *not* done so is late 1948. Among Catholic curate respondents the tendency is even more pronounced: the average year of ordination of curates who have advised their congregations in this way is 1960, as against late 1968 for their colleagues who have not offered their advice in the party political sphere.

The next question is designed to measure how priests perceive their ability to affect the voting behaviour of their respective congregations, should they wish to do so. Certainly, respondents seem to perceive their influence to be greater in this regard than the findings of Birrell and Roche to a similar question would suggest. In this latter study, respondents were asked how they perceived their influence over their congregations' political views. Only 26 per cent of Roman Catholic priests felt they had influence in this sphere. This figure was easily the lowest among clergymen of the various denominations, and indeed, fell well below the overall average of 40 per cent among clergymen of the main denominations.[16] By contrast, table 5

Table 5 (question 18) If you were to advise your congregation as to which way they should vote in an election, do you think that such an appeal would

have a strong effect on their voting behaviour	5.2%
have a slight effect on their voting behaviour	42.2%
have no effect on their voting behaviour	26.3%
have a counter-productive effect on their voting behaviour	10.8%
no answer	15.5%

shows that almost half of all respondents believe that they could exercise at least some influence over the voting behaviour of their congregations, if they wished to do so.

While as we have seen from replies to question 17 that only 3.9 per cent of respondents have consciously advised their congregations as to which way they should vote in an election, 12.5 per cent disagree with the statement in part of question 19 that 'you would never advise your congregation as to which way they should vote in an election'. Part of this *apparent* discrepancy, however, can be partly attributed to the absolute nature of the question, for a number of respondents felt it necessary to make their answers conditional by referring to specific circumstances. Thus, for instance, four of those twenty-nine respondents or 13.7 per cent made it clear under what circumstances they would disagree with the statement that they would never advise their congregations as to which way they should vote in an election.

In any event, the most important variable for this part of question 19 is the respondents' birthplace. While 20.8 per cent of Southern-born respondents disagree with the proposition that they would never advise their congregations as to which way they should vote in an election, only 8.9 per cent of Northern-born respondents subscribe to this view. It is difficult to account for this finding. Certainly, when the results of question 17 on whether priests have *actually* used their influence in this way are cross-tabulated with the variable of birthplace, no statistically significant relationship is perceptible; on the contrary, only one out of eighty-five respondents born in the Republic of Ireland indicates that he has given advice to the congregation as to which way they should vote in an election. Still, it is possible to attribute the above finding to one or both of the following reasons. First, if one accepts the earlier the date of ordination, the more likely it is for clerics to perceive their influence to be greater than do those ordained in a later period, it is interesting to note that 46 per cent of Southern-born respondents are members of religious orders. The average year of ordination for respondents of this status is mid-1958, *some ten years* earlier than the average year of ordination of those Catholic curates who participated in this questionnaire. Second, it is possible to argue that as most priests born in the Republic of Ireland have spent at least their formative years there, they are inclined to equate their influence with priests presently residing in the South, a state whose Roman Catholic ethos is frequently seen as the mirror image of the Protestant ethos in the Northern state.

The other two parts of question 19 measure the perceptions of respondents in two areas: if they perceive the troubles as having reduced their political and social influence over the Roman Catholic community; if they believe any advice they might give to people about how they should vote in an election would have a greater impact on older members of the congregation than younger members. In both instances a small majority of respondents agree with such statements. 57.8 per cent of respondents agree with the supposition that 'priests have less political and social influence over their people nowadays as a result of the troubles',* 21.1 per cent disagree and 14.7 per cent express no opinion. 54.7 per cent of respondents agree with the statement 'if you gave advice to your congregation as to which way they should vote in an election this would have a stronger impact on older members of the congregation than younger members'. 16.4 per cent of respondents take the opposite view, while 18.5 per cent fail to express an opinion.

Over one-fifth of respondents are clearly unhappy with the response of the hierarchy to the troubles. In answer to question 21, 'on balance, how do you feel about the response of the hierarchy to the troubles?', 20.3 per cent describe themselves as 'generally unsatisfied'. A similar number of respondents (17.7 per cent) are 'very satisfied' with the hierarchy in this regard. A majority of respondents, however, (60.8 per cent) describe themselves as 'reasonably satisfied' with the response of the hierarchy to the troubles since 1968.

As table 6 shows, respondents are more critical of the hierarchy in response to specific questions than they are in their *overall assessment* of hierarchical policy in question 21. This is especially true in two areas: state violence and the use of more Church resources to help relatively deprived communities most affected by the troubles. Certainly, that 43.1 per cent feel the hierarchy ought to have done more to criticise various forms of state violence points to a deep division of opinion over this issue. (See chapter 3 for substantive treatment of this theme.) Respondents are most critical of hierarchical policy, however, in relation to whether more of the Church's resources ought to be used to help relatively deprived communities most affected by the troubles. This finding is significant not only because of the involvement of the Catholic Church in a number of social

---

* This tendency is implied by the findings of a field-trip which was conducted in Derry in December 1973. See *Doctrine and Life*, vol. 25, no. 1, January 1975, especially pp. 8–11.

Table 6 (question 22)

	Agree	Disagree	No opinion	No answer
the hierarchy has not done enough to discourage republican violence	16.4%	76.7%	4.7%	2.2%
the hierarchy has not done enough to criticise various forms of state violence	43.1%	47.8%	6.5%	2.6%
the hierarchy has not done enough to encourage reconciliation between Protestants and Catholics in Northern Ireland	27.6%	62.9%	6.0%	3.4%
the hierarchy ought to use more of the Church's resources to help those relatively deprived communities which tend to be most deeply affected by the troubles	52.2%	29.7%	11.6%	6.5%

projects* but the way in which the hierarchy has argued that social and economic deprivation has helped to foster alienation and violence in Northern Ireland.[17]

Those respondents who believe that the hierarchy ought to use more of the Church's resources to help those relatively deprived communities which tend to be the most deeply affected by the troubles are then asked in question 23 to choose between two distinctive policy options in this area. These

---

* Bishop Edward Daly of Derry estimates that there are Church projects going on in his diocese which involve expenditure of around £5 million. In an interview in Derry, 3 March 1988.

options are designed to distinguish between those respondents who broadly support a traditional charity-orientated approach to these problems, and those priests who endorse a more radical approach. 54 per cent of respondents support 'a redistribution of funds from the wealthier parishes in the dioceses to the socially deprived areas for the purpose of expanding Church charities'. A slightly smaller percentage of respondents (46 per cent) endorse a more radical plan which involves 'a major redistribution of Church funds so that such money could be invested (perhaps jointly with other interested organisations) in community projects/investments which are regarded as too risky by orthodox financial institutions'. When these figures are considered in terms of *all those who responded to the questionnaire*, approximately 26.3 per cent approve of expanding Church charities, while 22.4 per cent believe there ought to be a major redistribution of Church funds to tackle the problems affecting those relatively deprived communities that tend to be most deeply affected by the troubles.

Clerical status and period of ordination are crucial in understanding answers to question 21, which identifies three levels of satisfaction among respondents towards the hierarchy's response to the troubles, viz. 'very satisfied' (17.7 per cent), 'reasonably satisfied' (60.8 per cent), and 'generally unsatisfied' (20.3 per cent). Thus, for example, while only 8.9 per cent of parish priest respondents describe themselves as 'generally unsatisfied' with the hierarchy's response to the troubles, the corresponding figures for curates and members of religious orders are 20.6 per cent and 29.6 per cent respectively. Similarly, respondents' period of ordination to a considerable extent predetermines their view of the hierarchy's response to the troubles. While only 11.4 per cent of respondents ordained prior to 1955 and 16.3 per cent of those ordained between 1955 and 1964 are generally unsatisfied with the hierarchy in this area, the corresponding figure for 1965–1974 ordinations is 22.9 per cent and for those ordained in the 1975–1986 period, 40.9 per cent.

Similar trends emerge in three of the four statements made in question 22 to which respondents are asked to indicate their agreement or disagreement. The three statements express the view that the hierarchy's record on criticising state violence, encouraging reconciliation between Catholics and Protestants and the use of Church resources to help socially deprived communities deeply affected by the troubles have all been inadequate. In all three instances, parish priests are less critical of the hierarchy than either Catholic curates or members of religious orders. Thus, while 30.2 per cent of parish priest respondents agree that the hierarchy has not done enough to condemn state violence, 45.9 per cent of curate respondents and 65 per cent of religious order respondents share this view. While only 17.6 per cent of parish priest respondents believe that the hierarchy has not done enough to encourage Protestant–Catholic reconciliation in Northern Ireland, the corresponding figures for curates and members of religious orders are 29.9 per cent and 41.9 per cent respectively. Similarly, among respondents who feel that the hierarchy ought to use more of the Church's resources to help relatively deprived communities, 38.8 per cent of parish priests accept this view, while 69.7 per cent of curates and 76.9 per cent of members of religious orders support this call. Likewise, the year of ordination is important for each of the same three statements. Thus, to cite a few examples, the average year of ordination among respondents who believe the hierarchy has not done enough about state violence is early 1962, while the corresponding figure for those who take the opposite view is early 1958. Similarly, the average year of ordination for those respondents who feel the hierarchy has not done enough to encourage Protestant–Roman Catholic reconciliation in Northern Ireland is late 1962, while the corresponding figure for those who disagree is early 1959. This tendency is even more pronounced with regard to the use of more Church resources to help those relatively deprived communities which tend to be most deeply affected by the troubles: while the average year of ordination among respondents who endorse the above idea is late 1963, the corresponding figure for those who disagree is mid-1955.

Only the first statement of question 22, i.e. 'the hierarchy has not done enough to discourage republican violence' is not significantly affected by either the status of respondents or their mean average year of ordination. Such critics of this aspect of the hierarchy's response to the troubles are 'evenly spread' in terms of these two variables.

The importance of variables relating to present status and average year of ordination in the Church is underlined yet again by the results from question 23. The question asks those respondents *who have already indicated* their belief that the hierarchy ought to do more for relatively deprived communities most deeply affected by the troubles in Northern Ireland, whether it would be preferable for the hierarchy to pursue the charitable or the project-orientated option. While only 16.7 per cent of parish priest respondents prefer the project-orientated approach, 48.1 per cent of curate respondents and 56.1 per cent of religious order respondents share this preference. Moreover, the mean average year of ordination among respondents who prefer the 'charity' model is early 1960, while the corresponding figure for those who approve of the other model is late 1966.

There are only two pieces of evidence from this section of the questionnaire which suggest the existence of cleavages between critics of the hierarchy's response to the troubles in Northern Ireland. First, respondents hold contrasting views of the hierarchy's record on criticising state violence and discouraging republican violence. Thus, only 24.7 per cent of those respondents who feel that the hierarchy has not done enough to criticise various forms of state violence also feel that the hierarchy has not done enough to discourage republican violence. Second, among those respondents who are 'generally unsatisfied' with the response of the Catholic hierarchy to the troubles in Northern Ireland, the level of support for two of the four statements critical of the hierarchy in this regard is especially high. Only 45.2 per cent of such respondents believe the hierarchy has not done enough to discourage republican violence, while 66.7 per cent of this group believe the bishops have not done enough to promote Protestant–Roman Catholic reconciliation in Northern Ireland. By contrast, an overwhelming majority (84.1 per cent) of the same group feel the hierarchy has not done enough to criticise various forms of state violence, while 84.4 per cent of this group take the view that the hierarchy ought to use more of the Church's resources to help those relatively deprived communities that tend to be the most deeply affected by the troubles. More than anything else, such findings indicate that 'generally unsatisfied' respondents have a tendency to identify the most tangible effects of the Northern Ireland troubles as areas in which the hierarchical response has been particularly disappointing.

A substantial minority of respondents perceive religiously segregated education as in some way socially and politically divisive. This is underlined by the fact that 32.8 per cent of respondents 'agree that integrated education would reduce some of the problems in Northern Ireland'. 56.5 per cent of respondents disagree, 4.3 per cent have no opinion and 6.5 per cent fail to provide a valid answer.

Table 7 (question 25) 'Are you opposed *in principle* to integrated schools for Protestants and Catholics in Northern Ireland?'

Yes	53.0%
No	40.9%
No opinion	3.0%
No answer	3.0%

Such perceptions clearly influence answers to question 25. While 56.5 per cent of respondents disagree that integrated education would help to reduce some of Northern Ireland's problems, it is significant that a similar number of respondents (53 per cent) are opposed in principle to integrated education in Northern Ireland (see table 7). Likewise, while 32.8 per cent of respondents believe that integrated education would reduce some of the problems in Northern Ireland, 40.9 per cent are not opposed to the principle of integrated schooling.

Question 26 is designed for those respondents who are not opposed in principle to integrated education, and asks this group to choose one out of three possible answers. 59.5 per cent feel that 'under the present circumstances in Northern Ireland nothing can be done to change the present schools system except to increase contacts between children attending Catholic and Protestant schools'. 18.9 per cent feel that 'the Church

ought to give greater encouragement to new non-denominational schools such as Lagan College, for instance', while 21.6
per cent believe that 'the Church and State ought to launch a
campaign for integrated education in Northern Ireland'. *In terms
of the overall numbers of respondents to this questionnaire,* just over
half are opposed in principle to integrated education. Of the
remainder, 28.4 per cent feel that nothing can be done to change
the system under the present circumstances, 9.1 per cent believe
that the Church should give greater encouragement to non-
denominational schools, while 10.3 per cent advocate the
launching of a campaign for integrated education by Church
and State.

On the basis of these findings, the Catholic Church in
Northern Ireland appears to be *relatively monolithic* in its position
on the educational question. Despite the different contexts
involved in questions 13 and 26, for example, while 10.3 per cent
of respondents support the idea of launching a campaign for
integrated education in Northern Ireland, 50.4 per cent feel that
the state ought to legalise divorce and/or that the Church ought
to liberalise its position on mixed marriages in a united Ireland
situation. To cite yet another example, respondents are more
deeply divided over their criticisms of the hierarchy's response
to the troubles in Northern Ireland than they are in seeking
actual change in the educational *status quo.*

Such relatively solid support for the educational system
among my respondents, however, points to a deep divergence
of opinion in this area between the clergy and laity in Northern
Ireland. Indeed, results from every survey conducted on this
subject show that a large majority of Northern Catholics support
integrated education. (For further details see chapter 5, pp.
175–176).

When average year of ordination and present status are cross-
tabulated with questions 24–26, there is a strong tendency for
respondents ordained in later years to take a less negative view
of integrated education. Thus, while the average year of ordination among respondents who believe that integrated education
would help to reduce some of the problems in Northern Ireland
(question 24) is late 1964, the corresponding figure for those
who take the opposite view is early 1958. Similarly, while the

average year of ordination among respondents opposed to the principle of religiously integrated education (question 25) is mid-1958, the corresponding figure among those who take the opposite view is early 1963. Again, a not dissimilar pattern emerges for those respondents *not opposed* in principle to integrated education (question 26). For instance, while the mean average year of ordination among respondents who believe that nothing can be done at present to change the schools system is late 1958, the corresponding figure for those who advocate the launching of a campaign for integrated education is late 1963. Moreover, in terms of respondents' status within the Catholic Church, parish priests are most attached to the present educational system, while monks are least attached. Catholic curates occupy a central position. Thus, for example, when respondents are asked in question 24 whether they believe integrated education would reduce some of Northern Ireland's problems, only 14.5 per cent of parish priests agree, as against 31.2 per cent of Catholic curates and 66.1 per cent of members of religious orders. A possible explanation for this particularly weak attachment to the Catholic school system in Northern Ireland among members of religious orders is the relatively limited involvement of such priests in the educational system there. Certainly, most of those priests listed in the *Irish Catholic Directory 1986* as working in Northern Ireland schools are not members of religious orders.

It is important to note that both respondents born in Northern Ireland and those who have not lived outside that region since their eighteenth birthday tend to be more supportive of the educational *status quo* than their colleagues. While only 25.8 per cent of all respondents born in Northern Ireland believe that integrated education would help to reduce some of the North's problems, 54.1 per cent of those born in the Republic of Ireland take the same view. Similarly, while 67.2 per cent of Northern-born respondents are opposed *in principle* to integrated education for Northern Ireland, the corresponding figure for their Southern-born colleagues is only 39.7 per cent. Likewise, while 75 per cent of respondents who have not lived outside Northern Ireland since their eighteenth birthday are opposed in principle to integrated education, the corresponding figures, for example, among those who have lived in the Republic of Ireland and Great Britain, are 57.1 per cent and 51.6 per cent respectively. One possible explanation for this relatively deep attachment to the Catholic school system in Northern Ireland on the part of the respondents born there and those who have not lived outside the region since their eighteenth birthday is that they feel the system has served them well. Equally, it can be argued that living outside Northern Ireland has affected the views of many respondents on the education question.

Finally, given the relatively small number of respondents advocating changes in the educational system of Northern Ireland, it is hardly surprising that this group is critical of the hierarchy's response to the troubles in Northern Ireland. It is significant, moreover, that there is a strong relationship between respondents' answers to question 24 and their views on changes needed in Church and State in the event of a united Ireland coming about (question 13).

Before bringing this chapter to a close, it is imperative to highlight the fact that the closely related variables of year of ordination, age-group and present status affect *all* aspects of political opinion among respondents.[18] As each of these variables is synonymous with age, what this means, in effect, is that younger respondents are inclined to have what might be described as a less traditional political outlook than their older colleagues. To take just one of these variables as an example, i.e. year of ordination, respondents ordained in more recent years tend to be relatively pessimistic about when Irish unity is likely to come about. Similarly, more recently ordained participants are more open to changes in Church and State in a united Ireland context and they are more tentative than their fellow-priests about the Anglo–Irish Agreement. Although it has been rare for respondents to advise their congregations as to how they should vote in an election, those who have done so tend to have been ordained in an earlier period. Finally, more recently ordained participants are more inclined to be critical of the hierarchical response to the troubles and are less likely to support Catholic education in Northern Ireland.

The Church and
the Administration of Justice

THE ADMINISTRATION of justice has led to the political alienation of many Catholics in Northern Ireland throughout the period of this study. Consequently, the Church's record *vis-à-vis* the administration of justice is extremely important. During the course of the analysis which follows, salient aspects of what might be broadly described as the Church's position on security policy and the judiciary in Northern Ireland are analysed at length.

Before doing so, it is necessary, however briefly, to acknowledge that among the most active human rights campaigners in Northern Ireland have been priests, especially Fr Denis Faul of Dungannon and Fr Raymond Murray of Armagh. In terms of publications alone, Fr Faul has either written or co-written eighty-seven brief works on all types of alleged violations of human rights by the authorities. Of these, Faul has been the sole author of twenty-one such publications, while he and Fr Murray have co-authored sixty-one other works. (The five remaining pieces have been written by Faul, Murray and Fr Brian Brady of Belfast.)* Whatever one thinks of the claim once made by Fr Faul that 75 per cent of his colleagues supported his work in this regard (see *Hibernia*, 16 December 1977, p. 6), my own empirical research shows a widely-held perception among priests that the Catholic hierarchy has not done enough to protest against violations of human rights by the state. In my questionnaire to all the priests in Northern Ireland in April/May 1986, for example, some 17.7 per cent of the respondents were, on balance, 'very satisfied' with the response of the hierarchy to the troubles, with a further 60.8 per cent describing themselves as

---

* These figures have been calculated from the author index in the library of Trinity College Dublin, dated 1/1/87.

'reasonably satisfied' in their reply to the same question. By contrast, 43.1 per cent agreed with the statement that 'the hierarchy has not done enough to criticise various forms of state violence'. However one conceives of state violence, such data certainly implies widespread sympathy for what Fr Faul has been doing.

(i) *Security Policy*

Inherent in the statements of the Catholic hierarchy is a deep respect for the *impartial* implementation of the law. For instance, the leaders of the four main Churches in Ireland, including Archbishop Tomas O'Fiaich* for the Catholic Church, issued the following statement, quoted in Peter Taylor's *Beating The Terrorists? Interrogation at Armagh, Gough and Castlereagh*, pp. 233–234, in December 1977:

> We have been disturbed that serious allegations are being made of ill-treatment of suspects and prisoners; though at the same time we recognise that some persons opposed to state authorities can be expected to attack their security forces not only with physical violence, but also malicious accusations.
>
> A grave responsibility, therefore, rests on all law-abiding citizens to seek to strengthen the duly constituted forces of law and order both by constructive criticism and personal support, saving in mind the following points:
>
> 1. It is a basic responsibility of the forces of law and order to seek to protect not only the general public as they go about their lawful business but also persons who may be in custody.
> 2. Confidence in this protection is vital to a free society; and anything which would undermine it from within those forces is a serious threat just as are attacks from without.
>
> For this reason, the declared policies of the Chief Constable and the Government in Northern Ireland and the Government of the Republic of Ireland must effectively be implemented and adequate precautions taken against abuse.

* O'Fiaich was not made Cardinal until 1979.

Such *conditional* support for the security forces has been an almost constant feature of hierarchical pronouncements on the subject. Thus, to cite another good example, Bishop Cahal Daly, in *Violence in Ireland and Christian Conscience* in 1973, and in *Peace The Work of Justice Addresses on the Northern Tragedy 1973–1979*, especially pp. 100–110, has adopted the same approach to these problems. (The only member of the hierarchy to offer *unconditional* support for the security forces was the former Bishop of Down and Connor, Dr Philbin, who in October 1974, urged Catholics to help the security forces, saying that there was no way that they could help themselves. Despite the fact that Philbin's statement was made during a wave of sectarian assassinations, he appeared to effectively isolate himself from most members of the Catholic community. The SDLP, for one, was quick to emphasise that it found the RUC unacceptable.) (See *Irish News*, 31 October 1974)

Within the political community of Northern Ireland, such conditional support is, not surprisingly, interpreted in radically different ways. For most loyalists and the authorities in Northern Ireland, any criticism of the security forces is seen in some sense as an attempt to undermine the Northern State. On the other hand, the hierarchy's position is regarded by republicans as collaborationist with the authorities, a dominant theme in republican publications throughout the period of this study.*

In any case, the Catholic Church does not have a uniform policy on whether Catholics ought to contact the authorities if they have information concerning paramilitary violence. Thus, when Bishop Cahal Daly was asked in an interview with *Magill* in January 1985 (p. 77) as to whether Catholics had a moral duty to pass such information to the police, he replied that: '. . . While there is a *prima facie* obligation to co-operate with the police in suppressing subversive crime, we churchmen recognise the grave risks suffered by people who could be suspected of passing information. There is a moral obligation to prevent murder, but it's difficult to require people to expose themselves to immediate risk of death.' Whatever else might be said about this reply, it was certainly an imprecise judgment on whether a

* The way in which republicans have coped with clerical denunciations of the IRA will be examined in chapter 4.

specific person ought to inform the police about a specific act carried out by paramilitaries. By contrast, in April 1982, Bishop Edward Daly of Derry made an urgent appeal to people in the city who might have information about persons who had committed any type of murder to make this information available to the authorities. Ultimately, of course, it is debatable if a uniform Church policy on the question of whether Catholics ought to inform the authorities about paramilitary violence would actually result in more information of this kind being provided. If nothing else, such a Church policy would clarify the *moral* complexities that such a question might hold for many Catholics.

Consistent with the Catholic Church's deep respect for the *impartial* implementation of the law has been its perception of the alleged acts of violence by the security forces. On occasions, bishops have clearly alluded to the violence of the state security forces. Thus, during a lengthy denunciation of violence in Newry during the early 1970s which was overwhelmingly directed against local republicans, the then Bishop of Dromore, Dr O'Doherty, as reported in the *Irish Times*, 3 January 1972, pp. 1 and 9, also said: '. . . We cannot blame the military for all the destruction and loss of life. Undoubtedly they were responsible for some of it . . .' While for his part, Bishop Edward Daly of Derry once said that the British Army had made a major contribution to the violence in Derry. It must be emphasised, however, that such statements did not imply the military or the security forces in general were actually engaged in a separate *campaign of violence*. This was made explicit in a document released by the Irish hierarchy of the Catholic Church in 1975. The document, entitled *Thou Shall Not Kill*, and issued as one part of a four-part pastoral, denounced violence. In the bishops' view, however, there were only two campaigns of violence being waged in Northern Ireland, viz. those of republicans and loyalists: '. . . We do not close our eyes to the fact that there have been two campaigns of violence—the one aimed at achieving a united Ireland by force—the other a campaign of sectarian assassination . . .' (*Irish News*, 9 May 1975)

There have been frequent allegations of killings by the security forces during the period of this study. The scale of the problem can be gleaned from *Shoot to Kill? International Lawyers' Inquiry into the Lethal Use of Firearms by the Security Forces in Northern Ireland*, which was led by Kader Asmal (chairman) in 1985 (see p. 17, paragraphs 18 and 19):

> ... The Irish Information Partnership, an independent, non-profit research group based in Belgium provided the inquiry with extensive data on the killings of civilians by members of the security forces. Their evidence shows ... at least 269 persons killed by members of the security forces on duty in Northern Ireland between August 1969 and January 1984.
>
> The Irish Information Partnership testified that over 155* people shot dead in this period by British soldiers and the Royal Ulster Constabulary had no manifest connections to paramilitary organisations or activities ...

Obviously, such claims have been worrying to many people in Northern Ireland, including the Catholic Church. As the report says:

> ... Since 1972 there has been no Government inquiry into the killing of civilians by members of the security forces. Recently a number of leading figures in the Catholic Church[†] and the nationalist community have called on the Government to institute such a public inquiry, but to no avail. The refusal of the Government to appoint its own inquiry is one of the factors which have led us to undertake our inquiry ... (see *Asmal*, pp. 22–23, paragraph 36)

Moreover, in gathering evidence for their investigation the lawyers interviewed Fr Raymond Murray of Armagh, one of the priests most active in human rights affairs in Northern Ireland. Fr Murray has kept detailed records of over 120 victims whom he described as: '... completely innocent people not shot dead

---

* There is a list of civilians killed by the security forces in disputed circumstances in (Asmal: 1985). Totalling 177 cases in all, it is drawn from a variety of sources.
† These leading figures in the Catholic Church were Cardinal O'Fiaich and Frs Faul and Murray. (In an interview with Kader Asmal in Dublin, 1 December 1986)

in crossfire or anything like that, but whom I would regard as deliberately shot dead in cold blood by British Army, UDR and RUC . . .' (*Asmal*, pp. 26–27, paragraph 45) (In addition, it ought to be noted that in a statement issued by sixty-five priests from the diocese of Down and Connor in November 1972, it was claimed that in some areas of Belfast 'innocent and unarmed civilians, regardless of sex or age, are being shot by soldiers, in and out of uniform'.)*

A salient feature of the hierarchical response to the killings of civilians has been the tendency of bishops in the earlier part of the period to remain publicly silent on the issue. Indeed, with the exception of the 'Bloody Sunday' case (which will be examined on pp. 98–101), it was extremely rare for any ecclesiastical leader to accuse the security forces of such killings. A notable exception was, as reported in the *Irish News*, 1 March 1973, the call by Bishop O'Doherty of Dromore and the priests and principal teachers of voluntary schools in Newry, for a full public inquiry into the death of a local schoolboy, Kevin Heatley, who had been shot dead by the army. Eventually, such local pressure led to the prosecution of a member of the security forces for the youngster's death which was the first of its kind in Northern Ireland. However controversial, the findings of Asmal provide us with a broad picture of not only the scale of the killings, but more pertinent still, the dates and locations of such incidents. Although 109 of the 177 disputed killings or approximately 61.6 per cent of the total took place in Belfast, and 35 of them or approximately 19.8 per cent occurred in Derry respectively, neither Dr Farren, Bishop of Derry (1939–1974) nor Dr Philbin, Bishop of Down and Connor[†] (1962–1982) expressed their concern (at least publicly) about the specific circumstances surrounding any of these shootings. Moreover, it was during their periods as bishops that most of the controversial shootings took place. Of the Belfast shootings listed, for instance, approximately 91.7 per cent (or 100 out of 109) of them occurred when Dr Philbin was bishop of the diocese. In the Derry City area, approximately 66 per cent (or 23 out of 35) of the disputed

---

* The rest of this statement alleges army harassment/violence against large sections of the civilian population. It is analysed in pages 103–107 of this chapter.
† These dioceses include the areas of Derry City and Belfast.

killings occurred there while Dr Farren was bishop of the diocese.[1] Cardinal Conway (1963–1977) was, with the exception of Bloody Sunday, equally silent about such killings.*

Apparently sensitive to possible criticism of the Northern bishops' response to the troubles, Bishop Cahal Daly said the following in *Violence in Ireland and Christian Conscience*, p. 35, in 1973 (Daly was then Bishop of Ardagh and Clonmacnoise which is in the Republic of Ireland but part of the ecclesiastical province of Armagh):

> ... The bishops in the North have not failed in what is clearly their Christian duty—to condemn policies and acts of violence ... But neither have they failed in their related Christian duty—to condemn the brutalities and inhumanities of military repression which provokes further injustices out of which the violence grew. They have not been cultivating a public image, but trying to perform a duty in conscience before God—and have therefore not sought to publicise the constant and insistent representations they have been making to the responsible authorities to impress on them the need to abandon ruinous policies and be seen to be implementing radical structural reforms ...

Within this wide description of the hierarchy's position towards Government policy in Northern Ireland at this time lies the *possibility* that killings of civilians in disputed circumstances were among 'the brutalities and inhumanities of military repression' about which the bishops were making 'constant and insistent representations' to the authorities.

Whatever about bishops trying to cultivate public images, the successors to Bishops Philbin and Farren, as well as Cardinal Conway, have shown a greater readiness to publicly condemn

---

* As the dioceses of Armagh, Clogher, Dromore and Kilmore all cut across county boundaries, I have not attempted to quantify the number of killings in disputed circumstances which have occurred in these respective dioceses. On a county basis, however, most of the remaining incidents occurred in Counties Tyrone and Armagh. There were fifteen such killings listed in Co. Tyrone (8.47 per cent), while the corresponding figure for Armagh City and county was fourteen (or 7.91 per cent).

specific shootings by the security forces. While Bishop Cahal Daly (Down and Connor 1982–) is, on balance, less vocal than his colleagues Dr Edward Daly (Derry) and Cardinal O'Fiaich on this subject, he did not, for instance, hesitate to condemn the shooting to death of Sean Downes with a plastic bullet in Belfast in August 1984, describing it as an act of 'RUC violence'. Moreover, in a week following the killing of a joy-rider by the British Army in west Belfast, Bishop Daly said during the course of a lengthy statement quoted in the *Irish News*, 15 August 1984, that: '. . . There must be independent and impartial investigation of all incidents of suspected departure by security forces from the restraints of law . . .'

For his part, Dr Farren's successor in the diocese of Derry, Dr Edward Daly, has frequently criticised the security forces for carrying out various shootings in the area. Some examples of such protests were his response to the shooting of Mr Paddy Duffy, who had been shot dead by the army in 1978 while he was in a house being used to store arms and ammunition. Bishop Daly claimed at the time that British soldiers had been given the power to 'act as judge, jury and executioner'. Following the acquittal of two soldiers who had been charged with the murder of two Derry youths on Easter Sunday 1981, Bishop Daly said that he 'shared the great disgust of many people in Derry at the verdict'. Later in 1982, Bishop Daly condemned the killing of Eamonn Bradley, who it was claimed, had been shot dead by the army as he left a public house in Derry. Daly described it as an act of callous murder. Perhaps best remembered of all, however, was Bishop Daly's protest at the killing of two IRA men near Altnagelvin Hospital in December 1984, who had been ambushed by the British Army. The bishop expressed the view that it had not been necessary for the army in the circumstances to kill the men (see *Irish News*, 8 December 1984). Equally, Cardinal O'Fiaich has not hesitated to criticise shootings in the Archdiocese of Armagh. In 1983, for instance, he accused a member of the Ulster Defence Regiment of murdering Martin Malone, an eighteen-year-old youth, who had been killed by a single shot at point-blank range. With regard to the six killings which occurred in late 1982 in the Armagh area which later became the subject of the controversial Stalker report,* Cardinal O'Fiaich spoke of 'disturbing aspects' to the incidents in question. He pointed out that as two of the men were shot in his own parish, he had been able to get first-hand accounts from priests who had been called to the scene. The Cardinal claimed that: '. . . One of the men who had been killed previously had come to the parochial house to say that he had been threatened with death by the security forces . . . there is no doubt that the other was stopped at a road-check and threatened with death and one of the priests had to go out to try to save him . . .' (*Irish Press*, 3 January 1983, p. 1)

Nationalist opinion surrounding the events of 30 January 1972, when thirteen civilians were shot dead by the British Army at a civil rights march in Derry, was uniform: the British Army had murdered these people in cold blood. Within hours of the shooting, Cardinal Conway had clearly subscribed to this view when he said:

> I am deeply shocked at the news of the awful slaughter in Derry this afternoon. I have received a first-hand account from a priest who was present at the scene and what I have heard is really shocking.
>
> An impartial and independent public enquiry is immediately called for and I have telegraphed the British Prime Minister to this effect.
>
> Meantime, I call upon the whole Catholic community to preserve calm and dignity in the face of this terrible news. If an impartial and independent public inquiry is held the world will be able to judge what has happened. (*Belfast Telegraph*, 31 January 1972)

The most remarkable feature of the Cardinal's statement was that he had formed a definite and immediate opinion of the tragedy. Indeed, after speaking with uncharacteristic bitterness

---

* John Stalker, the Deputy Chief Constable of Greater Manchester, appointed to investigate these shootings, was taken off the assignment and suspended from the police force for three months, but was later re-instated in his old job. In December 1986, Stalker resigned. See *Irish Times*, 20 December 1986. The West Yorkshire Chief Constable, Colin Sampson, took charge of the NI investigation. For accounts of this major controversy see, Frank Doherty, *The Stalker Affair: including an account of the British Secret Service*, Dublin: The Mercier Press, 1986, and John Stalker's own version of events, *Stalker*, London: Harrap, 1988.

about the slaughter that had occurred in Derry, the Cardinal's demand for an 'impartial and independent public inquiry' was clearly designed to expose the guilt of the authorities in the matter. A war of words had begun: a senior British Army officer said it was absolute rubbish to suggest that there had been no gunmen at the scene of the shooting and that they had not first opened fire on the troops. The next day, seven local priests took the unprecedented step of calling an international press-conference to repudiate the version of events given by the British Army. Stressing that six of the priests had been at different points in the Bogside at the time of the shooting, the clerics issued a statement. Accusing the colonel of the Parachute Regiment of 'wilful murder', the statement (see *Irish Times*, 1 February 1972) went on:

> . . . We accuse the Commander of land forces of being an accessory before the fact . . . we accuse the soldiers of shooting indiscriminately into a fleeing crowd, of gloating over casualties, of preventing spiritual and medical aid reaching some of the dying . . . it was untrue that shots were fired at the troops in Rossville Street before they attacked. It was untrue that any of the dead that we attended were armed.
>
> We make this statement in view of the distorted and indeed conflicting reports put out by army officers. We deplore the action of the army and Government in employing a unit such as the Paratroopers who were in Derry yesterday. These men are trained criminals. They differ from terrorists only in the veneer of respectability that a uniform gives them.

This statement was not merely a more detailed and bitter version of events than that given by Cardinal Conway: it simply underlined the fact that Northern Ireland was looking down an abyss. Despite the patent anger of the priests' statement, its last two sentences were quite striking viewed from either a Unionist or nationalist position: for the Unionist population, of course, the priests' refusal to distinguish between terrorists and members of the security forces bordered on the treasonable; for the nationalists, on the other hand, what had been perpetrated in

Derry by the British Army still *could not justify* the violence of the IRA. Both sets of antagonists had been seen as 'criminals'. Polarisation between the Catholic and Protestant communities had become more complete than ever. Even the most moderate strands of Protestant opinion in Northern Ireland had taken offence at what Cardinal Conway had said about events in Derry. In their opinion, the Cardinal had presented a 'one-sided view' (*Belfast Telegraph*, 2 February 1972).

Within the Catholic Church in Ireland, however, there was total solidarity on the issue. The influential Dominican publication, *Doctrine and Life*, vol. 22, no. 3, March 1972, had the following to say: '. . . Why write an editorial about this in a review which normally confines itself to other matters? Because the lies of British officialdom are, alas, carrying the day in Britain and abroad . . . one feels that the fair-minded British public is being betrayed; that if it knew the facts it would condemn outright the outrages that have been perpetrated in its name by the Paratroopers especially . . .' With a clear view to mobilising Catholic opinion on an international scale, moreover, the Northern Irish Branch of the Association of Irish Priests prepared an account of the shootings for distribution to priests' associations all over the world.

More important still was not only the decision of local priests to testify at the official inquiry under Lord Widgery (*Report of the Tribunal appointed to inquire into the events on Sunday, 30th January, 1972, which led to loss of life in connection with the procession in Londonderry on that day*, paragraph 10, p. 38), but also the way in which this decision was endorsed by the families of the victims.[2] Ultimately, the conviction of civilians most familiar with the events of Bloody Sunday, i.e. that the army had murdered thirteen unarmed and innocent people, was clearly not upheld by Widgery. Among his conclusions were that: 'None of the deceased or wounded is proved to have been shot whilst handling a firearm or bomb. Some are wholly acquitted of complicity in such action; but there is a strong suspicion that some others had been firing weapons or handling bombs in the course of the afternoon and that yet others had been closely supporting them.'

Disappointment and frustration were widespread among the

nationalist community at the outcome of the inquiry. One eye-witness, Raymond McClean, in *The Road to Bloody Sunday*, pp. 139–141, has argued, however, that the Catholic Church was to some extent responsible for this unhappy sequel to the tragedy of Bloody Sunday: '. . . I was extremely disappointed to hear that a group of local clergy, headed by Fr Mulvey, had made a public statement in favour of attendance at Widgery and that the immediate families were in agreement with their statement. Our case for a truly independent enquiry had been sterilised at birth* . . . In my opinion the clergy had seriously underestimated the devious nature and political manoeuvring skills of the British establishment machine . . .'

However one wishes to interpret the role of the clergy in all this, the refusal of the Church to accept Widgery's conclusions was, however, obvious more than two years after Bloody Sunday. When the relatives of those killed in Derry were paid a total of £42,000 in compensation, Bishop Edward Daly (who as a local curate had been among those to testify at the Widgery Inquiry), challenged the British Government to tell the whole truth about Bloody Sunday. He then asserted 'the full truth is that all the victims were completely innocent' (*Irish News*, 20 December 1974).

As some of the deaths of civilians in disputed circumstances have been caused by plastic bullets, it is hardly surprising that the use of this weapon has proved controversial. The lethal nature of plastic bullets is clearly reflected by the following statistics in an article which appeared in *Fortnight*, no. 182, July/August 1981, p. 5: '. . . Thus, there have now been seven deaths from an estimated 17,000 rounds of plastic bullets fired—a fatality rate that is far higher than the 1 per 18,000 for rubber bullets, which were dropped partly because their tendency to kill people was politically unacceptable.' Given the frequency of these fatalities, human rights activists, Fr Denis Faul and Fr Raymond Murray, co-authored two publications denouncing the use of these weapons, viz. *Rubber and Plastic Bullets Kill and*

---

* At the instigation of the NCCL, a legal report was produced which drew widely different conclusions from those of Widgery. See Samuel Dash, *Justice Denied—A Challenge to Lord Widgery's Report on Bloody Sunday*, London: National Council for Civil Liberties, 1972.

Maim—Violations of Human Rights by RUC and British Army in Northern Ireland and *Plastic Bullets, Plastic Government—Deaths and Injuries by Plastic Bullets, August 1981–1982.*

As for the hierarchy, the earliest and most frequent critic of the use of plastic bullets has been Bishop Edward Daly of Derry. As early as 26 May 1981, Bishop Daly said that in the wake of the deaths of four people from plastic bullets, there was a need for an enquiry into their use and the manner in which they were being fired. In August 1982, moreover, Dr Daly spoke out against the continued use of plastic bullets in two consecutive days.[3] As if to leave the authorities and the general public in no doubt as to the attitude of the bishops towards these weapons, the hierarchy of the ecclesiastical province of Armagh issued a statement on the matter in July 1983 (see *Irish Times*, 5 July 1983, p. 7). Part of that statement read as follows:

> . . . Over many years we have repeatedly pointed out the immorality of violence in all its forms. It is precisely because we reject violence and are deeply concerned to prevent anything which might lead to its increase, that we feel obliged now to refer to two major issues*: the first is the use of plastic bullets.
>
> Many people have been killed by these weapons, some of them very young. Each of these deaths has caused deep grief to the family of the victims. The deaths have generated resentment throughout whole communities and have been the cause of growing alienation among wide sections of the population . . . Rioting is morally wrong but the methods used to control it must also be subject to the moral law. There cannot be one law for the security forces and another for the public. The use of plastic bullets is morally indefensible. The plastic bullet should be withdrawn as a riot control weapon . . .

Despite such a clearly enunciated position on the matter by the

* The other issue was the proposed re-introduction of capital punishment in the United Kingdom for certain types of killings, including those of paramilitary organisations in Northern Ireland. The proposal was defeated in the House of Commons.

Catholic Church and a host of other institutions,* plastic bullets are still being used by the security forces for riot control.

Given the level of violence in Northern Ireland and the top priority given to security by the authorities, it is hardly surprising that widespread accusations of military harassment of civilians have been made throughout most of the period in question. In the course of his testimony to the international lawyers' inquiry (see Asmal, pp. 26–27, paragraph 45) into killings by the security forces in disputed circumstances, Fr Murray of Armagh claimed that with regard to harassment: '. . . Over the years, I'm sure Fr Faul and I have made a thousand complaints and nothing ever comes of these complaints. There's no outlet, there's no opening for justice and this harassment and intimidation have increased in these last few years, especially because of the withdrawal of the other British regiments from the area . . . We have found that with the 'Ulsterisation', harassment has increased a lot and we just couldn't do anything about this because complaints fell on deaf ears.'

For its part, the hierarchy has acknowledged harassment of the civilian population by the security forces, albeit in an unsystematic way. For instance, both bishops of Down and Connor during the period of this study have referred to this problem. When still Bishop of Ardagh and Clonmacnoise, Bishop Cahal Daly spoke about this on a number of occasions. His predecessor in Down and Connor, William Philbin, arguably one of the most conservative Northern bishops of this period, also referred to this aspect of life in certain parts of his diocese. In his most substantive ever address on the situation in Northern Ireland, whose dominant theme was condemnation of IRA activities, Philbin also said at one point in *Ireland's Problem*, 1974, p. 5, that: '. . . in relation to all this [IRA violence] there has been greatly intensified military activity, the brunt of which often was directed to whole districts rather than to the persons who were directly involved. There were many instances in which reaction went far beyond legitimate limits . . .'

* Among these institutions, for example, was the European Parliament which voted a ban on the use of plastic bullets. See Alfred McClung Lee, *Terrorism In Northern Ireland*, New York: General Hall, 1983, p. 175.

In November 1972, a large group of priests in the diocese of Down and Connor organised an international press-conference at which they exposed 'military violence' in poorer areas of Belfast. The more important passages of their prepared statement were the following:

> We have condemned violence in the past when it was carried out by private citizens. We cannot now remain silent in the face of the violence now being used by the British Army, particularly in the poorer Catholic areas.
>
> No military victory could justify this campaign of attacking a civilian population . . . Homes are raided over and over again, at all hours of the day and night. People are arrested daily in their homes, places of work, social clubs and on the streets . . . This campaign of violence by the regular army became all the more intolerable when it is claimed that there are not enough soldiers to protect the population in other parts of the city from murder gangs. The army must be made to recognise that its first duty is to protect all innocent lives.
>
> Redress for these injustices has been refused even when full details have been given of military violence against people who have no involvement in any political movement. Indeed, if they were so involved, they ought not to be treated in such a way. People in the depressed areas of Belfast feel bereft of the protection of the law . . . We intend to make known in every place in which we can do so the consequences of this campaign, and especially in those countries which are soon to be our partners in the Common Market.
>
> We believe that the truth of what is happening must be told. We also propose immediately to organise direct non-violent action in the worst affected areas and to be present in some numbers with the suffering people. (*Irish Times*, 21 November 1972)

Obvious differences of perception and response existed within the clergy *vis-à-vis* the conduct of the British Army. As we have already seen, for example, the Irish hierarchy spoke of two campaigns of violence in a statement in 1975, viz. those of republican and loyalist paramilitaries, (see p. 93). In contrast, the above statement, unlike any by members of the hierarchy, actually spoke of the British Army's *campaign of violence*. Moreover, only a week before the sixty-five priests held this press-conference, Bishop Philbin and the priests of the Belfast deanery had issued a brief statement on the political situation in the city (see *Irish News*, 15 November 1972). The most pertinent part of that statement read as follows: 'We offer our deepest sympathy to the people in so many areas who are suffering in the present situation, whether from assassination, harassment, intimidation from their homes, burning of their business premises and houses, attacks on their churches and schools or from the deeds of violent men . . .' Far from accusing the army of waging a campaign of violence, the above statement was so vague that its only reference to military activity, however oblique, was when it spoke of people suffering from harassment.

One interpretation of the protest by the sixty-five priests and the position of Bishop Philbin was that:

> . . . The compassion which had motivated the original impulse was deeply universal as it was decided that it was just not good enough to be seen to be compassionate but that a public declaration of feeling for and identification with the victims of brutality should occur. It was accepted that such a declaration would not prejudice the efforts of Dr Philbin, Bishop of Down and Connor, on his own at the level of higher political and military authority to mitigate the severity of the current army policy . . . (*Hibernia*, 1 December 1972)

Such a view, however, begs a number of questions. First, if compassion for the laity was so universal and equally deep throughout the diocese, why wasn't there a common statement of a hard-hitting kind similar to that of the sixty-five priests issued on behalf of *all* clerics in Down and Connor? Second, if Bishop Philbin was attempting to achieve the same goals as those sixty-five priests who issued the much more militant statement, and he felt it possible to achieve these goals by quiet diplomacy, his perception of political reality clearly differed from the same sixty-five priests who had claimed that redress for such injustices had been refused by the authorities. Above all, the findings of my questionnaire to all the priests of Northern Ireland in April/May 1986 revealed widespread dissatisfaction as to how they regarded the response of the hierarchy to state violence: no fewer than 43.1 per cent expressed the opinion that the hierarchy has not done enough to oppose state violence throughout the period in question. Moreover, the level of dissatisfaction among the priests of Down and Connor in this regard was 59.5 per cent, the highest of any Northern diocese.

The protest of the sixty-five Belfast priests merely reflected the widespread alienation of Catholics in the area and the frustration of local priests who felt it necessary to point out that 'redress for these injustices has been refused, even when full details of military violence against people have been given'. What this meant in practice was spelled out by Fr Brady, who claimed that one priest had made more than fifty official complaints to the police about army behaviour. Only in four cases had the police investigated, and of those, only two had resulted in court cases. In addition, some interesting background to the protest was provided by an article which appeared in *Hibernia* on 19 January 1973, on page 6, which claimed that prior to the sixty-five priests calling their press-conference, some of their colleagues had had a meeting with high-ranking military officers to discuss their grievances. In an earlier meeting between a lower-ranking officer and a group of priests, one of the clerics was represented as saying that: 'I have only one problem remaining—it is at what moment precisely to do all in my power to lead the people in my area in a massive uprising against you.'

While nothing quite so dramatic ever occurred, the priests certainly made good their threat to highlight their claims both in Europe and further afield. According to *Hibernia*, at least, not only did the priests believe that Britain would feel vulnerable with such adverse publicity at a time when that country was entering the EEC, but that the then head of the British Army in Northern Ireland, General Tuzo, would be equally sensitive to such criticism as he was about to take up a new military post in West Germany. The strategy chosen by the priests was to provide information about British Army conduct to journalists and other writers in America and other European countries.

Finally, while it is a moot point as to how more effective such a protest would have been with the clear support of all the clerics of Down and Connor, it was claimed that army harassment reduced substantially after the priests' protest (at least in the immediate term). While the correspondent who made this claim was not perfectly clear as to *why* this had occurred, it is apparent how determined the priests were in making their protest effective. Certainly, the article in question informs its readers that two of the protesting priests had met the then Taoiseach, Jack Lynch, to ask him to raise the matter of military harassment with his British counterpart, Edward Heath, the day before the two premiers were due to meet for talks in London (*Hibernia*, 19 January 1973, p. 6).

Loyalist violence has occurred during much of the period under examination. According to McKeown, in fact, loyalists have been responsible for 624 deaths between July 1969 and July 1984, or just over 25 per cent of the total figure killed in Northern Ireland. The overwhelming majority of loyalist targets, as he puts it, 'were essentially Catholic civilian groups'.[4] Not surprisingly, loyalist violence has been a major source of terror among Catholics, especially in the most affected areas of Northern Ireland viz. Belfast, East Antrim and North Armagh. The response of the Catholic Church towards security policy in this area is examined here.

Following the catastrophic events of August 1969 and the subsequent deployment of British troops in the North, the Northern bishops issued a lengthy statement, reported in the *Irish News*, 25 August 1969, the most pertinent passages of which read as follows:

> . . . They [the Northern bishops] deeply regret that the true picture of these events has been greatly obscured by official statements and by the character of the coverage given in certain influential news media.
>
> The fact is that on Thursday and Friday of last week the Catholic districts of Falls and Ardoyne were invaded by mobs equipped with machine-guns and other firearms. A

community which was virtually defenceless was swept by gunfire and streets of Catholic homes were systematically set on fire.

We entirely reject the hypothesis that the origin of last week's tragedy was an armed insurrection . . . In this context we regret that the full evidence available regarding the actions of some of the police in the early hours of the morning in the Bogside area of Derry last January, has never been made public. We are convinced that in the terror evoked in the people of Bogside that night lies the basic explanation of recent events in Derry . . .

We ask all concerned to realise that among Catholics, belief in the impartiality of the Ulster Special Constabulary is virtually non-existent. The future can hold out no hope whatever unless the whole community is able to trust the forces of law and order . . .

The most salient feature of this statement was that it clearly exonerated the Catholic community in Belfast of causing the violence which had just occurred, and instead, placed the blame on some of their Protestant neighbours. Implicit in the statement, however, was the failure of the security forces to prevent the loyalist violence that had occurred in the city. With regard to events in Derry, the bishops' criticism of security policy was even more explicit insofar as they clearly pointed to the behaviour of the RUC in the Bogside in January of that year as the cause of the August disturbances.

Underlying the bishops' statement was the realisation that the British Government had assumed much of the responsibility for governing Northern Ireland. Only days before the hierarchy had issued their statement, the so-called Downing Street Declaration had been made on 19 August 1969, which clearly pointed to this development. The importance of this radical change in the Government of Northern Ireland had been clearly grasped by the Catholic Church. As we have seen in chapter 1, it was at this time that Church influence was at its zenith, and an important part of that influence was enjoyed as a result of the working relationship that had been established between the Church (especially Cardinal Conway) and the Home Secretary,

James Callaghan. Despite such clerical influence, the bishops, unlike some other strands of non-Unionist opinion,[5] did not *explicitly* prescribe changes in security policy. Instead, the Church leaders *implicitly* called for reforms in this area by emphasising the perception among Catholics that the 'B' Specials were not an impartial force and that there was no hope for the future unless the whole community could come to trust the forces of law and order. Nonetheless, in saying that the Church was lending its voice to the reform of security policy in Northern Ireland, it must be admitted that such a voice was a relatively weak one.

An important purpose of the bishops' statement was to contradict the Unionist interpretation of events. In alleging how the events of August 1969 had been obscured by official statements, the hierarchy was responding to the claims of the Prime Minister, Chichester-Clark, who claimed during the course of a debate at Stormont on 14 August 1969, that: '. . . people in Britain and elsewhere who are watching these events should waken up to the reality of what is happening here. This is not the agitation of a minority seeking by lawful means the assertion of political rights. It is the conspiracy of forces seeking to overthrow a government democratically elected by a large majority . . .' For their part, the bishops in their statement entirely rejected the hypothesis that an armed insurrection had occurred.*

The hierarchy was slow to publicly articulate its concern about the loyalist campaign in the early 1970s. Indeed, it was only in November 1972, when approximately sixty Catholics had been assassinated by loyalists, that separate statements were issued on this matter by Cardinal Conway and Bishop Philbin (together with the priests of the Belfast deanery).[6] In neither case, however, was security policy criticised by the clerics. Indeed, Cardinal Conway suggested in his statement that republican violence had largely provoked the loyalist campaign. One year

---

* Almost a week before the hierarchy's statement, Bishop Philbin (who had earlier urged the prime minister to deploy troops in the Ardoyne area of Belfast) made it clear to him that 'the Catholic community cannot accept the implication of his recent statement that the origins of the present disturbances lie on a conspiracy on their side to subvert a democratically elected government'. Source: *Irish News*, 18 August 1969, p. 4

later, the Cardinal first criticised security policy in this regard, albeit mildly, when he said that while he was not suggesting the authorities were unconcerned about the loyalist campaign of violence, such concern did not appear to be reflected by the authorities' response to the situation. A few days later in a radio interview, Cardinal Conway made more specific criticisms of government policy towards the problem of loyalist assassinations when he claimed that there were more unsolved killings than available detectives. He continued: 'The first tangible measures taken were the setting-up of joint army–police patrols in Belfast but even that step was not taken until the campaign had been under way for eleven months and more than 100 people had been killed . . . the primary responsibility for taking steps rests with the authorities and there is an impression among the minority that not a sufficiently effective line is being taken in this matter . . . Greater vigilance is needed . . .' (*Irish Independent*, 12 November 1973)

While the decision made the next day to proscribe loyalist groups such as the Ulster Freedom Fighters and the Red Hand Commandos does not appear to have been influenced by the Cardinal's comments, such proscriptions in any event seem to have had no effect on the course of the loyalist campaign. So much so, that we find a recurrence of hierarchical criticism during the wave of sectarian violence in 1975. The most important pronouncement was one by Cardinal Conway and his fellow-bishops in the ecclesiastical province of Armagh, who, in a far-ranging message deplored the 'ghastly campaign of sectarian murders', claiming that in so many assessments of the Northern Ireland problem, this feature of it had been virtually ignored.

Given the gravity of the loyalist campaign, it is hardly surprising that some members of the Catholic laity have criticised their Church for not being more active in highlighting this problem. Thus, in 1973 the *Andersonstown News* reported that a group of Catholic lay people staged protests of this kind outside Catholic churches. Later in 1981, relatives of some of those people killed by loyalists (and security forces) formed a group called Silent Too Long, whose purpose was to highlight this aspect of the troubles in Northern Ireland.

In putting the Church's response to security policy *vis-à-vis* loyalist violence into perspective, two points ought to be made. First, it is a moot point whether the suggestion by such groups, i.e. the Church ought to have been more vocal in highlighting loyalist violence, would have led to changes in this area of security policy. Second, a positive response on the part of clerics towards the Silent Too Long group is significant insofar as such a response can be interpreted as tacit condemnation of the Church's past response to the problem of loyalist violence, especially since that campaign was at its height between 1972 and 1977. Thus, while it is hardly surprising that leading human rights activists such as Fr Denis Faul and Fr Brian Brady supported this group, it is interesting to note that Cardinal O'Fiaich was the sole member of the hierarchy to identify himself with the Silent Too Long group when he met them in late 1981. The Cardinal was said to have been 'horrified' by the statistics presented to him on the killings of Catholic civilians in Northern Ireland.[7]

When internment without trial was introduced in Northern Ireland on 9 August 1971, the response of the Catholic community was one of fierce resistance. In his book, *The Northern Ireland Social Democratic and Labour Party: political opposition in a divided society*, 1977, p. 99, McAllister describes the effects of internment on the Catholic community rather well:

> . . . The reaction in Catholic areas was immediate, violent and strengthened by the very obvious fact that the military capacity of the IRA had been left unimpaired. To many Catholics internment appeared not as a carefully planned and executed military operation against the IRA, but a punitive expedition against their community. As the stories of ill-treatment began to filter back, Catholics closed ranks around the single issue of internment. The raw statistics of violence before and after internment have been frequently quoted, but they attest directly to its failure. In the six months preceding August there were 288 explosions; in the succeeding six months, this increased three-fold. In the same two periods, shooting incidents multiplied six-fold, security deaths four-fold and civilian deaths over eight-fold respectively . . .

It was hardly surprising, therefore, that there were several

clerical statements on internment at the time of its implementation. The most notable of these were by Cardinal Conway in
August, a statement by the bishops of the Northern dioceses
and a separate statement by the entire Irish hierarchy in
September. In November 1971, there were two major statements
largely related to the alleged torture of internees by 387 Northern Ireland priests and a similar statement from their bishops
later that month.

The first detailed statement,* however, was issued by Cardinal Conway within a week of the introduction of internment.
His statement, reported in the *Irish News*, 16 August 1971, read
as follows:

> Internment without trial is a terrible power to give to any
> political authority. Catholic bishops have over and over
> again condemned killings and other forms of violence as a
> means to political ends and it has been acknowledged that
> this view is shared by the great majority of Catholic people.
>
> It is necessary to state that abhorrence of internment
> without trial and particularly its one-sided application, is
> especially deep and widespread among those same people.
>
> At the present time it is important that the strong light of
> publicity should be focused not merely on reasons put
> forward to justify internment but also on the manner in
> which it has been exercised.
>
> Already there is *prima facie* evidence that entirely innocent
> men taken from their homes in the early hours of Monday
> morning were subjected to humiliating and brutal treat-
> ment by security forces.
>
> This evidence should be open to rigorous and independ-
> ent examination.
>
> For an official spokesman to say, as he has done, that
> complaints should be forwarded to the police for examina-
> tion must inevitably seem to those concerned in the climate
> of Northern Ireland at the present time as bordering on
> cynicism.

* The Cardinal had issued a statement on the first day of internment, but this
had merely called on Catholics to control their feelings. See *Irish News*, 10
August 1971.

One hopes that British and world opinion will maintain close and impartial scrutiny over this terrible power.

To say this is not to condone in any way activities of anyone who has deliberately stimulated violence and who therefore must share with others responsibility for deaths and the terrible suffering of so many thousands of people in recent weeks.

Catholic people should not allow themselves to be persuaded into violent or sterile or self-destructive forms of protest.

The importance of the above statement was not only that its major focus of discussion was internment, but that it encapsulated the most salient features of clerical protest relating to internment during this period. Consequently, in identifying the dominant themes of the above statement, it is possible to put these matters into perspective through wider reference to other statements and developments of the time.

Given the Church's consistent condemnation of republican violence, it is hardly surprising that any criticism of internment would be accompanied by their stated opposition to the activities of the IRA. From the hierarchy's point of view, it was more important than ever to make their views known on republican violence, given the rapid escalation in the level of violence in Northern Ireland. This was reflected not only by the above statement, but by the fact that the two statements issued by the hierarchy in September 1971 dealt more with republican violence than any other aspect of the political situation. That said, however, both statements in September acknowledged that republican violence was not the only feature of the political situation at the time.[8]

In criticising Government policy, moreover, the Northern hierarchy demonstrated a remarkable sensitivity towards the feelings of Protestants in Northern Ireland. Certainly in a statement by the bishops of the Northern dioceses in which they had listed criticisms of the *status quo*, including the policy of internment, the statement went on: '. . . Many Protestants in Northern Ireland—good Christian people—will not like our mentioning these things. We ask them to realise that these facts are part of the total situation. What we want to emphasise is that we are painfully aware of these facts and *nevertheless* we condemn the violence . . .' (*Irish News*, 13 September 1971) More than anything else, the above passage highlighted the dilemma which confronted the Catholic Church. While, on the one hand, the bishops felt themselves obliged to condemn both internment and IRA violence, they were also aware of how community relations in Northern Ireland had deteriorated still further as a result of events at that time. However sincere such a gesture may have been, it was to little avail: Protestant attitudes had hardened to the extent that many members of that community did not want to understand the widely-held views of their Catholic neighbours. So much so, that during this period, according to two leading Methodists, Eric Gallagher and Stanley Worrall, in *Christians In Ulster, 1968–1980*, 1982, on page 64, during this period: '. . . criticism from within their own Churches of the Protestant leaders for being too accommodating to the other side became more vocal. Sermons of an increasingly belligerent character were reported in the newspapers . . .'

The manner in which internment was condemned by the Catholic Church in a variety of statements underlined an important difference in emphasis between the higher and lower clergy. While Cardinal Conway was only prepared, as we have already seen, to describe internment as 'a terrible power to give to any political authority' (see p. 112), a majority of priests in Northern Ireland condemned the policy as immoral. On the first day of its implementation, Fr Brian Brady of Belfast declared internment to be immoral,[9] while a few weeks later, Fr Denis Faul of Dungannon made the same judgment in an article which appeared in the *Irish News*. Faul based his claim on a Vatican II document entitled *Pastoral Constitution on the Church in the Modern World*, paragraph 27, which said: '. . . The Council lays stress on respect for the human person . . . all offences against human dignity such as arbitrary imprisonment, deportation, slavery . . . all these and the like are criminal; they poison civilisation and they debase the perpetrators more than the victims and militate against the honour of the Creator.'

It was, however, in November 1971, that this view was clearly seen to be held by most members of the lower clergy. In a statement by 387 priests, which was easily the largest protest of its kind throughout the period of this study, it was alleged that internees had been subjected to brutality and torture. The statement also argued that imprisonment without trial was immoral. Again, the basis of this judgment was paragraph 27 of the *Pastoral Constitution on the Church in the Modern World* which was quoted in part during the course of the priests' statement.[10]

It was not coincidental that while the hierarchy failed to address the intrinsic morality of internment, 387 priests declared it to be immoral. Indeed, in a letter dated 23 September 1971, the Ulster branch of the Association of Irish Priests had called on the bishops of Ireland to condemn internment as immoral *in se.** The importance of the hierarchy's failure to do so lies in the Roman Catholic view of society. As Hickey, in *Religion and the Northern Ireland Problem*, 1984, p. 86, correctly points out:

> ... Thus in Northern Ireland there are two groups who, apart from other characteristics are distinguished by an interpretation of Christian beliefs which has direct social consequences. On the one hand, there is the Protestant view of religion which sees Christians as coming together to form the 'city of the holy'. This city is created by the voluntary cohesion of believers who join together to form a society based upon the creed of a common belief. This common belief is adhered to voluntarily and does not have imposed upon it the dogmatic authority of a hierachically organised church basing its claim upon the transmission of grace throug'. its clergy. On the other hand, there is the Roman Catholic view of society based upon a world view which accords *authority* to higher powers vested in a privileged elite—the clergy. This group can dispense grace through the sacraments and can therefore operate the types of sanctions on the lives of individuals, which no other institution can do ...

Given this Roman Catholic view of the world, the implications for the Catholic community and the Catholic Church at the time

* For a copy of this letter, see appendix D.

of internment were enormous. Members of that community were simply not conditioned to making individual moral judgments, but instead, were predisposed to look to Church authorities to make pronouncements of this kind. Important also were the possible political effects on the Catholic community, had the bishops declared internment to be morally wrong. While I would not argue that such a hypothetical pronouncement would have in any way altered the level of nationalist violence at the time, I would contend, however, it could only have further strengthened opposition to internment within the Catholic community. Moreover, the failure of the bishops to address the morality of internment could only have eroded the *hierarchical view of moral authority among the more perceptive members of the Catholic community in Northern Ireland.* In effect, what had happened was that 387 members of the lower clergy had referred to one of the Vatican *II* documents to justify their view on the immorality of internment, while their ecclesiastical superiors had chosen not to make a moral judgment on the matter at all. Arguably, at least, a large body of priests in Northern Ireland had, by default, assumed the role of moral leadership for the Catholic community at a critical time.

In any case, following the series of hierarchical condemnations of internment in late 1971, the bishops tended to be less vocal in their opposition to this measure in subsequent years. Certainly, it was only when Edward Daly became Bishop of Derry in 1974 that the question of internment was *clearly* made a top priority yet again by any member of the hierarchy. These activities included calls from Daly in April and October of 1974 for an end to internment and a direct appeal to the Secretary of State, Merlyn Rees, to this effect when the two men met in April 1975. In addition, Bishop Daly and his clergy led thousands of people in Derry City in a candlelight procession in which prayers were said for internees and the ending of internment.[11] Despite such activities, Rees has failed to acknowledge any of the opposition to internment as a factor in his decision to end this emergency measure at the end of 1975. Rather, he asserts that one of his main priorities from the beginning of his period as Secretary of State (in February 1974) was to end internment as soon as possible.[12]

Whatever tensions within the Catholic Church of Northern Ireland were caused by internment, it was the diocese of Down and Connor which was most visibly affected in this way. Two of the priests who resigned from this diocese between 1973 and 1975 gave what they saw as the disappointing response of the local church to internment as one of the reasons for their decision to resign from the priesthood. While this number may seem minuscule, it is interesting to note, however, that both men had been part of the diocese's intellectual élite. Fr Terry O'Keefe resigned from the priesthood in 1973 when he was ordered by Bishop Philbin to give up a lecturing post at the New University of Ulster and move to Ballymoney as a curate. According to other priests, this proposed transfer was the bishop's way of disciplining Fr O'Keefe after he had spoken out against internment and the local church's interpretation of Vatican *II*.[13] The other priest in question, Dr Gus McEvoy, issued a lengthy statement on the matter. McEvoy, who also lectured at NUU spoke among other things of the Church having fallen down on its duty to speak out against internment and other forms of state repression.[14]

While Cardinal Conway's statement was designed to discredit the policy of internment by highlighting the official justification for the measure, it was his call for a 'rigorous and independent examination' into allegations of brutality against internees that received an almost instantaneous response from the authorities. Although a government spokesman immediately called on the Cardinal to submit to the General Officer in Command any evidence he may have had of internees being subjected to brutal treatment, it was only a week later that the establishment of an independent inquiry was announced by the British Government. Arguably, at least, the Primate had been instrumental in persuading the British authorities to establish such an inquiry. Ex-internee, McGuffin, in *The Guineapigs*, 1974, p. 76, has referred to a meeting between Cardinal Conway and Prime Minister, Edward Heath, in mid-August: '. . . His meeting with Heath was and is to this day, secret, but obviously enough was said to worry the Prime Minister . . . On 31 August 1971, Reggie Maudling [the then Home Secretary] announced that he was appointing a committee to investigate allegations 'of physical brutality' by the 'security forces' during the initial forty-eight-hour detention period . . .'*

Although the Cardinal had, not surprisingly, welcomed the establishment of such an inquiry, this did not deter the hierarchy from repeating the earlier allegations of the Primate. In September 1971 the Northern bishops issued a lengthy statement on the political situation, which spoke of: '. . . the deep indignation which the recent internment swoops caused, the humiliation of innocent men, the allegations of brutality and worse, many of which we are convinced are well-founded . . .' (*Irish Times*, 13 September 1971, p. 1)

In another statement at the end of the same month, the Irish bishops referred to many of the injustices in Northern Ireland. Implicit in what they said about internment was that prisoners had been subjected to brutal treatment. The hierarchy's statement talked of: '. . . the reaction [of the Catholic community] to internment and to the one-sided and inhuman way in which it has been exercised . . .' (*Irish Times*, 30 September 1971)

The statement of November 1971, which was signed by most Northern Ireland priests and declared internment to be immoral, also alleged that internees had been brutalised by the authorities. Expressing their deep conviction that brutality, physical and mental torture and psychological pressure had been inflicted on men arrested under the Special Powers Act since 9 August 1971, the priests' statement went on:

> . . . We believe that these barbarities are still being inflicted on innocent people—convicted of no crime—at the Palace Military Barracks, Hollywood, under the protection of law by the Special Branch of the RUC. We base our conviction on substantial medical evidence: on the testimony of priests who saw the injuries and on the statements of men whose truthfulness is already known to us through our pastoral work.
>
> We note, too, that the authorities have failed to explain

* McGuffin (p. 136) also claims that Cardinal Conway and the Department of Foreign Affairs in Dublin made representations to Whitehall concerning a small number of internees who had been subjected to electric-shock treatment. Prime Minister Heath personally ordered that this electric-shock treatment was to be stopped.

where the 12 missing men were from August 11th to 17th; where Liam Shannon was from October 9th to 17th; or where Graham Rogers was from October 11th to 17th . . .

We, therefore, demand that brutality and torture* by the forces of law be stopped immediately. We call for a public impartial judicial tribunal to expose the full truth of what has been done to people arrested since August 9th under the Special Powers Act, and to ensure the punishment of those responsible and redress for the victims. We condemn the holding of prisoners incommunicado from their relatives for indefinite periods. We want an immediate end to imprisonment without trial which is immoral and unjust. (*Irish Times*, 2 November 1971, p. 8)

Such a statement was remarkable *vis-à-vis* the earlier statements of the bishops in a variety of ways. First, the priests' allegations were highly detailed in nature. Not only did they clearly establish the basis for their allegations (viz. medical evidence, the testimony of priests who witnessed some of the injuries and the known truthfulness of the prisoners themselves), but the priests had actually listed names of people who had 'disappeared' for a number of days. Second, this statement, unlike those of the hierarchy, had actually called on those responsible for the alleged torture to be punished. Third, while the statements of the hierarchy in September 1971 had certainly implied mistrust of the government enquiry being held during the period, the priests had clearly dismissed such an inquiry as an irrelevancy by calling for 'a public impartial judicial tribunal to expose the full truth of what had been done to people arrested since 9 August'.

A few weeks after the statement by the 387 priests, the findings of the Compton inquiry into allegations of brutality were made known. Compton denied that brutality or torture had taken place but admitted that some ill-treatment of internees had occurred, and that interrogation in depth of prisoners had been authorised at senior level.

* Such allegations were largely upheld by a ruling of the European Court of Human Rights after the Irish Government brought the case against the British Government. See Peter Taylor, *Beating the Terrorists?*, Harmondsworth: Penguin, 1980, especially pp. 19–28.

Only days after Compton had published his findings, the Northern bishops issued a lengthy statement, reported in the *Irish Times*, 22 November 1971, p. 1. While condemning IRA violence and rather vaguely calling for 'far-reaching political initiatives', much of the statement related to the treatment of internees. The most pertinent passage read as follows:

> . . . It is also our duty, however, to condemn another form of violence which is also shameful and contrary to the law of Christ. We refer to the process known as 'interrogation in depth' as it has been practised in Northern Ireland in recent months. Men have been kept hooded and standing with arms and legs outstretched practically continuously for days and nights on end until from exhaustion (leading to repeated collapse), darkness, noise and thirst, they felt that they were going out of their minds and prayed for death. These were men who had been imprisoned without trial. One of them who suffered most has since been released.
>
> We condemn this treatment as immoral and inhuman. It is unworthy of the British people. It is a test of a civilised people that the methods of its elected government remain civilised even under extreme provocation. We have also disturbing medical evidence of the physical beatings of arrested persons, even in recent weeks . . .

Inherent in the bishops' statement was a total rejection of Compton's findings. Ignoring Compton's distinction between 'ill-treatment' and 'brutality' of prisoners, for instance, the hierarchy referred to the technique of interrogation in depth as a 'form of violence'. Moreover, in emphasising that the beatings were still taking place the hierarchy could be seen as criticising the narrow terms of reference of the Compton Report, which, as we have already seen, only looked at allegations of brutality during the first forty-eight hours of internment (p. 118).

The statement was also important because of its uncharacteristically militant language. Certainly, by referring to interrogation in depth as a 'form of violence', the hierarchy was unusually equating an aspect of security policy with the activities of paramilitary organisations. Moreover, unlike their failure to address the morality of internment, they had clearly seen interrogation in depth as 'immoral and inhuman'. Indeed, the whole statement was a highly emotive one, not least in its vivid description of the hardships endured by the internees.

All this, of course, indicated that Church–State relations were at a low ebb. So much so, that the statement appeared to be aimed at the conscience of the British public rather than at that of the British Government. Speaking of the treatment of internees, the bishops had said: '. . . It is unworthy of the British people. It is a test of a civilised people that the methods of its elected government remain civilised even under extreme provocation . . . '

(ii) *The Judiciary*

The first cleric to publicly criticise the Northern Ireland judiciary during the period of this study was Fr Denis Faul. In an address delivered in Dungannon, Co. Tyrone, he suggested that some of the judges and magistrates in Northern Ireland be transferred to the English and Scottish circuits for between five and ten years so that they could be replaced by English officials during that period. The reasoning behind such a proposal was made clear by the following passage from Fr Faul's address:

> . . . The belief of many people of the minority is — and it has been vindicated by the Cameron report and strengthened by recent tragic events — that they can never trust a Unionist politician, certainly not of the old kind, now or in the future. These judges are felt to have to all appearances, acquiesced in, perhaps actively promoted, systematic discrimination against the Catholic minority, and to have been rewarded for this and other services to Unionism by seats on the bench . . . (*Irish News*, 14 November 1969)

Such profound criticisms of the judiciary in Northern Ireland were met with predictable Unionist opposition. So much so, that three Unionist MPs and members of the legal profession, Robin Baillie, Basil McIvor and Robert Babington, put down a motion for debate in Stormont condemning Fr Faul's remarks (see *Newsletter*, 18 November 1969). In addition, Fr Faul's address was attacked by two members of the Northern Ireland Cabinet, the Minister for Home Affairs, Mr Porter, and the

Minister for Commerce, Mr Bradford. The latter called for Fr Faul's religious superiors to take the priest to task for what he had said (see *Irish Times*, 18 November 1969, pp. 1, 4).

It was against this background of mounting Unionist criticism that Cardinal Conway condemned Fr Faul's address. If one looks at the political stance adopted by the Cardinal at the time, however, his response was hardly surprising. As we have already seen in chapter 1, Cardinal Conway was endorsing the promised reform programme of this period, and indeed, only weeks earlier had enthusiastically welcomed the Hunt Report, describing it as 'important and far-reaching'. From the Primate's point of view, therefore, Fr Faul's address and the resultant Unionist criticism could only have added to the difficulties of securing reform within Northern Ireland. This was reflected by the Cardinal's statement, which, while critical of Fr Faul's comments, did not directly address the content of his priest's remarks. Indeed, apart from a brief introduction, the Cardinal's message was conveyed by a single sentence: '. . . The Cardinal deprecates these remarks which he considered both unfortunate and unwarranted.' (*Newsletter*, 18 November 1969) In effect, the Primate's statement was so vague that it would prove extremely difficult to misquote or distort, even in the unending war of words that is such a prominent feature of political life in Northern Ireland. This is precisely what occurred on a television programme shortly afterwards, when a guest attempted to use the Cardinal's statement as a *complete* defence for the legal system in the North. In a subsequent reply reported in the *Irish News*, 5 December 1969, it was stated that:

> In view of the use of the Cardinal's name in a television discussion on Tuesday night, it is pointed out that the statement issued in the Cardinal's name on November 17 did not refer to the whole field of justice in Northern Ireland. It dealt solely — as the introduction to the statement made clear — with certain remarks couched in general terms about 'the Northern Ireland judiciary' . . . to interpret the Cardinal's statement of November 17 as a blanket approval of the whole system and practice is incorrect . . .

Reaction to the controversy among the anti-Unionist population was anomalous: while there appeared to be a good deal of underlying support for Fr Faul, his views were only explicitly endorsed by a few scattered voices. Certainly, the pro-nationalist newspapers were quite sympathetic towards Fr Faul's position. The editorial of the *Irish News*, 19 November, pointed out: '. . . Father Faul has since been rebuked by his Ordinary—a rebuke which unhappily does not specify what in a lengthy address at Dungannon, was both 'unfortunate and unwarranted'. Father Faul said many things with which there will be widespread agreement among the minority . . .' For its part, the *Mid-Ulster Observer* claimed that it had held a 'spotcheck', indicating that a majority of Catholics in mid-Ulster sympathised with Fr Faul's address. Despite all that, Fr Faul appeared somewhat isolated in his views *vis-à-vis* political activists and clerical colleagues. The only parliamentarian who openly lent his support to Fr Faul's address was Austin Currie[15] and he was joined in this by the usually anti-clerical *United Irishman*, December 1969, p. 10. Faul also received the endorsement of the Campaign for Social Justice and the Armagh Labour Party, as well as the Dungannon Tenants' Group and the Cookstown branch of the Civil Rights Association. More significantly, Fr Faul appeared almost totally isolated within the Church. The only priest to publicly comment on the matter was Fr Des Wilson of Belfast. Moreover, while Fr Wilson was sympathetic, it must be emphasised that he did not necessarily agree with Faul's comments. Rather, Fr Wilson's address stressed the need for freedom of speech within the Catholic Church. He said he had read of the intervention of Church authority with horror and dismay. Fr Wilson insisted that a statement from a person such as Fr Faul should be listened to, made the subject of critical examination, objected to if necessary. He went on to say that everyone had a lot to learn about the value of open discussion.[16]

When seen in the light of Fr Faul's comments in November 1969, the refusal of many priests to complete their census forms in 1971 merely underlined how radicalised the Catholic community had become in the intervening period.

In April 1971, twenty-seven priests from the diocese of Down and Connor issued a statement, the most important parts of which read as follows:

On the 18th of April last a young man offended some members of this community by shouting a political slogan 'up the IRA'. He was taken by the police, convicted of crime in a court of law, and sentenced to a year's imprisonment.

On the same day, very many men and youths offended some members of the community by shouting political and anti-religious slogans 'up the UVF' and 'to hell with the Pope'. None were taken by the army or the police who were present and certainly knew the law was broken, none were convicted of crime, and none imprisoned . . .

We believe that minorities in our community whether they be political or religious, are not accorded equality of citizenship. We believe that there is evidence of inequality before the law from the current practices of its enforcement agencies — the police and the judiciary . . .

On reflection we have decided that we have a serious moral obligation to protest against the perversion of justice. It would be futile at this time to resort to any of the legal means of protest available in a normal society.

We have therefore decided to make known our abhorrence of the present operation of the law by refusing to complete the Government census forms . . . (*Irish News*, 24 April 1971)

The refusal of the priests to fill out their census forms, of course, constituted an unashamed violation of the law. Their disdain for the said law in Northern Ireland was reflected by what the priests called 'the perversion of justice'. Significantly, moreover, this protest had far wider terms of reference than that of Fr Faul in 1969. Not only did these twenty-seven priests from Down and Connor point a finger of guilt at both 'the police and the judiciary', but made a more profound criticism by asserting that 'minorities in our community, whether they be political or religious, are not accorded equality of citizenship'.

Although the priests' ecclesiastical leader, Bishop Philbin, refused to comment on their protest,[17] positive reaction came from other quarters. The pro-nationalist *Irish News*, on 26 April, described it in the following terms: 'Massive support was forthcoming last night both from fellow clergymen and from anti-Unionist groups throughout the country for the stand taken by the 27 priests in the Down and Connor diocese against the partial administration of the law in Northern Ireland . . .' Eighteen priests from Co. Tyrone gave what they described as 'unqualified support' to their colleagues in Down and Connor. Moreover, in the concluding sentence of their statement, the Tyrone priests alleged that the protest in Down and Connor had been effectively ignored by television journalists: '. . . .We also note with regret the lack of coverage given to their statement by both ITV and BBC national news.'

On hearing of this protest in Co. Tyrone, Fr Faul immediately lent it his complete support. Two days later the protest spread still further when a total of twenty-five priests from the diocese of Derry pledged their support. Their spokesman added that apart from their own decision not to fill out their census forms, many Catholics, both clergy and laity, had made their feelings known 'on the selective operation of the law at all levels by writing their protests on their census forms'. In all, a total of seventy-one priests,[18] or approximately 11 per cent* of all Northern priests, had refused to fill out their census forms. Many more, in common with many other anti-Unionists had written a note of formal protest in fulfilling their duty as citizens.[19]

In putting this census protest into perspective, it is necessary to understand how widespread these feelings were within the Catholic community. The Westminster MP for West Belfast, Gerry Fitt, for example, viewed the situation so seriously that he met the then Lord Chancellor, Lord Hailsham, and told him of the 'raging discontent' which was building up over the operation of the judicial system in Northern Ireland. Certainly, the priests' protest gained support from many groups including the Central Citizens' Defence Committee, the Association for Legal Justice and the Campaign for Social Justice. The following day, thirty-nine Catholic schoolteachers announced that they would also refuse to co-operate with the holding of the census.[20] Less than a week before the priests launched their protest,

* Assuming that the total number of priests in Northern Ireland has remained relatively stable, this percentage is calculated on the number of priests in Northern Ireland as outlined by *The Irish Catholic Directory* (1985).

republicans and the Civil Rights Association were deciding what their respective strategies would be towards the census. A few days later, it was reported that the Comhairle Ceanntair, Sinn Fein, Belfast, had said that while census enumerators should be impeded in every way, it was not urging that the questions should not be answered. In contrast, various republican clubs indicated that their members and supporters were planning to publicly burn their census forms.[21] According to the *Irish News*, thousands of census forms were burned in Belfast, with bonfires being made with heaps of forms in Andersonstown, Ballymurphy, Ardoyne, the Markets area and Springfield Road. In addition, it estimated that thousands of other census forms were not going to be completed because of an organised boycott by the civil rights and other groups throughout the North. Whether through accident or design, the priests' protest had played a part in opening a pandora's box throughout the nationalist community. Most remarkable of all, however, was the way in which the militancy of the protesting priests appeared to rival that of the Civil Rights Association and many republican groups throughout the North.

Still feeling dissatisfied about the response of the authorities to their earlier protest, the same group of priests, numbering seventy-one in all, decided to call for an open inquiry into the administration of the law in Northern Ireland. The most important part of their statement, reported in the *Irish News*, 23 April 1971, p. 1, read:

> ... Despite the public outcry two months ago, the response of the legal profession, apart from some honourable exceptions, has been disappointing. The decision to set up a joint committee from the Bar Council and the Incorporated Law Society is only a small step forward. Internal inquiries are rarely satisfactory ... One can recall the unhappy experience of the Bailie inquiry into the activities of the police in Derry ... Only an inquiry of the kind conducted by Lords Cameron, Hunt and Scarman will restore confidence in the law.
>
> We call for such an inquiry into the administration of law in Northern Ireland.

Clearly, the most significant feature of this statement was that its signatories had made an important pre-condition for any inquiry into the administration of justice in Northern Ireland: that it be an open one. Moreover, by praising the inquiries presided over by Englishmen and Scotsmen (viz. those of Lords Cameron, Hunt and Scarman), it was clear that if any inquiry which examined the administration of the law were to be held, it was implied that an official from 'across the water' should be chosen to head such an investigation.

Following a statement on television by the then Minister of State at the Department of Home Affairs, Mr John Taylor, who had described the protesters as 'political priests' displaying 'an unco-operative attitude to the security forces', Cardinal Conway finally broke the silence of the hierarchy over the ensuing controversy. The *Irish News*, 26 June 1971, described the Primate's statement as follows:

> Cardinal Conway said last night that anxiety about the administration of justice in Northern Ireland ought to be taken seriously. But the Cardinal refused to comment on specific instances mentioned in a recent statement by the 71 priests who are calling for an inquiry into the administration of law. The Cardinal, however, said he felt that anxiety about some aspects of the administration of justice was very deep, sincere and widespread.
>
> He added that it was very important in the context of community confidence that this anxiety be taken seriously.

Although the Cardinal had not *actually* supported the call for an inquiry, he obviously regarded some initiative of that kind to be necessary. After all, how else could anxiety about the administration of the law be taken seriously? Once again, however, one is struck by the circumspect nature of the Cardinal's statement: while he had acknowledged the importance of the issue in question, there was no attempt on his part to become *directly involved*.

In putting the Cardinal's stance into perspective, however, it is necessary to understand the fundamental changes that had occurred in distinct, but interacting areas: the decline in the political influence of the Catholic Church between 1969 and

1971; the wider political context of Northern Ireland. As we have already seen in chapter 1, the strategy of the Church from August 1969 had largely come unstuck by mid-1970. The period of this census protest, as it turned out, was to mark the final phase of SDLP attempts to work within the framework of one-party rule in Northern Ireland, a policy that had been endorsed, albeit tacitly, by the Catholic Church when it appointed a chaplain to Stormont in February 1971. Second, it was against a background of escalating violence and a generally deteriorating political situation in Northern Ireland, that the Church had become radicalised to the point that such a large number of priests were prepared to take part in a protest of this kind. It was under these conflicting pressures, then, that the Cardinal had spoken on the issue but certainly one thing was clear: it was unthinkable that the Cardinal would react as he had done in November 1969 when Fr Faul's criticisms of the Northern Ireland judiciary had been dismissed by the Primate as being 'unfortunate and unwarranted'.

Naturally enough, the controversy surrounding the priests' refusal to fill in their census forms had not been forgotten by the authorities. In November 1971, eight of the protesting clerics were among twenty-one people who were fined £7 for their refusal to fill out their census. All the priests refused to pay their fines, but instead, said they intended to make a contribution equal to the amount of the fine and costs to the Association for Legal Justice. In a statement they issued outside the court, which was reported in the *Irish Times*, 26 November 1971, p. 11, it was said that the administration of the law had not improved since the time of their initial protest. The statement went on:

> . . . Internment without trial is wrong and its application has made a bad situation infinitely worse. Legalised brutality and torture, which accompany it, subverts all human-itarian conventions.
>
> We wish to identify with innocent people who have suffered and we will not thank anyone for paying our fines . . .

The disquiet felt by these priests at the possibility of someone paying their fines was given clear expression by all the protesting clerics shortly afterwards. With each of the priests facing mandatory jail sentences for non-payment of their fines, the Minister for State in the Prime Minister's Office, Dr G. B. Newe (a Catholic), approached the Bishop of Down and Connor, Dr Philbin, and Monsignor Arthur Ryan, with the intention of contributing to a fund for the payment of all such fines. Already, one of the offenders, Fr Gerald Park, had been arrested for his refusal to fill out his census form, but had been released five hours later. According to the authorities, an anonymous person had paid his fine. In an emotive statement issued at the time and reported in the *Irish Times*, 31 January 1972, the priests said:

> We have for some weeks past known of the efforts of Dr G. B. Newe to organise a fund for payment of fines. To add insult to injury, he approached some of our fellow-priests to contribute to the fund. This was calculated to undermine our protest . . . Since internment last August injustice against Catholics has increased . . . the need for more protests against these injustices is greater than ever, from the beginning we have been prepared to go to jail. We are even more determined now to identify ourselves with the suffering members of our community . . .

A few months later, one of the protesting priests, Fr Malachy Murphy of St Anne's, Derriaghy, was arrested by the police for having refused to pay his fine. Fr Murphy and his colleagues, however, were all saved from being imprisoned by an anonymous source who paid all their fines. According to *Hibernia*, 19 January 1973, p. 6, at least the benefactor was not Dr Newe* as many people had suspected.

Thus, the census protest, which had got off to such a strong start, ended in anti-climax. Whatever effect all this had on priests in Northern Ireland, it is interesting to note the lack of clerical protests at the time of the 1981 census when republicans dominated the opposition to the holding of the latter census.

A controversial aspect of the judicial system in Northern Ireland has been the use of the so-called supergrass system. Under this system, some people convicted of politically motivated

* The benefactor remains unknown.

offences have been offered a variety of inducements to turn informer on their accomplices. The official rationale for this policy was outlined in the annual report of the RUC in 1983 by its Chief Constable, Sir John Hermon:

> . . . Controversy concerning the use of converted terrorists as witnesses intensified in 1983. The fact that a number of former terrorists who admitted varying degrees of complicity in serious crime were given immunity from prosecutions is understandably distasteful to many people. It must, however, be borne in mind that the evidence so provided has contributed significantly to the removal from society of a considerable number of persons convicted by the courts of the most appalling crimes . . . [22]

Part of the wave of criticism directed at the supergrass system has come from the Catholic Church. Early critics of this policy were human rights activists, Fr Denis Faul and Fr Raymond Murray. In September 1983, Bishop Edward Daly of Derry and his Anglican counterpart, Dr James Mehaffey, both criticised the supergrass system on a BBC Radio Ulster programme. Dr Mehaffey called the practice morally questionable, while Dr Daly said the supergrass system brought the law into disrepute.[23] Not surprisingly, therefore, Bishop Daly reacted swiftly to the claim of one of the twenty-six people freed after the collapse of the Raymond Gilmour trial that the Catholic Church had turned a blind eye to the supergrass system and its victims. Not only did Bishop Daly say that he had condemned the use of paid informers on many occasions, but he also disclosed that he had raised the issue with the former Secretary of State, James Prior, and his officials at the Northern Ireland Office.[24] In a wide-ranging interview a few days later, Cardinal O'Fiaich condemned the supergrass system, saying that one of the factors he objected to most was that it was really becoming internment under a different name. The Cardinal estimated that about 400 or 500 prisoners had been arrested under the supergrass system and some had been awaiting trial for close on three years. He added that in his diocese alone, a group of people had been imprisoned for twenty months and were only released when the supergrass concerned would not go into court (see *Irish News*, 20 December 1984, p. 1).

Still, the failure of the hierarchy to issue a collective condemnation of the supergrass system has led some of the victims of that system to criticise the position of at least some of the bishops on this matter. As recently as June 1985, six men who had been granted bail in the Christopher Black informer trial[25] said that 'with the exception of a few individuals the Catholic hierarchy have been silent on the issue'. One of the men, Mr Jackie Donnelly, challenged the Bishop of Down and Connor, Dr Cahal Daly, to condemn the supergrass system outright, adding that Daly's silence 'can only otherwise be construed as condoning the system' (see *Irish News*, 29 June 1985, p. 3). Bishop Daly did not respond to this challenge and he has subsequently failed to clarify his position on the supergrass system in Northern Ireland.

Such has been the visible response of the Catholic Church to the supergrass system. By the end of 1986, however, the last people detained for trial on the evidence of a supergrass were released, and the system appears to have been ended.

On 5 June 1984, Lord Justice Gibson acquitted a sergeant and two constables of the RUC for the murder of Eugene Toman, one of three IRA men who had been shot dead by the security forces in an incident near Craigavon, Co. Armagh, in November 1982. In doing so, the judge criticised the Director of Public Prosecutions for bringing the case in the first place, calling the accused 'absolutely blameless' and describing the evidence against them as 'tenuous'. He went further however: he praised the policemen for their courage and determination in bringing the three IRA men to justice or to quote him, 'in this case to the final court of justice'.

The Catholic hierarchy was so upset about the judge's remarks that they decided to issue a statement on the matter. By doing so, this was to be the only occasion throughout the period of this study that any Catholic bishop had criticised a member of the judiciary by name. A statement signed by the six bishops and three auxiliary bishops of the Northern dioceses, said:

We wish to voice our grave disquiet at the remarks accompanying the judgment delivered recently by Lord Justice Gibson in the case involving certain members of the RUC. Such remarks, made in the context of a considered written judgment, seem to us inexplicable on the part of a senior member of the judiciary.

One of the greatest needs in our community at the present time is to restore respect for the law and public confidence in the administration of law. Judge Gibson's remarks have done a serious disservice in this regard. (*Irish Times*, 16 June 1984)

While the bishops had not referred to the judgment itself, their anxiety about Gibson's comments and the negative perception of these comments on the part of the Catholic community was self-evident. Moreover, it was widely believed that the timing of the bishops' statement was highly significant insofar as it was issued just after the holding of the election to the European Parliament. During that electoral campaign, the Sinn Fein candidate, Danny Morrison, had alluded to Gibson's comments quite often, while his SDLP opponent, John Hume, had decided not to use the judge's comments as an issue in his campaign for re-election. It was widely believed that had the bishops issued their statement prior to polling day, this could have given a certain electoral advantage to Sinn Fein. As it turned out, however, a Catholic Church spokesman failed to explain why the hierarchy had only issued the statement a few days *after* it had been drafted.[26]

Timing apart, the bishops' statement merely tended to re-echo the criticisms of nationalists throughout the country. The deputy-leader of the SDLP, Seamus Mallon, described Justice Gibson's comments as a 'licence to murder simply and solely', adding that the Northern Ireland judiciary had reached a 'new low'. The editorial of the *Irish Times* pointed to the affair as a need 'for a root and branch reform of the administration of justice and the conduct of the security forces in Northern Ireland'. The following day, Senator Brid Rodgers of the SDLP spoke of a collapse of confidence in the judiciary in Northern Ireland as a result of the judge's comments. In a speech a few days later, the Minister for Foreign Affairs, Mr Barry, disclosed that the British Ambassador to Ireland, Mr Allan Goodison, had been called in over Judge Gibson's remarks and that the Minister himself had made strong representations to the then Secretary of State, Mr Prior, on the matter.[27]

More significant still was the decision of one of the bishops, Edward Daly of Derry, to give a television interview on the Judge Gibson controversy. Like the hierarchy's statement, the bishop's interview on Ulster Television was not broadcast until after the election campaign. In that interview, reported in the *Irish Times*, 16 June 1984, Bishop Daly said that in any civilised society, respect for the law depended not only on justice being done but a perception of it being done. He went on: '... My perception of that decision is that it almost gives people a licence to kill ... I believe that this judgment has done great, great, great damage ...' An interesting feature of Bishop Daly's criticisms was not only that they had gone further than those of his ecclesiastical colleagues, but that in one sense they had gone further than many of the comments made by constitutional nationalists. For instead of limiting his criticism to the judge's remarks accompanying the judgment, Bishop Daly said that he had perceived Gibson's *judgment* itself as almost giving people a licence to kill.

In the face of such widespread criticism, Lord Justice Gibson went to the extraordinary length of defending what he had said in court. In what was believed to be the first public statement by a Northern Ireland judge in a case over which he himself had presided, Justice Gibson said: 'I would wish most emphatically to repudiate any idea that I would approve or that the law would countenance, what has been described as a shoot-to-kill policy on the part of the police ... (*Irish Times*, 23 June 1984) The war of words, at least, seemed to come to an end on the matter with Seamus Mallon calling for the resignation of Lord Justice Gibson. No such resignation was made.*

* In April 1987, Gibson and his wife, Cecily, died instantly when the car in which they were travelling was blown up by the Provisional IRA.
Source: *Irish Times*, 27 April 1987

4

The Catholic Church and Republicans*

IN EXAMINING Church–Provisional relations between late 1969 and 1970, it must be borne in mind that this brief period was one in which Catholic self-defence became a crucial issue. In Belfast, for instance, between July and September 1969, 82.7 per cent of displaced households were those of Catholics (see Scarman Report, *Violence and Civil Disturbances in Northern Ireland in 1969 Report of Tribunal of Inquiry*, April 1972, vol. 1, 31.23, p. 248). Events in these months (especially August) were central to the subsequent republican split and the role of several clerics in these disturbances became a source of some controversy.

While earlier in 1969, priests in areas such as Dungiven, Co. Derry,[1] and Ardoyne in Belfast,[2] had played an important peace-keeping role, this became impossible in mid-August 1969. In the worst trouble spots in parts of Derry and Belfast, a recurring pattern emerged: when the RUC or 'B' Specials made baton charges into Catholic areas, they were followed by loyalist crowds. Not surprisingly, this led many Catholics to believe that they were under attack from a combination of authorised and unauthorised loyalist forces. Once this happened in Derry, for instance, Scarman, pp. 140–143 and 181, admitted: 'Parleys between police and well-intentioned priests could do no immediate good in the situation that now developed'.

Indeed, on the following evening (13 August), when Catholics thought that St Eugene's Cathedral was under threat of loyalist attack, a local curate, Fr Mulvey, and other respected figures of the Derry community were among those who threw a barricade across the street in order to defend the building.[3] It

* The term 'republican' refers throughout this chapter to Provisional republicans, unless otherwise stated.

was in two areas of Belfast, however, where the most nakedly sectarian clashes were to occur and where the behaviour of Catholic clergy was to come under most scrutiny. In Ardoyne, local priests tried to calm their parishioners as late as 5 p.m. on 14 August. The events of that night and the next morning, however, proved to be the point of no return for local Catholics. Twelve men were shot in this period, two of whom died. All the gunshot victims were Catholic. On the following afternoon, a local priest, Fr Gillespie, was among a group of men who commandeered a bus for use as a barricade on the Crumlin Road. More serious still have been claims made about the behaviour of priests in Ardoyne at this time. Rev Ian Paisley, for one, claimed that he had seen a police statement saying that the belfry of Ardoyne monastery had been used as an arsenal and that the priests there were handing out bullets. Such claims were firmly rejected by a subsequent Government inquiry.[4] Nonetheless, the local account of events given to Burton three years later was that Catholics had only one gun, and that the weapon was rushed from corner to corner by a priest to create an impression of fire power (see Frank Burton, *The Politics of Legitimacy—struggles in a Belfast Community*, 1978, p. 17). At around the same time as these events in Ardoyne, Clonard Monastery received an anonymous phone call which warned that the building was to be burned down. As a result, the rector, Fr McLaughlin, raised a vigilante group to protect the property. The next day, Catholic fears were aggravated by reports that a loyalist sniper was firing on the monastery. When Fr McLaughlin was offered help from two armed men, he gave them access to the monastery on the strict condition that they confine their role to a purely 'defensive' one. When Protestants living nearby heard of these 'IRA gunmen', as they immediately called them, there was an invasion of the building, followed by a gun battle. The loyalist crowd retreated from the site of the monastery, but then proceeded to burn down rows of Catholic houses in the area.[5]

It was against this background of intense sectarian violence and widespread Catholic fear that *ad hoc* defence committees were to be formed in Catholic areas of Belfast. Within a matter of days of the arrival of the British Army in Northern Ireland, this informal network of defence groups was given a semblance of cohesion by becoming part of an umbrella group, the Central Citizens' Defence Committee.

As we have already seen in chapter 1, while the CCDC was quickly marginalised by wider events and especially the emergence of two militarily active IRAs, it was during this brief period that the political influence of the Catholic Church in Northern Ireland reached its apex. We shall now consider the nature of Church–republican relations within the CCDC, although such a task has been rendered problematic by the lack of documentary evidence of that organisation's activities. Consequently, it has been necessary to rely on interviews for information in this general area. Two salient questions arise from such investigations.

First, while there is no consensus regarding details of the CCDC's requests to the Dublin Government for arms, there is no evidence to suggest that Catholic priests were involved in such activities. Indeed, the unanimous view among my interviewees was that priests in the CCDC were never party to smuggling arms into Northern Ireland. By contrast, there is sharp disagreement over the circumstances surrounding the change of leadership within the CCDC in mid to late 1970. Put briefly, the first chairman of the organisation, Jim Sullivan, was later replaced by Belfast businessman, Tom Conaty. Such a change begs the question whether Sullivan, a known Official republican, resigned or was forced out by anti-socialists. One interpretation given to me was that Sullivan resigned after he had become an embarrassment to the organisation because of his republican background.[6] There is, on the other hand, substantial evidence that suggests otherwise. The then secretary of the group, Paddy Devlin, (who resigned at the time of Sullivan's departure), insists that Sullivan was forced out of the chairmanship of the CCDC by a number of anti-socialists, including Catholic clergy and known Provisional republicans.[7] What is not in dispute is that after the change in leadership, the CCDC was given use of diocesan property and office equipment for its new headquarters on the Falls Road. Ultimately, it is impossible to make a definitive judgment about such conflicting interpretations of events, although there is no doubt that the

Church was at best apprehensive about the CCDC having a Marxist-orientated chairman. Certainly, in his Lenten Pastoral of 1970, the local bishop, Dr Philbin, launched a blistering attack on socialism—an attack which *could* be seen as one directed at the Officials.

In the absence of empirical research, it is impossible to quantify how much sympathy there may have been among Catholic priests towards Provisional republicans in 1970. It can be said, however, that the interests of the Catholic Church and the Provisional IRA converged more clearly on 27/28 June 1970, than at any other time during the period of this study, when fierce sectarian rioting occurred in various parts of Belfast. In the east of the city, loyalist crowds attempted to burn down St Matthew's Church. In response, some armed Provisionals decided to defend the building and took up positions in the churchyard. In the confrontation that followed, four loyalists were shot dead and the chapel was saved. Local priests later showed their gratitude to the Provisionals by being part of the CCDC group who invited a Provisional IRA contingent to tea.[8]

Despite appearances, it must be stressed how fragile Church–republican relations actually were at this time. Some weeks before the St Matthew's incident, for example, the Northern bishops had issued a statement in which the decision of any individual or group to 'deliberately provoke violence' was described as 'a betrayal of the Catholic community—a stab in the back'. (For the full statement of the bishops, see *Irish News*, 22 May 1970, p. 1.) While no explicit reference had been made to Provisional republicans, it is highly significant that the statement had been issued following clashes between Catholics and the British Army—amidst widespread allegations that Provisionals had helped to orchestrate such disturbances. Thus, well before the Provisionals' campaign had even got under way, the hierarchy had indicated its position on violence. Overall then, whatever distinction clerics may have been prepared to make between *defensive* and *offensive* operations by the Provisionals, it was obvious that they would condemn any military-style campaign that might ensue.

Since the emergence of that military campaign, in fact, the most visible response of the Church has been its virtually incessant condemnation of republican violence. Moreover, the frequency of hierarchical condemnation of republican violence has been consistently matched by its ferocity. Thus, to cite but one example, in June 1974, the then bishop of Down and Connor, Dr Philbin, spoke of the men of (republican) violence as being 'wholly in the grip of the powers of evil—devil people'. If anything, hierarchical opposition to republican violence has become even more granite-like since the republican split of 1970. This is certainly reflected by how Bishop Cahal Daly has differentiated between the Provisional IRA of 1970 and 1980. While Dr Daly is not totally explicit about this, the leftward shift of the Provisional IRA in more recent years is one of the reasons for such a view: 'I go further and contend that the IRA movement at this beginning of 1980, is a quite different reality even from that of 1970. Almost only the name has remained unchanged. The leadership is new. The structures are new. The ideology is new. The ultimate aims are new. The mentality and the methods have a new and amoral ruthlessness.' (*Irish Times*, 1, 2 January 1980)

Underlying such criticism of republican violence, however, is the lack of an effective Church teaching on the morality of war. This is hardly a new problem. Indeed, while the early Christian Church was, for the most part pacifist in outlook,[9] much of this changed following the conversion of Constantine to Christianity in AD 312.[10] As Bishop Edward Daly of Derry points out in 'In Place of Terrorism' in *The Furrow*, vol. 26, no. 10, October 1975, p. 598: 'Ironically, it was only when the persecution of Christians ceased that they began to justify the use of violence against others. Since that time, Christians have waged war in every century, against pagans, sometimes in the cause of Christianity and against fellow Christians over some worldly advantage.' It was in the face of such violence that the so-called doctrine of the just war began to evolve. As theologian, Enda McDonagh, in 'Modes of Human Violence' in *The Irish Theological Quarterly*, vol. xli, no. 3, July 1974, p. 193, puts it: 'the conditions for a just war or revolution which had been elaborated in this tradition were highly sophisticated and went through considerable refinement from their first adumbration by Ambrose and Augustine through the classical authors such as Aquinas and Vitoria down to the recent discussions about the possibility of a just war today.'* Still, despite the putative sophistication of the just war doctrine, it has generally failed to be meaningful in the real world, something which McDonagh points out in the same article: 'The just war theory and its extension to the just revolution embodies a long tradition of reflection on the problems of political violence. Yet its limitation in practice—and ethics is about practice—are only too obvious. The riposte that it hasn't failed but simply has never been tried is not convincing.'

Within the local Church, moreover, there is an apparent lack of agreement as to the status, meaning and possible application of the just war theory to the contemporary situation in Northern Ireland. Bishop Edward Daly, for one, is certainly dismissive of the just war doctrine in its present forms and points to the theological inadequacies of the Church's position on contemporary violence in 'In Place of Terrorism', p. 597: 'The theology of the just war, for example, is vague and ambiguous in the extreme, and almost every two-bit revolutionary has his own version of it. We need far greater development of the theology of the morality of violence and of institutional injustice and of the theology of the just war. It is a crying need in the Churches today.' By contrast Bishop Cahal Daly has argued that the just war cannot be invoked to justify physical-force republicanism as the theory had not been designed to justify wars, but rather to *restrain* war-making.[11] No other member of the Irish hierarchy has discussed the just war *vis-à-vis* contemporary Northern Ireland.

As a result of all this, it is hardly surprising that the local hierarchy has never provided a precise exegesis as to why republican violence in Northern Ireland is morally wrong. In the view of Bishop Cahal Daly (see *Peace The Work of Justice Addresses on the Northern Tragedy 1973–79*, 1979, p. 85), most certainly, there is no need to do so: 'The reflections one advances in support of the proposition that human life is sacred, that

---

* There are six conditions for a modern just war: (i) a just cause; (ii) force must be the only way left of affecting change: (iii) there must be a properly constituted authority to direct the action; (iv) there must be a feasible goal; (v) the means must be appropriate to the end; (vi) reconciliation must be sought as the ultimate end.
Source: *Violence In Ireland—A Report to the Churches*, Dublin: Veritas, 1976, p. 61

deliberate killing of the innocent is evil, are not given as "proofs": in a real sense, one *sees* the truth of these propositions rather than waits for them to be proven before assenting to them.' Consequently, bishops have done little more than *assert* that such violence is immoral. The following passage which is from a statement by the Irish hierarchy on 12 September 1971, typifies this approach: 'Our main purpose in this statement, however, is to repeat, unreservedly and without qualification our condemnation of violence . . . [violence] is grievously wrong and contrary to the law and spirit of Christ.'[12] The above position, moreover, contains an important ambiguity, i.e. the failure of the Catholic hierarchy to *define* violence within the Northern Ireland situation. As already seen in chapter 3, this has meant in practice that the bishops' use of the term 'violence', *for the most part*, has referred to paramilitary (and especially) republican activities.

Surely, it is due to the lack of an effective moral teaching on political violence that serious criticism of hierarchical statements in Northern Ireland has been possible. Certainly, if the Catholic bishops could have pointed to a uniform policy of non-violence throughout the history of the Church or at least to a well-formulated and commonly accepted theological position on the issue, their position would not suffer from the deficiencies outlined above.

Irish history also poses difficulties for the credibility of the Church's position *vis-à-vis* contemporary republican violence. While Bishop Cahal Daly is the only Irish bishop to have explicitly justified the republican violence of the period 1916–1921 in the context of an address on the present phase of IRA violence, such reasoning is fraught with difficulties. An illustration of this is the following passage from Dr Daly's statement in *Violence in Ireland and Christian Conscience*, 1973, p. 31: 'I am personally convinced that our fight for national freedom was just and necessary. The heroism both of soldiers and civilians in that struggle wrote a glorious chapter in our history.'

What the above passage overlooks is the uncertain position of the Catholic Church on the violence that occurred during the period of what Cahal Daly calls 'our fight for national freedom'. Certainly, Professor Whyte has pointed out the most striking thing about the Church's response to the 1916 rising was, that of thirty-one bishops and auxiliary bishops in Ireland, twenty-two of them failed to make their views publicly known on the matter. Seven members of the hierarchy published 'emphatic condemnations' of the rebellion, while Dr Fogarty issued a hesitant condemnation. Bishop O'Dwyer of Limerick appeared to have condoned the Easter uprising.[13] Moreover, the Catholic Church was not monolithic in its judgment of the violence which occurred in Ireland between 1919 and July 1921. Instead, the main tendency among bishops was to criticise all forms of violence, or in other words, whenever IRA violence was condemned it was rarely done without equally (and sometimes more emphatically) pointing to the excesses of the British forces. More generally, Bishop Daly's acceptance of republican violence between 1916 and 1921 points to a central problem for contemporary anti-Unionists who reject the present campaign of republican violence. Until comparatively recent times, history in Ireland has, for the most part, meant political history. Moreover, such political history has tended to be both teleological (Ireland's struggle for independence) and unilinear (a struggle which is said to have been a constant feature of Irish life for centuries). Indeed, I would contend that such precepts are central to nationalist ideology in the post-independence period. The problem, therefore, for modern nationalism is how such an ideological tradition can be accepted by people who simultaneously condemn contemporary republican violence whose intended effect is, *inter alia*, to complete the 'final phase' of the Irish struggle for freedom?

Central to Bishop Daly's position, of course, is the argument that there is *discontinuity* between contemporary republicans and those of the early twentieth century. This is underlined in the following passage in *Peace The Work of Justice Addresses on the Northern Tragedy 1973–1979*, p. 85:

There is no historical continuity whatever between the present, largely faceless, leaders of the self-styled 'republican movement' and their honourable forbears; there is no moral continuity between their methods and those of the earlier struggle for independence. One of the aims of the

present 'republican movement' is to overthrow the very
institutions of democracy which earlier republicans sacri-
ficed limb and life to establish . . . In short, the present
'republican movement' has nothing but the name in common with the earlier tradition described by that title.

Such a passage not only reflects a mainly unsubstantiated view
of history but points to a problem that is neither confined to
Cahal Daly nor the Catholic Church, i.e. the fact that many
historical assumptions have been shared by republicans and
constitutional nationalists alike has hardly been conducive to a
better understanding of Ireland's past or present. Above all, the
failure of academics to deal substantively with the continuity or
otherwise of past and present republican violence has hardly
enhanced the quality of such debate.

Whatever about hierarchical condemnation of republican violence, more tangible forms of clerical opposition to republicans
have taken place within various communities. As we shall now
see, clerical behaviour has varied between being explicit and
relatively subtle. Three broad examples will be considered here.

The most explicit example of such clerical opposition occurred
in Ardoyne, Belfast, in the early 1970s. In mid-1972, Fr Aquinas,
the editor of the parish bulletin, denounced the IRA in the name
of 85 per cent of his congregation. This attack, in turn, provoked
a response from the IRA which included a protest outside the
church.[14] In early 1973, Fr Aquinas returned to this theme, and
yet again, the IRA responded to the priest's criticisms. Second,
in his fieldwork in west Belfast, Darby found that since the late
1970s, the Catholic Church had become increasingly active in
the parish of Kileen,* where among other things, the clergy had
helped to establish a community workshop and attracted positions for about forty ACE workers (see *Intimidation and the
Control of Conflict in Northern Ireland*, 1986, p. 109). In another
west Belfast parish, for instance, New Hull/Avoca, the clergy
became more involved in the life of the community by having
the church hall used for a plethora of social and recreational
purposes. Finally, in the wake of the UWC strike, the Church
set up a relief network in Belfast for any future emergency. It

* The various place names in this study are fictitious.

was believed at the time that Cardinal Conway and the bishop of the diocese, Dr Philbin, had instituted the organisation.[15]

Underlying these activities is an awareness that the Church has been engaged in a struggle with republicans for the allegiance of local Catholics. Thus, Burton, in *The Politics of Legitimacy*, p. 104, describes the dispute between Fr Aquinas and the IRA in Ardoyne as follows: 'These claims and counter-claims represent ideological struggles within a discourse of legitimacy. They are political arguments striving for moral authority in the community.' In his analysis of increased clerical involvement in Catholic west Belfast during the 1980s, Darby similarly contends: 'It was part of a struggle for power within the Catholic communities, and the main antagonists were often the Catholic Church — conservative, paternalistic, non-violent — and Sinn Fein, radical, anti-clerical and supporters of the IRA. The clergy in Kileen regarded radicals and republicans as greater threats to the stability of the area than any external enemies. The antipathy was mutual.' (See *Intimidation and the Control of Conflict in Northern Ireland*, p. 156.) Last but not least, the background to the Church's decision to establish a relief network in Belfast in 1974 implies that clerical authorities were, at least in part, responding to what they perceived as a republican initiative. A similar group had been set up earlier by lay community workers, but had come under criticism from the Central Citizens' Defence Committee which by this time was seen as having become increasingly influenced by the clergy.

Despite all these signs of clerical opposition towards republicans, it ought to be noted that the Church has not, by and large, imposed theological sanctions on the Provisionals. First, the IRA custom of providing paramilitary honours at its members' funerals has been a consistent source of embarrassment to Catholic clergy. Indeed, it has produced something of a quandary for priests, who, on the one hand, are quite naturally anxious to accord Catholic burials to all members of the Church, but are sensitive that by doing so may in some vague way identify the Church with the republican movement. In practice, no Church policy *per se* was publicly enunciated on this issue until late 1981[16] and the vast majority of deceased Provisionals have received conventional Catholic burials. On a few rare occasions, however, priests have refused to allow the remains of IRA volunteers into their churches, but instead have said prayers for the deceased at their graveside.[17] Second, the excommunication of Provisionals (the most severe ecclesiastical punishment within the Catholic Church) has never been a real issue for the Northern bishops. While the question has come up for discussion among the hierarchy, none of the Northern bishops seems to believe that excommunication of the IRA would be meaningful in the Northern Ireland situation.[18] In any event, some hierarchical statements on the IRA have virtually amounted to the same thing. In a homily given in 1986, for instance, Bishop Edward Daly said that while he was not formally excommunicating anyone, the people in question had to realise that by their activities, they were excommunicating themselves. Certainly, if history has served as any guide to the judgments of bishops on this matter,[19] they must have been aware of how the general excommunication of republicans in the civil war in 1922 had no visible effect on the course of events.[20]

Before considering other aspects of Church–republican relations, it is necessary to examine the persistent belief that there is a significant number of priests who have been sympathetic towards contemporary republicans. Such a belief has sometimes been held by unlikely people, such as Garret FitzGerald TD,[21] for instance. Yet, all available evidence points in the opposite direction—that only a tiny minority of priests in Northern Ireland[22] are sympathetic towards republican groups. First, there have only been two Catholic clerics in Northern Ireland who have been convinced of physically assisting the IRA. In late 1971/72, two Cistercians, Fr Thomas O'Neill and Brother Patrick Skehan, were arrested and convicted of attempting to drive escaped IRA prisoners across the border. Moreover, only three priests in Northern Ireland have *openly* refused to condemn IRA violence there: Fr McVeigh, Fr McEvoy and Fr Wilson. In late 1985, Fr Joe McVeigh of Irvinestown, Co. Fermanagh, said the Catholic hierarchy had no right to condemn those who took up arms to fight for freedom in Northern Ireland when they themselves remained unwilling 'to take on' the British establishment (see *Irish Times*, 2 December 1985, pp. 1 and 8). In an article, 'A Northern Analysis' in *The Furrow*, vol. 23, no. 10, 1972, pp. 607–610, Fr McEvoy's position on republican violence was one of *at least* implicit support. For his part, Fr Des Wilson concluded by the mid-1970s that condemning IRA violence involved the adoption of a position devoid of moral and intellectual credibility. It is surely significant, moreover, that two of these priests have found their former position within the Church untenable: Fr McEvoy resigned from the priesthood,[23] while in 1975, Fr Des Wilson resigned from his curacy but not his priesthood in the diocese of Down and Connor. As if to confirm the minuscule level of support for republicans among members of the clergy, it ought to be noted that in my question-naire which was circulated to every priest in Northern Ireland in April/May 1986, only nine priests or 3.9 per cent of respondents indicated the likelihood of their voting for Sinn Fein in a future general election.

The remainder of this chapter examines three salient features of Church–republican relations. First, there is an analysis of the Church's position on the prisons question, prison protests and the hunger-strikes which have occurred during the period of this study. Second, an assessment is made of the Church's response to the electoral rise of Provisional Sinn Fein. Finally, there is an examination of how republican literature has coped with the constant and resolute condemnation of IRA violence by the Catholic Church.

Before discussing the prisons question in detail, it is necessary to put this matter in context by referring to key events in the recent history of Northern Ireland prisons. When on 9 August 1971 the Northern Ireland Government introduced internment without trial under the Provisions of the Special Powers Act (1922), the prison population soared. During the course of negotiations between the Provisional IRA and the British Government which led to a short-lived truce in 1972, republican prisoners were accorded special category status. Although internment was later ended in 1975, the Government phased out special category status for those convicted of offences committed after March 1976. This policy of 'criminalisation' was immediately resisted by republican prisoners. Such protests continued and escalated throughout the remainder of the 1970s until, in late 1980, a number of republican prisoners went on hunger-strike to seek the so-called five demands. Shortly afterwards, the hunger-strike was called off when an agreement was reached between the prisoners and the authorities. Amid allegations that the Government had broken its word, however, a second series of hunger-strikes was started on 1 March 1981, the fifth anniversary of the first Diplock-style conviction. This second round of hunger-strikes lasted 217 days and ended only after ten of the strikers had died and some of the other protesters were taken off their fast by relatives. The unanimous view of the three major works on the hunger-strike is that the prisoners' demands were largely met by subsequent changes in the prison regime.[24]

Whatever about the official status of republican prisoners or indeed the state of Church-republican relations, available evidence points to a significant degree of religiosity among republican prisoners. Certainly, all the books published on the prisons question have contained religious imagery, language and symbolism which more often than not have been of a distinctively Catholic nature.[25] Significantly, according to Beresford, in *Ten Men Dead The Story of the 1981 Hunger Strike*, p. 429, prisoners tended to turn more to religion during periods of crisis and this was noted by different authors during the blanket protest and the hunger-strikes. Probably the most remarkable example of this was how the three prisoners of the Marxist-orientated INLA who died on hunger-strike became increasingly religious during their imprisonment.[26]

It is possible to put such religiosity into its proper context. Certainly, if one uses the most common yardstick of religiosity in the Roman Catholic tradition i.e. weekly attendance at Mass, it may be possible to establish how religious republican prisoners are *vis-à-vis* the Catholic community in Northern Ireland. Two major surveys have shown a high level of weekly Mass attendance among Northern Catholics. Thus, Rose discovered that 95 per cent of Catholic respondents claimed to attend Mass at least once a week, while some ten years later, Moxon-Browne found the corresponding figure in a Co. Derry town to be 89.8 per cent (see *Nation, Class and Creed in Northern Ireland*, p. 125). Such levels of religious observance clearly exceed that of republican prisoners. In 1975, Bishop Edward Daly of Derry ruefully observed that in one of Northern Ireland's prisons, less than half of republican prisoners attended Mass.[27] In an interview almost ten years later, reported in the *Irish Times*, 26 April 1984, p. 11, Fr Denis Faul (who has been saying Mass in Long Kesh since 1972), said that only 50 per cent of Provisional prisoners attended Mass there at all. Yet, in the absence of more detailed research on this subject,[28] it might be argued that a more valid basis of comparison is between the religiosity of prisoners and that of *specific* Catholic areas from which they may have come. In Catholic parts of west Belfast, for instance, Darby found there was a marked decline in religious practice.[29] Certainly, during the course of a recent interview, Fr Des Wilson estimated that weekly Mass attendance in the west Belfast parish of Corpus Christi is somewhere between 25 per cent and 38 per cent. In any case, that approximately 50 per cent of Provisional prisoners attend Mass still reflects a considerable degree of religiosity among that group. Certainly, that particularly critical periods within the prisons should be accompanied by increased religiosity among republican prisoners clearly points to Catholicism as a powerful agent of socialisation within the minority community of Northern Ireland.[30]

In any broad assessment of the hierarchical position *vis-à-vis* republican prisoners, it must be acknowledged that more recently appointed bishops have tended to be more involved in this area than their predecessors. For example, while the Catholic hierarchy condemned internment in 1971 (and such denunciations fell far short of those of a majority of the lower clergy, see chapter 3, pp. 114–116), the topic of internment failed to remain in the forefront of statements by the bishops of that period. Instead, it was a newly-appointed bishop, Edward Daly of Derry, who in 1974 was the most actively visible anti-internment campaigner within the hierarchy (see chapter 3, p. 116). Moreover, the reluctance of the hierarchy in the early 1970s to visit prisoners can be contrasted with the activities of more recently appointed Church leaders, especially Bishop Edward Daly and Cardinal O'Fiaich. For example, it was nine months after the introduction of internment before any member of the Catholic hierarchy visited internees.[31] It is inconceivable that such a thing would happen in more recent years. In *Magill* of January 1985, for instance, Bishop Daly of Derry points out that apart from his visits to prisons in Northern Ireland, he makes a point of visiting annually republican prisoners from the Derry area who are serving sentences in the Republic of Ireland and Great Britain.

In the same article, Daly admits that such concern for prisoners has created the suspicion on the part of the authorities that the Church is in some way sympathetic towards republicans. While Church leaders such as Cardinal Conway, for instance, made representations to the government earlier in the decade concerning specific prisoners, overall hierarchical involvement in the prisons issue provoked little or no controversy. In any case, on the basis of available evidence, it *appears* that Bishop Edward Daly and Cardinal O'Fiaich in particular have been much more involved in the area of general prisoner welfare than any of their predecessors.

As there is an impressive body of literature on the prison protests and hunger-strikes (including substantial detail of Catholic Church involvement in these events) the following examination of these themes has a dual purpose: first, to provide a synopsis of the Catholic Church's involvement in the controversy surrounding prison protests and the hunger-strikes; second, to analyse such Church involvement in terms of the wider perceptions and motivations of the Catholic hierarchy as well as to assess the effectiveness or otherwise of the initiatives by various Catholic clergy.

At a time when the prison protests were more than a year in progress and the dirty protest was under way for some months, two ecclesiastical leaders registered their concern at the situation. Bishop Edward Daly of Derry called for a solution to the conditions of 'indescribable filth' in the H-blocks after he had made a visit there in June 1978. At the same time, the papal nuncio in Dublin, Dr Gaetano Alibrandi, granted an audience to relatives of blanket men at which he spoke of the Pope's concern over the H-blocks protest. In his second meeting with the then Secretary of State, Roy Mason, Archbishop O'Fiaich discussed the dirty protest which by then had been in progress for some three and a half months. O'Fiaich saw Mason's attitude as totally unyielding. Consequently, the Archbishop decided that on his next visit to Long Kesh, he would issue a strong statement on the matter. Such a statement was issued at the beginning of August 1978. Among the points Archbishop O'Fiaich made were the following: that he was preparing a report on conditions in Long Kesh for the Holy See; non-cooperation with the prison regime on the part of the prisoners should not entail their loss of physical exercise, free association or contact with the outside world; that prisoners had complained of being beaten and punished by the prison authorities; despite the claims of the authorities that such prisoners were no different from any others, everything about their trials and family backgrounds indicated otherwise. Perhaps the Archbishop's most emotive description was, however, reserved for H-blocks 3, 4 and 5: 'One would hardly allow an animal to remain in such conditions, let alone a human being. The nearest approach to it that I have seen was the spectacle of hundreds of homeless people living in sewer pipes in the slums of Calcutta.'[32]

The immediate effect of Archbishop O'Fiaich's statement was to transform the prisons protest from a relatively peripheral issue into a major international news item. Above all, that such a statement had been made by the Primate of the Catholic Church in Ireland also helped to provide the H-block protests with a new-found respectability.

Conditions in the prison remained unchanged, however, and O'Fiaich (now appointed Cardinal) was soon to be more involved in the events of 1980. (For a detailed account of clerical involvement in the crisis until the hunger-strikes of October 1980, and especially that of the cardinal and Bishop Edward Daly, see Collins, *The Irish Hunger Strike*, pp. 312–330.) As Beresford explains:

> The Catholic Primate of all-Ireland, Cardinal Tomas O' Fiaich was persuaded to throw his weight into the search for a settlement. He held a series of meetings through 1980 with the newly appointed Secretary of State for Northern Ireland, Humphrey Atkins, as well as meeting secretly with top Sinn Fein officials. To try to encourage the talks, the

IRA called off the attacks on prison warders. But by mid-1980 it was becoming obvious that little ground had been gained through negotiation. (*Ten Men Dead*, p. 34)

It was against this background that seven republican prisoners began a hunger-strike on 27 October 1980 which was soon joined by others in Long Kesh and by female prisoners in Armagh. The strike was called off on 17 December 1980, when one of the strikers, Sean McKenna, was close to death and after the Northern Ireland Office had issued a 34-page document which seemed to promise major concessions to the prisoners. During the latter part of this critical period the Church had played an important role as mediator. According to Clarke, this role was, in effect, a process that seemed to the prisoners to resemble negotiations with the British. In his book, *Broadening The Battlefield — The H-Blocks and the Rise of Sinn Fein*, p. 126, he goes on: 'The conduits for this process were the clergy and the civil servant in charge of prisons, John Blelloch, who made a visit to the jail on 10 December to explain to the seven hunger-strikers the reforms that were already available to them should they choose to abandon their protest.'

Prospects for a settlement faded, however, when prisoners claimed that the authorities had gone back on their word. In an effort to avert a second series of hunger-strikes, Cardinal O'Fiaich tried to mediate yet again, but to no avail.[33] The second round of hunger-strikes began on 1 March 1981.

Most attention now turned to the hunger-striker most likely to die first, Bobby Sands. The most notable clerical initiative at this point came from the Vatican when the papal envoy, Fr Magee, travelled to visit Mr Sands. The envoy also met British authorities and other hunger-strikers, but finding both parties to the dispute quite entrenched, he quickly returned to the Vatican. During the time of Bobby Sands' fast, the independent MP for Fermanagh and South Tyrone, Frank Maguire, died. There was a flurry of activity as nationalists of various kinds considered contesting the subsequent by-election. Prior to the nomination (and electoral success) of Mr Sands, the local clergy involved themselves by asking Maguire's brother, Noel, to stand for the seat (see Beresford, *Ten Men Dead*, p. 102). According to one source, the Bishop of Clogher personally intervened in this matter. For his part, Maguire asked the bishop not to make a statement about alleged intimidation of potential nationalist candidates by Sinn Fein. (Mr Maguire later backed Bobby Sands.) It was also during this period that divisions over the morality of the hunger-strikes between Catholic Church leaders in England and Ireland became apparent. As if to illuminate his earlier comments about hunger-strikes being forms of violence, Cardinal Basil Hume said a few days before Sands' death that if Mr Sands were to die, such a death would be suicide. Cardinal O'Fiaich failed to publicly respond to these comments but the senate of priests of the Armagh diocese sent a strong letter of protest to Hume.[34] In an oblique rejection of Cardinal Hume's judgment, Bishop Daly of Derry later said that Bobby Sands' death had not been suicide (*Irish Times*, 11 May 1981, p. 5). While the bishop in Sands' diocese of Down and Connor made no comment on whether the death was suicidal or not, it was decided at a meeting of local Canons that priests in the diocese would not be allowed to say public Masses for the deceased (*Irish Times*, 5 May 1981).

Before and for some time after Sands' death, the Catholic Church tried to encourage a settlement to the dispute in two ways. First, Cardinal O'Fiaich tried to persuade the Prime Minister, Margaret Thatcher, to make some concessions to the prisoners. This was done by sending her telegrams and then by expressing his view to her at a meeting in London where his auxiliary bishop, Dr Lennon, articulated similar sentiments. All such attempts proved fruitless (see Collins, *The Irish Hunger Strike*, pp. 337–348). Second, there were the attempts of the Church body, the Irish Commission for Justice and Peace, to intervene in the dispute. A delegation of the ICJP which was comprised of clergy and laity, included the auxiliary bishop of Dublin, Dr Dermot O'Mahony. The most hopeful moment for the Commission occurred at a critical point in the hunger-strike of Joe McDonnell when it seemed that a basis for an agreement with prisons' minister, Michael Allison, had been reached through their mediation. The authorities, however, delayed in making their proposals known and Mr McDonnell died (see Clarke, *Broadening The Battlefield*, pp. 170–175). The Commission felt that Mrs Thatcher had overruled any such agreement and called a press conference at which they revealed details of their unsuccessful talks.

Finally, it was against this background of mounting death among hunger-strikers that Fr Denis Faul of Dungannon decided to use his influence to have the protests ended.[35] Although Faul's involvement in the hunger-strike crisis had been negligible to this point, he was in a rather unique position to intervene. For probably more than any other cleric in Northern Ireland, Faul had worked tirelessly in exposing and protesting about alleged violations of human rights and not least questions surrounding the area of prisons/detentions. Not surprisingly, such activities gave Faul a certain standing among many prisoners' families.* In late July 1981, Fr Faul organised a meeting of prisoners' families and relatives at which he expressed the belief that the strikers should come off their protest and that the IRA had the authority to end the protest if they wished to do so. There then followed a meeting between Fr Faul, the relatives and Gerry Adams at which Adams was eventually persuaded by the priest to visit the prisoners to explain 'the situation'. The prisoners told Mr Adams the following morning that they would continue their hunger-strike.[36] Still, Fr Faul continued in his efforts to influence the families of hunger-strikers. Soon afterwards, families began to take their protesting relatives off their hunger-strike. The protest was officially ended on 3 October 1981.

From the outset, the Catholic Church saw its involvement in the prison dispute as a purely pastoral one. During the first series of hunger-strikes, for instance, the then MP for West Belfast, Gerry Fitt, said in the House of Commons, (see *Hansard, House of Commons Debates*, vol. 992, col. 140, 10 November 1980), that he had newspaper cuttings relating to Cardinal O'Fiaich and Bishop Edward Daly which appeared to show them on the side of the hunger-strikers. The two churchmen quickly issued a statement which was reported in the *Irish Times*, 12 November 1980, p. 1, in which they said they were deeply distressed by

* In terms of publications alone, Fr Faul has written or co-written over 50 pieces which deal at least in part with aspects of prison/interrogation.
Source: TCD: author index, 1987

Fitt's remarks. The statement went on: 'We wish to state that our discussions with Mr Atkins regarding problems in prisons were motivated solely and exclusively by pastoral concern.'

Be that as it may, there can be no doubt churchmen were quick to realise not only that the hunger-strikes had greatly increased the popularity of the IRA within the Catholic community, but *inter alia*, how this threatened to adversely affect the temporal authority of the Catholic Church in Northern Ireland. Certainly, in accounts of the meeting between Prime Minister Thatcher, Cardinal O'Fiaich and Auxiliary Bishop Lennon, the last mentioned pointed to the effect that the hunger-strike was having in alienating Irish youth both from the Church and moderate politicians.[37] Moreover, Church sensitivity to increased support for the IRA was manifest in different parts of the North. As already seen, in encouraging the nomination of independent Noel Maguire in the Fermanagh–South Tyrone by-election, the clergy of Clogher were, in effect, trying to impede the Provisionals from making electoral inroads in Northern Ireland. Similarly, while the decision of Canons in the diocese of Down and Connor to forbid priests from saying public Masses for Bobby Sands was primarily meant to distance the Church from the IRA, it was also an attempt to discourage increasing support for the Provisionals. In short, while Church involvement in the prisons dispute was indeed motivated by pastoral concern, there is no doubt that as events unfolded churchmen became increasingly aware of the possible political implications of the situation and reacted in a predictable way: directly and indirectly, they promoted 'constitutional nationalism'.

Within a month of the first series of hunger-strikes, the Northern bishops had outlined their position on the protest. They called on the hunger-strikers to end their fast and, almost inevitably, they took the opportunity to call on the IRA to end its campaign of violence. With regard to the Government, the bishops called for more flexibility on their part and added: '. . . the hunger-strike would probably never have arisen if a more urgent and sensitive attempt had been made long ago to prevent the prison situation from deteriorating'. (*Irish Times*, 28 November 1980, p. 1)

Overall, there are four closely related but distinctive factors which tended to undermine the effectiveness of clerical involvement in the hunger-strike crisis. First, the Church's prescription that the hunger-strike was to be ended and that the authorities were to show greater flexibility in the prison regime seemed less than credible because of events in late 1980 and early 1981. After the first series of hunger-strikes had been abandoned it was, according to prisoners, the failure of the authorities to be flexible that provoked the second round of hunger-strikes. Second, as the Catholic Church was not a party to the dispute, events were, of course, to be largely predetermined by the prisoners and authorities. Moreover, the position of the Catholic churchmen was hardly helped by the seemingly uncertain negotiating position of the authorities in general and the *apparently* inflexible position of Mrs Thatcher in particular. Third, despite outward appearances, the efforts of mediation by the ICJP were rendered meaningless by secret talks that were taking place at the same time between the Foreign Office and the Provisional IRA.[38] So much so, the Foreign Office appeared to be offering more generous terms for a settlement than the Commission seems to have been given by the Northern Ireland Office. When Gerry Adams revealed this to some members of the Commission, they were quite astounded. Last but not least, the different judgments of Cardinal Hume and the local Church as to whether the hunger-strike was a form of suicide merely underlined the lack of a clear moral position by the Catholic Church as a whole on this issue. That it was the head of the English Catholic Church who said that the hunger-strike was suicide, moreover, made it appear that such judgments had more to do with nationalism than morality.

Still, it can be argued that Church involvement was effective at two crucial points of the hunger-strike crisis. First, Church mediators were among those who had influenced the hunger-strikers to abandon their first protest. Indeed, in the prisoners' statement announcing the second series of hunger-strikes, Cardinal O'Fiaich and the bishops were condemned as part of the 'moral blackmail' exerted on the prisoners to end their first strike. Second, there was the late intervention of Fr Denis Faul in encouraging hunger-strikers' relatives to take their loved ones off their protest. While it is a moot point whether some relatives would have made this decision without Faul's involvement, one lasting effect of the priest's intervention was that he would be condemned by republicans for undermining the hunger-strike. This was explicit in the prisoners' statement of 26 September 1981, for instance, in which Fr Faul was described as a 'treacherous, conniving man'.

Despite earlier clashes with Sinn Fein spokesmen, the position of the church *vis-à-vis* Sinn Fein only became a burning issue when that party first involved itself in electoral competition during the 1980s. The electoral success of prisoners in both the Dail and Westminster elections in 1981 encouraged Sinn Fein to enter the electoral arena. The following year, Sinn Fein put forward candidates for election to the Northern Ireland Assembly.

Interestingly enough, none of the local bishops made any reference to republican candidates who contested elections during 1981 and 1982 in Northern Ireland. While this may appear anomalous in the light of subsequent controversies surrounding this development, it is worth noting two important points. First, it was the failure of the SDLP to nominate a candidate for the earlier by-elections in Fermanagh–South Tyrone in 1981 rather than the behaviour of the Catholic Church which provoked most Unionist criticism. Moreover, while the 1982 Assembly election was the first time Provisional Sinn Fein *per se* had entered the political arena, the campaign failed to generate much enthusiasm within the Catholic community. The mood of the electorate in Catholic areas of Belfast, for instance, where Sinn Fein was to make a big breakthrough, was reflected by the *Andersonstown News*, 16 October 1982, p. 4, which said of the campaign: 'Up until now it has been a rather low key affair in the nationalist areas of Belfast, which is not surprising given the number of elections held over the past ten years and the present state of despondency among the population.'

It was only after Provisional Sinn Fein captured just over 10 per cent of the overall vote that three members of the hierarchy made their feelings known on the subject: Cardinal O'Fiaich, Bishop Cahal Daly of Down and Connor, and Bishop Edward Daly of Derry.

The position of Cardinal O'Fiaich and Dr Cahal Daly on the

question of Catholics voting for Sinn Fein began to emerge, albeit tentatively, in early 1983 during an address for the world day of peace given by Daly and in a radio interview with the Cardinal. While both men expressed concern at the emergence of Sinn Fein as an electoral force, it was Cahal Daly who was more uncompromising in his opposition to such a development. In a direct reference to the Provisional IRA (which obviously applied to Sinn Fein as well) Dr Daly said: 'They must choose either physical force or democratic persuasion. They cannot have both. The armalite and the ballot box cannot both be carried together.' (*Irish Times*, 1, 3 January 1983, p. 5) In referring to the Assembly elections of October 1982, Cardinal O'Fiaich commented: 'It would have been wrong for the Church to have urged its people to vote in any particular way in the elections. I don't think that before the election any party or candidate was proposing any kind of violence. My memory is that clear support for violence came only later at the Sinn Fein Ard Fheis, when the statement was made that all elected candidates should give unambiguous support to the armed struggle.' (*Irish Times* 1, 3 January 1983, p. 1)

While the latter claim is debatable, the Cardinal went on to say that if the Provisional IRA did not rescind the statement made at its recent Ard Fheis which had instructed its elected representatives to give unambiguous support to the IRA's armed struggle, then a vote for Sinn Fein would be a vote for a continuation of the IRA campaign. This position, however, was qualified still further when he added rather meaninglessly: 'one would have to judge each election as it came along'.

On the basis of statements made in May 1983 and January 1984, the positions of both Cahal Daly and Tomas O'Fiaich appeared to have shifted from those of January 1983. By the time of the Westminster general election in 1983, for instance, Cahal Daly had not only resigned himself to the fact that Provisional republicans could indeed have both the armalite and the ballot box, but called on Catholics to think seriously before voting for Sinn Fein and called on them to consider that such a vote *could be* interpreted as support for violence.[39] Speaking on the RTE radio programme *This Week*, at the beginning of 1984, Cardinal O'Fiaich clearly accepted that Sinn Fein had ratified

IRA violence but pointed out that people both joined and voted for Sinn Fein for a variety of reasons. The Cardinal did stress, however, that if one either joined or voted for Sinn Fein as an act of support for the violent activities of the IRA, then in his view such an individual was morally wrong in doing so. The Primate added that the Church should make it clear that in voting for Sinn Fein, the voter was supporting a group very closely associated with violent people and people who were guilty of crimes. Before voting, the individual had to weigh this against any other consideration and also had to take into account that their vote might be misrepresented.

During the general election campaign of 1983, Bishop Edward Daly of Derry called on Catholics to examine their consciences before voting for general election candidates associated with violence. In doing so, he made his feelings known towards Sinn Fein candidates by declaring his opposition towards what he called 'aspiring public representatives' who would justify acts of violence.

Two immediate observations can be made about the Church's position on the question of Catholics voting for Sinn Fein. First, the hierarachy's failure to issue a common statement on the issue* and the apparent shifts on the part of Cardinal O'Fiaich and Bishop Cahal Daly only made the Church's stance less credible than was necessary. Second, despite this obvious weakness in their position, the bishops' apparent assumption that a vote for Sinn Fein *is not necessarily* an endorsement of violence is shared by Sinn Fein MP, Gerry Adams. In an interview in *Magill* Mr Adams said of the Sinn Fein vote in the 1983 general election: 'A large percentage . . . was a vote for the armed struggle, but I don't know how to quantify that.'

For many anti-republicans, of course, the bishops' response to the electoral rise of Sinn Fein in this period was inadequate. In putting such a response into perspective, however, there are three major reasons why members of the hierarchy did not adopt a stronger position on the matter. First, the Church sees

* When this was put to Bishop Edward Daly in an interview on 3 March 1988, he argued that a common statement by the Northern bishops could have proven to be 'anaemic'. Implicit in this statement, of course, is that bishops have been inclined to adopt different approaches to the electoral rise of Sinn Fein.

itself as a teaching Church which assists in the development of
'enlightened conscience'. Thus, in a recent doctrinal statement
by the Irish Episcopal Conference on conscience and morality, it
was stated that:

> Our purpose in issuing this statement is to deepen the
> awareness of moral values among our people . . . In offer-
> ing these guiding principles on the relationship between
> conscience and morality, and in referring, however briefly,
> to the respective roles of love, freedom and authority in the
> Christian life, our aim is to help Catholics to grow in moral
> insight and freedom, as they become progressively more
> responsive to the guidance of an enlightened sure and
> sensitive conscience.[40]

Certainly, as the bishops would see the question of Catholics
voting for Sinn Fein in mainly moral terms, any attempt on their
part to adopt a stronger position on the issue would have been
inimical to the development of an 'enlightened' conscience. That
the use of individual conscience was emphasised in the bishops'
response to the electoral challenge of Sinn Fein merely under-
lines the importance of this theme within the Church's teaching.
Second, as already seen in earlier chapters, Church leaders have
conceived of politics in narrow party political terms. It is within
this narrow conception of politics that the Church's position on
Sinn Fein must be considered, and it is because of such a
conception, for instance, that Cardinal O'Fiaich said it would be
wrong for the Church to urge its people to vote a particular way.
(Indeed, such a move would have been unprecedented in the
history of Church–republican relations in Ireland.) Finally, even
if the bishops had wanted to issue some type of directive
instructing Catholics not to vote for Sinn Fein, there is little
reason to believe that such a statement would have had the
desired effect. It ought to be borne in mind that after some of the
above statements were made by bishops, Sinn Fein went on *to
increase* its share of the vote in the 1983 general election by over
3 per cent from its level of electoral support gained in the
Assembly election the previous year. (Source: *Fortnight*, June
1983, no. 195, p. 5.)

Having analysed the response of the Church to contemporary republicanism at some length, it is appropriate to end this chapter with an examination of how republican publications have coped with the constant and resolute clerical condemnation of IRA violence throughout the period of this study. The view is posited here that republican publications on the matter accurately reflect the state of Church–republican relations at any given time. While it can be said that republican literature has become increasingly hostile towards the Catholic Church with the passage of time, it is possible to identify three broad phases in this evolution. First, in the period 1970 to early 1971 the republican view of the Church was muted. Second, from the early to the late 1970s, republican criticism of the Church was predictably fierce but in some ways qualified. Finally, reflecting the Provisionals' ideological shift to the left in the late 1970s/ early 1980s and an increasingly secularised view of the world, republican opposition to the Church became more straightforward than it had been in previous years. It is within this general framework that two distinctive but broadly related features of the republican view of the Church will be discussed here: (i) the changing forms of criticism of the Catholic Church by republicans, and *ipso facto* republican self-justification; (ii) how the general tendency of earlier republican literature to distinguish either between the political position of different bishops on the one hand, or that of prelates and priests on the other hand, became increasingly blurred in later years.

It was only in early 1971 that republican publications became openly critical of the Church. *An Phoblacht*, for instance, condemned a sermon by Bishop Philbin of Down and Connor in which he criticised republicans (and which provoked a protest by residents of Belfast's Ballymurphy area outside the bishop's home).[41] For its part, *Republican News*, January/February 1971, p. 1, criticised the decision of the Catholic Church to appoint a chaplain to Stormont, though this was qualified by implying that not *all* clerics have been hostile to nationalist aspirations in Ireland: 'We read with deep regret that the Roman Catholic Church in Ireland has appointed a chaplain to the Six County parliament. Not because we believe that the Roman Catholic Church in Ireland were anything but hostile to the National aspirations of the Irish people with the exceptions of such as the late Cardinal MacRory, Archbishop of Armagh.'

Later in 1971, republican criticism had, if anything, become even more bitter. Thus, the editorial of the *Republican News*, 30 October 1971, stated that:

> Since August '69 Catholics in the North have been looking to the Hierarchy for some indication of leadership. They looked in vain. As the repression gained in intensity, they found the twisted speeches of their Bishops becoming more and more irrelevant . . . However, the back-stabbing edict issued this week by the Irish Hierarchy's Commission must rank as the greatest act of premeditated treachery against innocent people since Judas betrayed his Saviour with a kiss . . . An effective excommunication could leave the Catholic Churches practically empty.

For our purpose, at least, the crucial feature of this passage is how the Provisionals' position is defended in moral, and not least Roman Catholic terms. This was a far from unusual practice in republican writings of this period. Thus to cite a few examples, one Fr Art O'Neill* wrote a number of articles in *Republican News* during mid- to late 1973 in which the IRA campaign, in effect, was justified by referring to the morality of the Northern Ireland situation. As if to add to the moral importance of such pieces, it was claimed that they were based on discussions among a group of Catholic priests.[42] As late as January 1974, *Republican News* was responding to criticism of the IRA campaign by Cardinal Conway in terms of a statement which had originally been issued by the republican leadership in September 1971. The statement endorsed the Provisional campaign by juxtaposing historical, political and moral considerations. With regard to the moral aspect of the republican campaign and the Northern Ireland situation, it accused clerical condemnation of having implied dual standards of morality. It even resorted to quoting a pro-republican priest, Fr Sean

---

* I have been unable to discover anything else about Fr Art O'Neill. He certainly did not live in Ireland as no such priest is listed in the *Irish Catholic Directory* of either 1971 or 1973.

McManus, as a means of self-defence (*Republican News*, 19 January 1974, p. 6).

In later years, Provisional self-justification would be increasingly based on specific historical, social and political perspectives of Ireland. While inherent in all republican writing is the morally justifiable position of the IRA, there has been no attempt to argue this *explicitly* in a later period. If there had been such an argument, it is difficult to imagine that it would have invoked the statement of a Catholic priest.

Such change has been equally reflected by the different treatment of the hierarchy in republican literature at different stages of the period. Thus, a number of articles in *Republican News* during 1974 criticised the position of Bishop Philbin while implying that his views on the IRA campaign were somehow different from those of his ecclesiastical colleagues. In the 11 May edition of *Republican News*, p. 2, for instance, Dr Philbin was described as 'the most outspoken churchman in Ireland in support of the British forces', while two months later the 6 July edition of the same newspaper portrayed Dr Philbin, on p. 8, as 'an extreme right-wing churchman'. In its November edition it was claimed that the British authorities were using Bishop Philbin to fight republicans.[43] Similarly, two successive editions of *An Phoblacht* in September 1975, implied that the then newly-appointed Bishop of Derry, Dr Edward Daly, held different political views from those of his fellow-bishops. In sharp contrast to the practice of trying to distinguish between the political views of individual bishops in the mid-1970s, by the 1980s *An Phoblacht* was responding to the criticism of IRA violence by *individual* bishops as though such statements constituted hierarchical policy *per se*. Examples of this can be found in *An Phoblacht*'s treatment of statements by Cardinal O'Fiaich and Cahal Daly in January 1983 and May 1983.

For much of the period, republican writings have tended to distinguish between the behaviour of the hierarchy and the lower clergy. So much so, on a number of occasions republican literature gave maximum coverage to priests who identified with the republican cause. Thus, in June 1974, *Republican News* made the case of one Fr Connolly, a priest who had been suspended from the diocese of Birmingham because of his IRA sympathies, its lead story. Similarly, when Fr Sean McManus* made a pro-IRA statement in 1971, the item became headline news in *An Phoblacht* (October 1971). By drawing attention to such cases there was at least the implied belief that there was widespread support for the IRA among the lower clergy. At one point, in fact, *An Phoblacht* actually asserted that priests in Ireland were beginning 'to take up arms with the risen people'.[44]

This would-be bond between priests and the IRA began to break down in republican literature, however, during the late 1970s. Consequently, the view of Berman *et al* in 'The Theology of the IRA' in *Studies*, vol. lxxii, no. 286, summer 1983, p. 138, which identified in *An Phoblacht* a 'bad religion' of prelates and a 'good religion' of priests needs to be qualified. As early as 1977, a lead story in *An Phoblacht* accused one Fr Agnew of St Michael's Parish, Belfast, of preaching 'crown politics from a Belfast pulpit'. The article went on to quote a statement from Sinn Fein which described Fr Agnew's sermon as a 'political diatribe forced on the congregation' which reflected a 'wholly pro-British stand'. In late 1981, moreover, Fr Denis Faul of Dungannon was repeatedly subjected to fierce criticism in *An Phoblacht*. This was no doubt due to the belief among republicans that Faul had played an important role in undermining the hunger-strikes of that year.[45] Perhaps the most definitive example of this breakdown in the 'good religion' of priests, however, was the claim in *An Phoblacht* of January 1983, that no fewer than fifteen priests and ministers had issued condemnations of the IRA during the previous week.[†]

* As Fr McManus is not listed in the *Irish Catholic Directory* (1971), he was not resident in Ireland at this time. Unfortunately, *An Phoblacht* does not make it clear where Fr McManus was working when he made this statement.
† In defence of Berman *et al*, the authors made it clear that they had not examined 1983 copies of *An Phoblacht*.

5

The Catholic Ethos in Ireland:
an analysis

IT IS frequently argued that the Catholic ethos has important repercussions for political life in Ireland. Consequently, this chapter analyses the nature and effect of the Catholic ethos in Ireland with particular reference to how it impinges on the Northern Ireland situation. As the Catholic ethos in Ireland can be best understood in terms of clerical *influence* and clerical *authority*, this chapter is divided into two such sections.

The first section is presented in two parts. In part one, clerical influence is taken to mean the ways in which the politico-moral attitudes, behaviour and perceptions of Irish Catholics are influenced by their Church, and how in turn this affects the outlook of Protestants in Ireland, especially those in Northern Ireland. As the Catholic Church's influence is stronger in the Republic of Ireland than in Northern Ireland, contentious areas of Church–State relations in the South form the main background to the discussion in the first part of this section. Given the considerable influence of the Catholic Church in these areas of Irish life, it becomes pertinent to consider the hierarchy's underlying position on the rights of Protestants in Ireland. This is done in the second part of the section.

The second and more lengthy section of this chapter analyses two areas over which the Catholic Church exercises authority, viz. education and mixed marriages. Many people believe the Catholic school system in Northern Ireland to be divisive. In the face of such criticism, members of the Catholic hierarchy have defended their educational system on several occasions.[1] The most substantive defence of that system on behalf of the *entire* hierarchy is contained in one of the papers submitted by the Irish Episcopal Conference to the New Ireland Forum in 1984 (Veritas, Dublin). Consequently, the first part of this section offers an empirically-based assessment of the main arguments put forward in that paper. The latter part of the section analyses Catholic Church policy on mixed marriages in Ireland. While Church policy in this area is determined by canon law, *Matrimonia Mixta* (1970) has been interpreted and applied in different ways in different countries. Thus, the record of the Irish Catholic Church on mixed marriage since 1970 is assessed within a broad comparative framework.

Clerical influence

There is unanimous agreement among major studies on the subject that the Catholic ethos plays an important part in the political life of the Republic of Ireland. Indeed, works on the Church's political influence south of the border only differ with each other over the extent of such influence. Thus, while Whyte, in *Church and State in Modern Ireland 1923–1979*, 1980, p. 416, concludes that the Catholic hierarchy's position lies somewhere between the extreme model of a theocratic state and that of just another interest group, Blanshard, in *The Irish and Catholic Power—An American Interpretation*, 1953, p. 296, takes the view that the influence of the Catholic Church is so great that the Southern state 'is an exhibit of mutilated democracy'. While other authors such as Clarke, Cooney and Inglis are less emotive in their treatment of this subject than Blanshard, they are nonetheless critical of the extent of clerical influence.[2]

The influence of the Catholic Church in Ireland (especially in the South) has clearly affected the political attitudes and perceptions of many people on both sides of the border. This is particularly true of Northern Irish Protestants. Indeed, the results of two surveys in the 1970s indicate that the Protestant perception of clerical power in Ireland is an integral part of Unionist ideology. Thus, in a major attitudinal study of people in Northern Ireland, Moxon-Browne found among his Protestant respondents that fear of the power of the Catholic Church was their third most common reason for opposing a united Ireland.[3] The same fear is inherent in a study of Northern Ireland stereotypes conducted by O'Donnell in 1977 in which a word list technique is used on pp. 69–83 to discover how respondents describe various groups in their region.

Significantly, the third most popular phrase used by Protestants to describe Catholics is 'priest-ridden'. The fourth most popular expression in this category is that Catholics 'breed like rabbits'.

Such results point to how Catholicism is seen by many Northern Protestants as part of a political conspiracy. While the term 'priest-ridden' speaks for itself, the expression 'breed like rabbits' is more than just a derisory remark about the Roman Catholic Church's policy on artificial birth-control. In the context of Northern Ireland, in fact, it implies the ultimate Unionist nightmare: that Catholics might become a majority in Northern Ireland and succeed in bringing about a united Ireland.[4] In any case, many Irish Catholics acknowledge the existence of the widely-held fear of Protestants towards their Church. Consequently, 58.3 per cent of Moxon-Browne's Northern Catholic respondents in *Nation, Class and Creed in Northern Ireland*, p. 38, perceive Protestant fear of the Catholic Church's power as one of the reasons for Protestant opposition to a united Ireland. In his survey of Dubliners, moreover, Mac Greil, in *Prejudice and Tolerance in Ireland—Based on a survey of intergroup attitudes of Dublin adults and other sources*, 1977, p. 337, found that 40.8 per cent of his participants agreed with the statement that 'the position and influence of the Catholic Church in the Republic is a real obstacle to Irish unity'. While the above findings are significant in themselves, it can be argued that such perceptions have lowered the expectations of many nationalists *vis-à-vis* Irish unity, and in this sense at least, have contributed to the feeling of hopelessness felt by many anti-Unionists during all or at least much of the period of this study.

The position of the Catholic hierarchy towards possible change in those state laws which relate to public morality* has been rather anomalous. As Professor Ryan has pointed out in 'Church and Politics: The Last Twenty-five Years' in *The Furrow*, 30, 1 January 1979, pp. 13–14, there have been four distinctive policies adopted by different bishops in this area despite the existence of a commonly stated position by the hierarchy since November 1973. At that time, the hierarchy publicly stated for the first time in Ireland that what is considered wrong by the Church need not be prohibited by the state. Alongside this clear

---

* This term is used here in the rather narrow sense of sexually-related morality.

distinction between what can be called 'Church morality' and 'State morality', however, are a number of other positions which have been espoused on occasions by a small group of bishops. Ryan categorises these as follows: (i) that the state cannot enact something contrary to the moral law; (ii) the state laws ought to reflect majority opinion;[5] (iii) the Church ought to appeal to the loyalty of the people. Consequently, while *collective statements* by the Irish hierarchy on the constitutional amendment of 1983 and the divorce referendum of 1986 openly supported one side in each of the respective debates, they also clearly acknowledged the right of Catholics to exercise their conscience in voting.[6] Yet, some individual bishops went further in their approach to these matters. Thus, at the time of the 1983 amendment the late Archbishop Ryan of Dublin and the then bishop of Kerry, Dr McNamara, took what one commentator has described as 'an unqualified stance' on the issue (see Cooney, *The Crozier and the Dail*, p. 69). Less than a week before polling day in the divorce referendum, Dr McNamara (who in the interim period had become Archbishop of Dublin) issued a totally uncompromising statement on the subject (see Inglis, *Moral Monopoly*, p. 87). The reaction of bishops to the Family Planning (Amendment) Bill of 1985 (which was narrowly passed into law by the Dail) was, for Whyte, at least, the clearest evidence of divergence within the Catholic Church over such matters in recent years. The bill, which legalised the sale of contraceptives to all people over eighteen years of age, was opposed by various bishops on an individual basis. Whyte not only finds this lack of a collective statement significant in itself but argues: 'at least nine bishops issued individual statements over a ten-day period, and the differences in tone between some of them were sufficiently marked to attract attention.' ('Recent Developments in Church–State Relations' in *Seirbhis Phoibli—Journal of the Department of the Public Service*, vol. 6, no. 3, 1985, p. 9)

Whatever about the distinctive positions of certain bishops on the plebiscites, the constitutional referendum to ensure the continued prohibition of abortion was passed in 1983, while the proposal to end the constitutional ban on divorce was defeated in 1986. While it is a moot point as to how important clerical intervention was in determining the outcome of these referenda, there can be no doubt that what can be called the 'moral dimension' was an important factor in both campaigns.[7] Whatever else one can say about the results of these plebiscites, moreover, it can be argued that the almost identical outcome to both of these referenda indicates a major cleavage in Southern Irish society which can be broadly labelled as one of traditionalists versus modernists.

The effect of these events on Northern Ireland can be characterised in the following way. First, there must have been deep disappointment among those nationalists in the North who believe that different outcomes to the referenda would have at minimum reduced some of the divisions between North and South. Yet, according to Moxon-Browne's findings (see Moxon-Browne, table 2.1, p. 21), it seems that in relation to the divorce issue at least, such nationalists constitute no more than a large minority: only 47.6 per cent of his Catholic respondents believed that the Irish Government should take the steps necessary to make divorce legal in the Republic. In any event, the position of this group is an anomalous one as it relies exclusively on the political behaviour of the Southern electorate to introduce change of this kind—an electorate which does not necessarily relate constitutional change to the Northern Ireland situation. Second, while many Unionists and nationalists would argue that a different outcome to recent referenda would in no way alter the attitude of Northern Protestants towards the Republic or the question of Irish unity, there is empirical evidence which suggests that some such change would at least improve North–South relations. To cite Moxon-Browne yet again, 77.3 per cent of his Protestant respondents supported the idea that Dublin should take the steps necessary to legalise divorce in the South. It can be hypothesised, moreover, that the legalisation of divorce in the Republic or some other constitutional changes there, might eventually erode the perception among Northern Protestants that there is necessarily a symbiotic relationship between Catholicism and Irish nationalism.

It is in the light of the Catholic Church's influence in Ireland that it becomes important to consider the hierarchy's underlying position on the rights of Protestants in Ireland. This is done by referring to the most substantive insights to hierarchical thinking in this area which are contained in two recent documents, viz. the written submission of the Irish Episcopal Conference (Veritas, Dublin) and the oral submission of the Irish Episcopal Conference Delegation to the New Ireland Forum in early 1984 (see *New Ireland Forum No. 12: Public Session, Thursday 9 February 1984, Dublin Castle: Report of Proceedings,* Dublin: Stationery Office, 1984).

Just as divisions appear to have developed within the Catholic hierarchy over the referenda and the Family Planning (Amendment) Bill, so too, apparent differences emerged in the area of Protestant rights in the written and oral submissions to the New Ireland Forum. This is exemplified by the adoption of a majoritarian approach to minority rights in the Irish Episcopal Conference's paper (pp. 18–19) on pluralism. Thus the paper argues: 'Every legal system throughout the world bears the trace of majority opinion and of the public ethos and the majority consensus . . . A Catholic country or its government, where there is a very substantial Catholic ethos and consensus, should not feel it necessary to apologise that its legal system, constitutional or statutory, reflects Catholic values.' Not only does such a passage reflect a majoritarian approach, but it appears in a paper which is addressing itself to a *new Ireland*, and yet makes no explicit reference to the rights of Northern Ireland Protestants. The failure of this paper to be specific about its unit of analysis, therefore, gives rise to confusion over whether the present rights of Northern Protestants are to be safeguarded in the context of a new Ireland. By contrast, the guiding principle of the bishops' approach to Church–State relations in the oral submission to the Forum is that embodied by the Irish hierarchy's statement of November 1973, i.e. what is considered wrong by the Church need not be prohibited by the State. Unlike its written submission, moreover, in which no explicit reference is made to the rights of Northern Ireland Protestants, the episcopal delegation to the Forum meeting repeatedly expressed its support for Northern Protestants to have their present religious and civil liberties safeguarded in a new Ireland.[8]

Yet the basis of this hierarchical support for the rights of Northern Ireland Protestants remains unclear, especially when seen in the wider context of Protestants' rights in the Republic of Ireland. The most detailed explanation of the bishops' defence of Northern Protestant rights certainly sheds little light on hierarchical reasoning. In reply to a question from Brian Lenihan TD at the New Ireland Forum, Bishop Cahal Daly said that the Catholic Church's defence of Northern Protestant rights in a new Ireland would be 'a matter of plain justice and not just of political expediency' (*New Ireland Forum No. 12*, especially pp. 2, 13, 23, 35, 37–38). In contrast, none of the delegates from the Episcopal Conference made any such pledge on behalf of *the present rights* of Protestants in the Republic of Ireland. Instead, when questions were posed by Senator Mary Robinson and Deputy John Kelly about changing those laws in the Republic which presently prohibit some of the liberties enjoyed by people in Northern Ireland, the bishops' replies invariably pointed to the fact that different opinions had to be taken into account and that legislators or the electorate had to make any ultimate decisions in these areas (pp. 23, 39–40). What such answers overlook, of course, is that the Catholic Church's views are so influential in the Republic of Ireland that the most likely outcome of any such debate is the maintenance of the *status quo*. In effect, the hierarchy holds divergent views on the rights of Northern and Southern Irish Protestants. If, as Cahal Daly insists, those rights that are presently enjoyed by Northern Protestants are supported by the Catholic Church out of a sense of justice and not out of political expediency, one is left to speculate about the basis of such support and why the same support is not readily accorded to Southern Irish Protestants.*

Clerical authority: Catholic education

The controversy over whether Catholic children in Ireland should attend a Catholic-run or a state-controlled school is one which has raged for well over a century. While the Irish bishops co-operated with the national school system established in 1831,[9] clerical opposition to these *technically non-denominational* schools according to John Mescal in *Religion in the Irish system of*

---

* I have written to Bishop Cahal Daly for clarification of his position on this matter, but I have not received a reply from him.

education, 1957, p. 107, where he described the system as 'un-denominational in theory but denominational in practice', increased within a generation.[10] The increasing power of the Catholic Church during the latter part of the nineteenth century rendered the national school system increasingly denominational in nature (see Donald H. Akenson, *The Irish Education Experiment—The National System of Education in the Nineteenth Century*, 1970, pp. 4–5). It is hardly surprising that since the establishment of Northern Ireland, the Catholic Church has insisted on maintaining its own school system.[11] For one thing, canon law virtually prohibits a non-Catholic education for a Catholic child (Donald H. Akenson, *Education and Enmity—the Control of Schooling in Northern Ireland 1920–1950*, 1973, pp. 105–106). In the context of Northern Ireland, moreover, Protestant clergymen have held similarly segregationist views on education (*Education and Enmity*, pp. 193–194), while widespread Catholic mistrust of the state has hardly been conducive to the development of non-denominational education in that region. Indeed, as already noted in this chapter (p. 163), members of the Catholic hierarchy have staunchly defended the Catholic educational system. In addition, commitment among the lower clergy to that system is not in doubt: in a questionnaire circulated to all the priests of Northern Ireland in 1986, only 10.3 per cent of respondents supported the proposition that Church and State ought to launch a campaign for integrated education in that region.

In assessing the bishops' defence of the Catholic school system in Northern Ireland, two preliminary points ought to be made about the integrated education issue. First, many advocates of both integrated education and the *status quo* have failed to provide empirical evidence for their respective arguments[12] and by doing so have contributed to the mainly unsatisfactory nature of this debate. Second, it must be stated from the outset that there is no way, at least at this point,[13] of actually proving that the present schools system is divisive or otherwise. Put simply, it is not possible to establish the wider political effects of segregated or integrated education in Northern Ireland, unless a precise response to a number of hitherto unresearched questions can be found. As one commentator has correctly pointed out: 'Only if one has information on the children's attitude *before* they began schooling *and* on other influences upon their developing attitudes *and* upon their attitudes when they finish schooling can one claim to have established what the effects of integration are.' (Donald H. Akenson, *Education and Enmity*, p. 270)

The most substantive defence of Catholic education in Northern Ireland on behalf of the *entire* hierarchy is contained in one of the papers submitted by the Irish Episcopal Conference to the New Ireland Forum in 1984. Consequently, the main arguments contained in that document form the basis for the analysis which follows.

In the main part of that paper which is entitled 'the charge of divisiveness', pp. 26–32, especially pp. 27–30, the bishops argue that four broad points must be considered before any honest evaluation can be made about the possibly divisive effects of the Catholic school system in Northern Ireland:

- a comprehensive assessment of the most significant causes of division in Northern Ireland;
- an analysis of the values of the Catholic schools system and their likely effect in promoting or frustrating reconciliation;
- a consideration of the assumption implicit in this view that schools can unite a community which is otherwise deeply divided;
- a review of relevant empirical research.

Arising from these four broad points, it is possible to identify five explicit tenets of the bishops' argument. In addition, there are two implicit, albeit important tenets of the Church's position contained in this paper. The following assessment will deal with all seven parts of the ecclesiastical argument. It will begin by looking at the two implicit points of the argument.

The bishops state that the charge of divisiveness levelled at Catholic schools in Northern Ireland 'is not only unjust but deeply offensive to the religious principles of the Catholic community'. If one refers to an earlier section of this brief paper (p. 26), it becomes clearer what this means: 'The Catholic school system is therefore a religious system of education cherished as such by Catholic parents who see themselves as supported by their teachers and priests in their task of "handing on the faith" to their children.'

Most obviously, this assumes that Catholics solidly support the Catholic school system in Northern Ireland. Moreover, inherent in the above statement is that integrated education might undermine the belief and practice of Catholicism among schoolchildren. Neither assumption, however, appears to be borne out by empirical investigation. First, results from every study concerned with people's attitudes towards integrated education have indicated that a large majority of Catholics (and Protestants) welcome such a development. In his investigation, 'Opinions on School Desegregation in Northern Ireland' in A. E. C. W. Spencer, H. Tovey (eds), *Sociological Association of Ireland—Proceedings of the First and Fourth Conferences*, 1978, p. 50, Miller found that 77.4 per cent of Protestants and 88 per cent of Catholics expressed at least a moderate degree of support for integrated education. Keane discovered in his sample of schoolchildren in the South Down area that while Catholics expressed a greater willingness to share schools with Protestants than vice-versa, 'it could be reasonable to conclude that the sample as a whole would welcome integration' ('Attitudes To The Religious Integration In Schools In A Sample Of Secondary School Children In The Newry And South Down Area' in *Proceedings Third Annual Education Conference of the Educational Studies Association of Ireland*, 1978, p. 24). For his part, Rose, in *Governing Without Consensus: an Irish Perspective*, 1971, p. 336, found that 69 per cent of Catholic respondents in his survey approved of integrated education. Moxon-Browne, in *Nation, Class and Creed*, pp. 134–135, found even greater support for integrated schooling among his respondents: 81.8 per cent of Protestants and 84.5 per cent of Catholics disagreed with the proposition that it is a bad idea to educate Catholic and Protestant children in the same schools. In a 1980 opinion poll, moreover, only 15 per cent of Protestants and 12 per cent of Catholics said they would 'definitely' continue sending their children to a single religion school if mixed religion schools became available (Moxon-Browne, *Nation, Class and Creed*, pp. 134–135).* Despite this

---

* It is interesting to note that 60.7 per cent of participants in a major attitudinal survey in Dublin perceived segregated education as a major cause of division in Northern Ireland. See Michael Mac Greil, *Prejudice and Tolerance in Ireland*, Dublin: College of Industrial Relations, 1977, p. 377.

apparently emphatic desire on the part of the Northern Ireland public (and not least the Catholic community) for integrated education, two influential educationalists have warned against accepting such findings at face-value.[14] Whatever about such reservations, however, the above empirical findings do not, as the hierarchy suggests, indicate a commitment on the part of Catholics to religiously segregated education in Northern Ireland. On the contrary, such studies point to an overwhelming majority of Northern Catholics who, at a minimum, subscribe to *the principle* of integrated education. Second, it must be admitted that there is inadequate research carried out on whether integrated education might undermine the transmission of the Catholic faith to the younger generation in Northern Ireland. That said, however, research carried out in one of the few religiously mixed schools in Northern Ireland concluded:

> That the Roman Catholic children were found to have significantly more favourable attitudes to religion than the Protestants, is in line with the findings of research carried out in local denominational schools by Greer, Turner and research elsewhere . . . As the present study concerned only some fifty children attending a school which must be considered unusual, if not unique in a Northern Ireland setting, any conclusions drawn must be highly tentative. Nonetheless, the pattern of the findings appear to be consistent and to support those who have argued for the primacy of the home in the development of religious attitudes.[15]

The other main finding of this kind can only be regarded as relevant *if* one accepts that the effect of friendship between Catholic and Protestant schoolboys is analogous to that of integrated education. If so, it is interesting to note that the recurring conclusion of three major surveys was that such interreligious friendships did not weaken the religious beliefs and behaviour of those concerned (James Russell, 'Integrated Schooling—A Research Note' in *Secondary Teacher*, autumn 1977, p. 11). In short, while it is not possible to draw any firm conclusions about this matter, none of the existing research points to integrated education (or friendships between young

Catholics and Protestants) as having any deleterious effect on the religiosity of young Catholics.

An important part of the hierarchy's argument is that there must be a comprehensive assessment of the most significant causes of division in Northern Ireland before one can draw conclusions as to the possibly divisive effects of segregated education in the region. For their own part, the bishops, in their *Submission to the New Ireland Forum*, p. 28, argue:

> While recognising that there is a tendency to identify the Protestant with the loyalist tradition and the Catholic with the republican/nationalist tradition and that, in that sense, it might be claimed that there is a religious element in the situation in Northern Ireland, we would reject the view that religious differences *qua* religious differences play a part in the sad divisions in our society. We would therefore dispute the charge of divisiveness levelled against the existence of Catholic schools.

The above position is problematic for two broad reasons. First, there is no consensus as to what the most significant causes of division are in Northern Ireland. Instead, there is a plethora of conflicting explanations of the Northern Ireland problem — something which is more likely to complicate rather than clarify one's understanding of the conflict in Northern Ireland.[16] An interesting symptom of this dissensus is, moreover, how most Protestant clergymen generally conceive of the Northern Ireland conflict in more religious terms than their Roman Catholic counterparts. This is clear from interviews with Protestant churchmen conducted by John F. Galliher and Jerry L. De Gregory, *Violence in Northern Ireland: Understanding Protestant Perspectives*, 1985, pp. 55–58. Second, even if one accepts that religion *qua* religion does not play a part in the divisions of Northern Ireland society, it does not necessarily follow that Catholic schools are not divisive. Certainly, those researchers who have relied most heavily on interviews and observations in their work have found that Protestant criticism is based more on the perceived political indoctrination of children within the Catholic system than either the putatively religious (D. Murray,

Worlds Apart, p. 110) or cultural effects (Galliher and De Gregory, p. 76) of such an education.

The education document goes on to defend the Catholic school system in terms of an analysis of the values of that system and their likely effect in promoting or frustrating reconciliation. It continues: 'More positively, we would wish to claim that the values which are the inspiration of the Catholic school system are incompatible with violence, hatred or intolerance.'

Obvious difficulties exist with regard to the above approach. Not only are 'values' as described above impossible to analyse empirically, but one assumes that similar claims can be made by the apologists of virtually any educational system. Less obvious is that such a narrowly-conceived defence of Catholic education overlooks two broad considerations: (i) that acculturation in schools is a largely unconscious process; (ii) that mutual stereotyping within the present school system, rather than the system *per se*, is the problem in Northern Ireland. These are major points in the findings of one researcher who is unique for having spent a year participating in neighbouring Catholic and Protestant schools (Murray, *Worlds Apart*, pp. 107, 144). Consequently, he found that: 'In the schools it seemed that the transmission and reception of cultural mores and attitudes was, in fact, largely an unconscious process.' (*Worlds Apart*, p. 115) While this mainly unconscious process may be disturbing enough in the same author's view, the conscious process of mutual stereotyping which occurred in both schools is even more alarming (pp. 120, 122): 'The two most striking findings with regard to the stereotypes articulated by individuals in both schools was their unanimity and their almost invariably unfavourable nature . . . it is not segregated schools *per se* that are the problem in Northern Ireland, but rather the meanings and stereotypes which are attributed to them by members of that society.'

The fifth major part of the Church's argument as outlined in this paper is a consideration of the implicit assumption on the part of some people that schools can unite a community which is otherwise deeply divided. In considering this assumption, the bishops claim that there is a virtual consensus among educational theorists that the reconstructionist view of education, i.e. that schools should be principal agents of cultural or social changes, is invalid. As part of this argument, the paper quotes Russell who has written that 'the community, rather than the school is the chief socialiser of divisive political content'. In assessing such claims, it is, first of all, quite untrue that a 'virtual consensus' exists among educationists concerning the invalidity of the reconstructionist view of education in Northern Ireland. Thus, while the paper quotes from Salters[17] and Russell,[18] for instance, who have rejected the 'reconstructionist' thesis, it overlooks the findings of other educationists such as Robinson, (see 'Education and Sectarian Conflict in Northern Ireland' in *The New Era*, vol. 52, no. 1, January 1971, pp. 384–388, especially p. 388), who has subscribed to this view *in principle*, and in more recent years, Murray, who has written in *Worlds Apart*, p. 123, that 'it seems schools can, and should, provide the setting for social reconstruction'. Russell's quotation that the community rather than the school is the chief socialiser in Northern Ireland, which is used to support the Catholic Church's position, points to a central problem in the debate surrounding integrated education: namely, the impossibility of satisfactorily establishing the relative importance of segregated education *vis-à-vis* other factors in the socialisation process in Northern Ireland. Indeed, this has been highlighted by a number of sources such as Fraser, for instance, in *Children in Conflict*, 1973, p. 135, who has described this process as a 'curious exercise of tracing a "vicious circle" back to its source'. Only one educationist, in fact, has tried to trace this 'vicious circle' back to its source in a methodological way: Russell, in *Some Aspects of the Civic Education of Secondary Schoolboys in Northern Ireland*, 1972, especially p. 27, has used the technique of multiple regression and through such means has concluded that the schools cannot be the chief determinant of the attitudes that most youths have towards government. The value of such an exercise is debatable, however, as any application of multiple regression to this problem is based on the dubious belief that it is possible to control *all* the variables relevant to the education debate in Northern Ireland. In any event, even if one accepts that schools cannot be the chief determinant of youths' attitudes towards government, this *does not* necessarily invalidate a reconstructionist view of education.

A crucial part of the bishops' 1984 paper is the empirical evidence it adduces to show that Catholic education is not socially divisive. Two types of evidence are provided: studies conducted outside and inside Northern Ireland.

First, studies are quoted from the United States of America which claim that Catholic education in that country is not divisive. Surely, even if Catholic education is not socially divisive there, it is a *non sequitur* to use such evidence as part of an argument to show that the same can be said of Northern Ireland. In any event, that religion is a less salient cleavage than race in the United States renders such an example an inappropriate one. Still, even when one draws parallels with more analogous cases such as Austria, Belgium, Holland and Switzerland, it becomes obvious that it is impossible to view Catholic education as either *intrinsically* integrative or divisive. Certainly, the religious cleavage has diminished in all these countries against the background of differing approaches to the education question. In Austria and to an even greater extent in Switzerland, education policy has become more decentralised, leaving it more of a local or regional issue rather than a national one.[19] In Belgium and Holland Catholic education has experienced a surprising degree of continuity despite *inter alia* a spectacular political realignment in both countries.[20] While in Belgium a consensus on the education question was to emerge with the signing of the *pacte scolaire* in 1959, Catholic education in Holland has, despite enormous changes within Dutch Catholicism, retained something of its institutional strength. (For a detailed analysis of the *pacte scolaire* see, Jaak Billiet, 'Secularisation and Compartmentalisation in the Belgian Educational System—an analysis of the problems relevant to the revision of the school pact' in *Social Compass*, vol. xx, 1973/74, pp. 569–591.) In short, no general conclusion can be made about the effects of Catholic education in one society by examining the effects it may have in another.

Second, with regard to research conducted in Northern Ireland, the bishops refer to the work of John Salters as evidence that there is a strong suggestion in Salters' findings, in fact, that as a group, Catholic schoolchildren are somewhat more tolerant than pupils in Protestant schools. If one accepts such findings, the problem of isolating the effect of an educational system from wider social influences comes into play yet again. For while the hierarchy apparently attributes this relatively high level of tolerance among Catholic schoolchildren to their educational system, it is more plausible to argue that this is merely a symptom of how Protestants and Catholics see the Northern Ireland problem in different terms: Protestants tend to perceive the conflict in more religious terms while Catholics are more likely to see it as a nationalist one. This has been clearly accepted by authors such as Heskin (*Northern Ireland: a psychological analysis*, pp. 22–51, especially p. 47) and Buckland (*A History of Northern Ireland*, 1981, p. 100). (In any event, anti-Catholic feeling among Protestants is noted by a variety of writers such as Bell (*The Protestants of Ulster*, 1976), Galligher and De Gregory (*Violence in Northern Ireland*, pp. 71–92) and O'Malley (*The Uncivil Wars*, 1983, especially pp. 133–203).)

The final tenet of the paper's argument is that even if one were to adopt the theoretical position that integration would be a possible step towards community harmony, a review of some practical considerations might suggest an alternative conclusion. The document goes on to list such considerations as the bussing of Protestant and Catholic children and teachers and argues that a majority of people in Northern Ireland would oppose integrated education when it became clear what such a process would involve. The view is also expressed that any attempt to integrate schools prior to the ending of the Northern Ireland conflict may only increase conflict in that society.

As all the above considerations are, of course, hypothetical, there is no empirical basis for evaluating them. The final point is of some interest, however, as a growing body of evidence exists in relation to how youngsters educated in a segregated system have responded to different forms of 'integration'. While such findings can be criticised because of the relatively small numbers involved, the authors' conclusions are all the more impressive, however, not only because the children in question come from highly segregated areas of Belfast but because they all have special problems. Lockhart and Elliott found in Northern Ireland's only religiously integrated institution for young offenders that friendships developed across the religious divide. A sample of thirty-seven boys participated voluntarily in the study which involved attitudinal measurement on arrival, five weeks later (just as the offenders were due for release), and five weeks after release. The researchers concluded: '... even within a relatively short period of exposure to each other attitudes can change and closer identification occur. Moreover the results indicate that such changes may be relatively enduring. Such results must support those who argue for integrated education.' ('Changes in the attitudes of young offenders in an integrated assessment centre' in Jeremy and Joan Harbison, *A Society Under Stress: Children and Young People in Northern Ireland*, 1980, p. 112) For his part, Crutchley, in 'Joyriding problem—West Belfast' in *Constabulary Gazette*, vol. lxix, no. 5, May 1982, p. 9, has reported on an auto project in west Belfast whose aim is to discourage actual or potential joyriders from engaging in such activities in future. While the centre caters for mainly Catholic boys, they have been joined by six Protestant youths. There has been no sign of sectarian bitterness between these groups of youths. Moreover, in an interdenominational day centre for maladjusted schoolchildren, 150 subjects between ten and sixteen years of age were observed. The author of the study, M. Blease, in 'Maladjusted School Children In A Belfast Centre' in Joan Harbison (ed), *Children Of The Troubles—Children In Northern Ireland*, 1983, p. 28, points out: 'Taking into account the sectarian nature of the violence with which the pupils live, staff at the Jaffe centre have been surprised by the lack of bitter, religious conflict between pupils.'

On the basis of the above evidence, it is only fair to conclude that if religious differences do not prove a source of friction among these young 'deviants' and that in some cases friendships develop within these 'integrated' environments, practical problems involved in devising ways of integrating mainstream schoolchildren in Northern Ireland are hardly insuperable.

To conclude, it is at present impossible to prove the divisiveness or otherwise of the Catholic school system in Northern Ireland. Yet, on the basis of the above assessment, the Church's *apologia* of Catholic education in Northern Ireland is a weak one. Not only is there little empirical evidence to substantiate any of the main arguments advanced in the hierarchy's paper but much of its reasoning is at best questionable.

Clerical authority: mixed marriages

The Catholic Church's policy on mixed marriages in Ireland is widely perceived as inimical to good community relations. This is pointed out, for example, by authors such as Edwards (*The Sins of our Fathers Roots Of Conflict In Northern Ireland*, 1970, pp. 190–196) and Barrit and Carter (*The Northern Ireland Problem: a study in group relations*, 1972, pp. 26–27 (2nd edition)). For their part, Protestants have criticised both the nature and wider social effects of the Roman Catholic Church's teaching in this area. The gravity of the problem has been acknowledged by the Catholic Church; certainly, Bishop Cahal Daly has gone so far as to call mixed marriage 'the crux of ecumenism' (*Irish Times*, 22 January 1981, p. 7).

Ecumenism apart, a number of writers have attributed great political significance in Ireland to the introduction of the *Ne Temere* decree of 1908, which for most of this century has been the basis of Catholic Church policy on mixed marriage. This papal decree, which imposed a variety of religious promises on *both* parties to a mixed marriage was perceived by many Protestants as a virtual assault on both their religion and community. In the context of early twentieth-century Ireland, this is said to have had consequences for the Home Rule movement. Thus, in his examination of Anglican–Methodist relations around this time, Frederick Jeffrey has argued that the decree did much to reinforce the fear that Home Rule would mean Rome Rule 'Anglican–Methodist Relations' in Michael Hurley, SJ, (ed), *Irish Anglicanism 1869–1969 — Essays on the role of Anglicanism in Irish Life presented to the Church of Ireland on the occasion of the centenary of its Disestablishment by a group of Methodist, Presbyterian, Quaker and Roman Catholic scholars*, 1970, p. 87. For his part, T. P. O'Neill, in 'Political Life: 1870–1921' in the essays mentioned above, claims that the provisions of *Ne Temere* helped to bring the question of 'Rome Rule' to the forefront of the Home Rule issue, while Barkley, in *St Enoch's Congregation 1872–1972—An Account of Presbyterianism in Belfast through the life of a Congregation*, 1972, p. 97, has even suggested that the decree proved decisive in swinging opinion among one Presbyterian congregation in Belfast against Home Rule.

In the light of earlier Church history and more recent Irish history, the effects of *Ne Temere* in Ireland proved ironic if rather unsurprising. The canonical form of the Roman Catholic Church as we know it today was first introduced by the Council of Trent in its Decree *Tametsi* in order to end the confusion and un-certainty resulting from clandestine marriages. For political and practical reasons, however, the law of the canonical form was not fully applied in some countries, including Ireland, especially in the case of mixed marriages.[21] What this meant in practice for earlier mixed marriages in Ireland is not altogether clear,[22] but that the full rigour of the *Ne Temere* decree was applied at such a crucial juncture in Irish political history almost ensured that it would be seen to have political overtones.

Deeply influenced by the spirit of Vatican *II*, the Roman Catholic Church modified its teaching on mixed marriage in 1970. Whatever can be said about the extent of such change,[23] the escalating violence in Northern Ireland tended to over-shadow this development. In any case, Unionists can and frequently do point to the mixed marriage laws of the Roman Catholic Church as a contributory factor to the decline of the Protestant population in the Republic of Ireland.[24]

During the course of the oral submission of the Irish Episcopal Conference Delegation to the New Ireland Forum, Bishop Cassidy of Clonfert found himself defending the position of the Roman Catholic Church on mixed marriage in Ireland. Much to the surprise of the general public, Dr Cassidy revealed that the Irish bishops had considered asking Rome for a derogation from the promise that all Roman Catholics entering a mixed marriage must make, i.e. that the Catholic partner will do everything in his or her power to bring up children from the marriage as Catholics. The bishop explained, however, that this was not done as there was little prospect that Rome would agree to such a derogation.

Assuming that any such derogation from *Motu Proprio*

Matrimonia Mixta is indeed not feasible, this still overlooks the fact that *Motu Proprio* acknowledges any type of uniform policy on the part of the Church towards mixed marriage to be impossible.[25] So much so, that the document encourages individual hierarchies to issue separate statements of their own. In practice, therefore, *Motu Proprio* is interpreted and applied in different ways in different countries. Thus, this brief section will examine the record of the Irish Catholic Church on mixed marriage since 1970 in a comparative perspective. This is done by referring to the following: the Irish bishops' statement on *Motu Proprio Matrimonia Mixta* and those of other episcopal conferences in the period 1970–1971; the Irish Episcopal Conference's Directory on Mixed Marriage (1983);* and certain practices on the part of the Catholic Church in different locations. Against this background, three important aspects of the mixed marriage question are examined: (i) the religious upbringing of the children of mixed marriages in different locations; (ii) the nature of the pastoral care offered by the Roman Catholic Church to partners in a mixed marriage in different countries; (iii) the contrasting positions of the Catholic Church on 'ecumenical Sacraments' in different locations.

Possibly the most contentious aspect of mixed marriage was the promise contained in the *Codex Iuris Canonici* (1918)† whereby both partners to such a marriage had to commit themselves to bringing up their children as Roman Catholics. Under *Motu Proprio* the Protestant partner is not asked to make any such promise, while it is implicitly recognised that all such children might not be brought up in the Roman Catholic faith. Accordingly, the Catholic partner is to promise to do 'all in his power' to have the children brought up as Roman Catholics. In their brief statement on *Motu Proprio*, the Irish bishops acknowledge this promise, but then go on to discuss the religious obligation of a Catholic in a seemingly inflexible way:

> This is why the regulations emphasise that the Catholic party at a mixed marriage must do all in his power to ensure

---

* These are the only statements of the Irish hierarchy devoted exclusively to the theme of mixed marriage. For a brief reference to this subject see, Irish Episcopal Conference, *Directory on Ecumenism in Ireland*, Dublin: Veritas, 1976, pp. 30–34.
† *Ne Temere* was central to this code of canon law.

the Catholic baptism and upbringing of all the children of the marriage . . . A Catholic can never be dispensed from the duty of handing on to his children the faith that is in him. Nor can he be authorised to withhold from the children the full riches of Catholic devotional and sacramental life. The Church's position in this matter flows from the very nature of Catholic faith. It constitutes no reflection on the sincerely held beliefs of others. (*The Furrow*, vol. 21, no. 11, November 1970, p. 733)

Put briefly, while the Irish bishops clearly accept the letter of the Roman law, i.e. that the Catholic has to do 'all in his power' to ensure a Catholic upbringing for his children, they do not explicitly acknowledge the possibility that such children might not be brought up as Catholics. Instead the above passage implies that the Catholic upbringing of children of a mixed marriage is something of a *fait accompli*.

By contrast, a number of episcopal conferences on the Continent clearly recognise the possible problems in this area and not least the conscience of the Protestant partner. Consequently, far from the religious upbringing of children being seen as an inevitably Catholic one, a number of Continental hierarchies leave this to the conscience of both partners of a mixed marriage. Thus, the German document concedes: 'But since the education of the children is always the task of both parents, and since one must not force either of them to act against his conscience, this duty means doing all that is possible, in the concrete situation, acting in the way which seems best in conscience.'[26] Similarly, primacy of conscience for both partners in a mixed marriage is stressed by other Continental hierarchies. Thus, the Swiss statement says that the couple must make a decision of which both partners can approve.[27] The French episcopal conference acknowledges that the 'promise' has to be carried out in the concrete circumstances of the couple's home and consequently a decision regarding the religious upbringing of that couple's children must be one that is acceptable to the conscience of each partner (*One in Christ*, pp. 232–233). For its part, the Belgian hierarchy's document says:

In a mixed marriage each has to confront his own conviction

with that of his partner, whose conviction is often as deep and as demanding as his own. Only honest and sincere reflection, undertaken together by the fiances before the marriage and carried on afterwards, can clarify the way little by little: it will lead them to decide upon a line of conduct which takes account of all the concrete possibilities of giving their children a truly faithful Christian education. (*One in Christ*, p. 233)

It is a moot point whether the Irish Episcopal Conference's *Directory on Mixed Marriages* (1983) represents an actual or apparent change in the position of the Irish Church on mixed marriage from that of their statement in 1970. Certainly, the 1983 Directory is more explicit than the statement of 1970 in recognising the possibility that children of a mixed marriage may not necessarily be brought up as Roman Catholic (Irish Episcopal Conference, *Directory on Mixed Marriages*, 1983, 8.5, pp. 20–21). Yet, unlike those Continental documents quoted above, for example, the 1983 Directory in no way implies that the exercise of the Protestant conscience in a mixed marriage is as valid as the Roman Catholic one. Unlike these Continental documents, for instance, the Irish Directory makes it perfectly clear in relation to the obligations of the Catholic partner to a mixed marriage that it is not the role of Catholic bishops 'to speak about the conscience of the other [Protestant] partner' (*Directory on Mixed Marriages*, 6.1, p. 13). More important, however, is the fact that the Irish hierarchy is virtually unique* in invoking divine law as the basis of the Roman Catholic's religious obligations in a mixed marriage. Consequently, equality or even apparent equality of conscience for a Protestant partner to a mixed marriage is impossible:

The obligations of the Catholic partner are not created by the declaration or promise which is required before marriage. Rather, they are rooted in his or her faith and in obedience to God's law. The promise simply reminds the Catholic and brings to the attention of the other partner, the

* Only the English and Irish hierarchies stress the Catholic's obligation in a mixed marriage on the basis of divine law. See *One In Christ*, vol. viii, nos. 2–3, 1971, p. 229.

obligations which the Catholic Church already has, independently of any promise, and establishes that the Catholic is committed to carrying them out. These obligations are not imposed by the Church's regulations, nor can the Church remove them; they come from God. It is simply the manner in which the obligations are to be acknowledged that is determined by the Church (*Directory on Mixed Marriages*, 6.2, p. 13).

The pastoral care offered to couples of a mixed marriage is another important area in which the policy of national hierarchies has contrasted enormously. Yet again, the Irish Church must be seen as being conservative in this area. As one authority on the subject has pointed out, in countries such as France, the Netherlands, Great Britain, Canada, Germany and Switzerland, co-operation between the Churches over mixed marriages is such that *a joint pastoral approach* to this question has been in operation there for some years.[28] The same author contrasts this with the situation pertaining in Ireland:

Since the required degree of co-operation, reached somehow in the countries named above at the beginning, seems to be only remotely attainable here at present, one must look for priests and ministers locally to come together, acknowledge each other's good faith and agree to be scrupulously fair in presenting both Churches' positions. At least, there might be an end to the conflicting explanations of the pre-marriage promise so often given, to the confusion of couples at present. (*The Furrow*, vol. 33, no. 6, June 1982, p. 362)

Consequently, in the absence of a coherent inter-Church policy on this issue, partners entering a mixed marriage in Ireland are vulnerable to possible misinformation about the theological implications of their union. Not only are such possible misunderstandings dysfunctional to improved community relations here, but the lack of urgency shown by the Irish Churches towards this problem is hardly encouraging. With specific regard to the Catholic Church, for instance, as late as 1983 the Irish bishops expressed the opinion that *there should be* a priest or priests designated in each diocese to specialise 'in mixed marriage counselling as part of the marriage advisory service' (*Directory on Mixed Marriages*, 4.10, p. 11).

With regard to the sharing of sacraments between Christians involved in mixed marriages, there is again variation between countries. In the *Irish Directory on Mixed Marriage* (1983), for instance, the idea of non-Roman Catholics receiving Holy Communion is virtually ruled out. Three conditions are listed on page 27 which must be satisfied before such a course would be sanctioned. It is pointed out, however, that it would be 'extremely rare' to find all these conditions fulfilled in this country. By contrast, in France inter-communion has become increasingly popular in mixed marriages (Joseph Hoffmann, 'Positions and Trends in France' in Michael Hurley (ed), *Beyond Tolerance— the challenge of mixed marriage—A record of the International Consultation held in Dublin 1974*, 1975, p. 124). The position in Australia varies between dioceses. In one of that country's largest dioceses and some smaller dioceses, the practice has arisen that Holy Communion is offered to the Protestant spouse and, if baptised, to his or her family (Paul Duffy, 'Positions and Trends in Australia', p. 149). Similarly, the Catholic Church in Ireland is relatively conservative with regard to baptism. This is clearly spelt out in 18.1, p. 32 of its 1983 directory: 'Concepts such as "concelebration" or "baptism into two churches" or "double baptism" must, however, be decisively rejected.' In France, certainly, such practices are not rejected by Catholic authorities. Indeed, what one authority describes as 'ecumenical baptism' has become commonplace for children of mixed marriages in that country (Joseph Hoffmann, 'Positions and Trends in France', pp. 122–123).

In putting the interpretation and application of *Motu Proprio* by these various hierarchies into perspective, it ought to be noted that, in general, the Irish policy is generally closer to that of the Church in the Anglo–American world than it is to the policies of the Church in Continental Europe. Thus, in distinguishing the Irish approach from that of the Catholic Church in many European countries, one commentator, Eoin de Bhaldraithe, in 'The Ecumenical Marriage' in *The Furrow*, vol. 32, no. 10, October 1981, p. 644, refers to the existence of a 'Continental interpretation' of *Motu Proprio*. Similarly, another article on this subject, 'Matrimonia Mixta' in *One In Christ*, identifies a cleavage between the Church in some Continental countries and those in English-speaking locations. Not only has the Catholic Church in Ireland been seen in a broad Anglo–American framework, but judging from the comments of different bishops it sees itself as primarily part of such a framework.[29] This in itself is hardly surprising: the Irish influence on Catholicism in the English-speaking world has been immense.[30]

Nonetheless, the effect of interpreting and applying *Motu Proprio* in an essentially Anglo–American and relatively conservative way can hardly be conducive to improved communal or political relations in Ireland. Certainly, the failure of the Irish bishops to adopt a more liberal policy on mixed marriage along the lines of many Continental hierarchies is inappropriate when one considers that Ireland's traditional sectarian problems are more similar to those of Continental Europe than other English-speaking countries. Above all, the seemingly endemic sectarianism of Northern Ireland would suggest that there is at least as great a need here for a relatively liberal interpretation of *Motu Proprio* as there is anywhere else.

Conclusion

THIS FINAL chapter considers the wider implications of this study. These implications are examined under four broad headings: (i) the nature of the Church's contribution to the search for political progress; (ii) the wider significance and impact of clerical protests on state policy in Northern Ireland; (iii) the nature of the Church's influence over the IRA: (iv) the Catholic ethos.

The Catholic Church's contribution to the search for political progress throughout the period of this study has been a paradoxical one. While the Church has had varying degrees of influence in promoting political change, the overwhelming tendency of clerics has been to limit their own influence in this sphere.

As seen in chapter 1, clerical influence of this kind is attributable to the special status of the Catholic Church within the Catholic community. This explains why, for instance, when Catholic politics was in a state of chaos from 1969 to 1970 the Home Secretary, James Callaghan, chose the Catholic Church to sell his package of reforms to the Catholic community. Even when this apparent political pre-eminence of the Church proved short-lived, see pp. 26–38, political prescriptions offered by the Church remained important. This was especially true for constitutional nationalism, although this type of clerical influence can only have been diminished by the fact that since the late 1970s the bishops have failed to provide a common political prescription for the future of Northern Ireland.

Whatever about the nature of such political influence, the overwhelming majority of clerics have consciously chosen not to intervene in the electoral process in Northern Ireland. Thus, among the findings in chapter 2 was the fact that only 3.9 per cent of respondents in my questionnaire indicated that they have given advice to their congregations as to which way they should vote in an election. This finding was all the more striking given that 47.4 per cent of respondents believed that they could exercise some type of positive influence in this sphere if they wished to do so. It is significant, moreover, that when some clerics called for a boycott of the Northern Ireland Convention elections in 1975, local bishops were quick to point out that the Catholic Church was recommending no such boycott.

This overwhelming tendency of Catholic clerics to exclude themselves from electoral politics points to an intention on the part of the Church to avoid 'politics' in the narrow party political sense of that term. Thus, while the Catholic Church and the SDLP have clearly shared many political ideas throughout the period of this study, the SDLP is a secular party.[1] Moreover, the overwhelming majority of clerics have distinguished between their political judgments as private citizens and their right as priests to influence the voting behaviour of their congregations. Indeed, only 3.9 per cent of respondents to my questionnaire indicated that they have advised their congregations as to which way they should vote in an election, while at the same time 87.9 per cent felt that they would be most likely to vote for the SDLP 'if a general election were to be held in the near future'. This does not mean, however, that the Catholic Church should be seen as necessarily neutral in party political terms. Even allowing for the fact that unfavourable clerical comments on the electoral rise of Sinn Fein were primarily of a moral nature (pp. 155–158), it is hardly difficult to understand the implications of such remarks in the political context of Northern Ireland. Put simply, not only are such comments politically unhelpful to Sinn Fein but if taken on board by nationalists, might be seen as effectively limiting their electoral options to either abstaining or voting for the SDLP.[2]

The tendence of the Catholic Church to criticise various aspects of state policy during the period of this study has two broad implications for political life in Northern Ireland: (i) the wider significance of clerical protest in the Northern Ireland context; (ii) the efectiveness of such clerical protest.

However many Catholic churchmen see such protests as merely a way of promoting social justice and protecting human rights, this aspect of clerical behaviour presupposes judgments about key institutions of the State such as aspects of security policy and the judiciary. Indeed, inherent in much of the clerical protest about state policy during the period in question are two closely related judgments. First, that the state has failed to implement the law in an impartial manner. Second, as such policies and especially aspects of security policy have increased alienation among sections of the Catholic community, they have also damaged prospects for political progress in Northern Ireland.[3] In effect, the Catholic Church has assumed the role of a pressure-group *vis-àvis* a wide range of government policies.

This in turn raises the question, how effective have such clerical protests been during the period of this study? If one chooses to judge the effectiveness of Church interventions of this kind in terms of whether the Government clearly responded to such criticisms, it must be said that there have been few tangible signs of success for clerical protest. Indeed, of the many protests we have examined, only a few appear to have led to a direct response from the authorities. First, it is claimed in chapter 3, p. 107, that army harassment decreased, if only temporarily, after sixty-five Belfast priests had protested about the conduct of the military in Catholic areas of their city in 1972. Second, it has been implied by ex-internee McGuffin that Cardinal Conway's allegations concering the brutal treatment of internees by security forces in 1971 proved instrumental in persuading the British Government to establish the Compton enquiry. Moreover, McGuffin also claims that Cardinal Conway was among those who made representations on behalf of a small number of internees who had been subjected to electric-shock treatment and that Prime Minister Heath personally ordered this practice to be stopped.

Of course, given the centrality of security policy, prisons and the judiciary to the administration of Northern Ireland, it is hardly surprising that the authorities rarely responded to clerical protests. Still, even if policy in these areas was not generally influenced by clerical protests, it must be admitted that, at a minimum, the authorities must have found major clerical protests more difficult to cope with than similar protests by other groups within the Northern Catholic community. After all, not only is the Catholic Church the most important institution in that community, but unlike the statements of formal pressure-groups or political parties, clerical protest cannot have been dismissed in narrow political terms.

The relationship between the IRA and the Catholic Church is rather anomalous. Not only does the Church enjoy a special status within the Catholic community but as seen in chapter 4, there is a considerable degree of religiosity among republican prisoners. Such religiosity, one might believe, should have rendered the IRA more responsive to the virtually incessant condemnation of violence by the clergy. Yet, such behaviour merely reflects a republican tendency to dichotomise between clerical authority in the areas of religion and politics. This tendency is hardly new. As seen in chapter 4, p. 144, for instance, even the Irish hierarchy's decision to excommunicate anti-treaty forces in the Civil War in 1922 failed to dissuade republicans from engaging in violent activities against their political opponents.

While the Church has failed to persuade the IRA to cease its military campaign, it is necessary to acknowledge that there has been a wider power struggle between the Church and the IRA over the hearts and minds of the Catholic people. Not only have we seen tangible examples of this struggle (see pp. 142–143), but it must be borne in mind that through constant denunciation of violence, the Catholic Church has been instrumental in creating an unfavourable moral climate in which the IRA has had to conduct its campaign. Ultimately, however, one can only speculate as to whether, and if so to what extent, the Church suceeded in limiting the IRA's appeal within the Catholic community.

Finally, two major implications emerge from this study concerning the Catholic ethos. First, the evicence indicates that the Catholic ethos is a divisive influence in Ireland and that this affects the Northern Ireland situation in a number of ways. Second, there is little prospect of the Catholic of the Catholic Church changing its position in this general area.

As seen in chapter 5, especially pp. 165–169, there is a widespread belief among both Catholics and Protestants that the power of the Catholic Church in Ireland is a real obstacle to Irish unity. The ramifications of such a belief are considerable for both nationalism and unionism. In a sense, many nationalists see the Catholic ethos as dysfunctional to the reunification of Ireland and, *ipso facto*, recognise a type of latent conflict which exists between Irish Catholicism and Irish nationalism. Indeed, the importance attached to the Catholic Church's submissions to the New Ireland Forum tacitly points to the belief that the Catholic ethos in Ireland is incompatible with the stated object- ive of constitutional nationalists to persuade Northern Unionists that they should see their political future in a united Ireland. (For reference to this objective see, *New Ireland Forum Report, 2 May 1984.*) For their part, Unionists can point to the results of the referenda of 1983 and 1986 as having effectively endorsed the Catholic orientation of the Irish Constitution. While it is a moot point whether changes in Church and State in Ireland would affect Unionsim *per se*, it would appear that at least some such change would contribute to a lessening of Protestant fear concerning the power of Catholicism in Ireland.

However people conceive of the Catholic ethos in general as a barrier to Irish unity, there is also little doubt that areas of life over which the Catholic Church exercises authority, viz. edu- cation and mixed marriages, are widely perceived as inimical to good community relations. Yet, findings in this thesis imply that there is little likelihood of the Church changing its policy in either of these areas. Certainly, given the hierarchical nature of the Catholic Church, such cange can only be sanctioned by the Irish bishops and there has never been any indication by the Irish hierarchy that a fundamental shift in either its position on Catholic education in Northern Ireland or mixed marriages in the whole of Ireland is forthcoming.* Underlying this position is a combination of ecclesiastical conservatism and an apparently limited level of debate concerning these issues. Such conservat- ism has undoubtedly been reflected by the way in which the Roman Catholic Church's policy on mixed marriage has been interpreted and applied by the Irish Church. Moreover, it is reasonable to assume that greater ecclesiastical discussion would be conducive to the development of a more sophisticated *apologia* for Catholic education in Northern Ireland than that presented by the hierarchy in its written submission to the New Ireland Forum. While bishops reassured questioners at the New Ireland Forum that they would resist any constitutional propo- sals in a new Ireland which might infringe or imperil the civil

---

* Indeed Bishop Edward Daly told me that it was difficult to see what the hierarchy could do to alter the tendency of many Protestants to perceive the Catholic Church in a negative fashion. (In an interview in Derry, 3 March 1988)

and religious rights of Northern Protestants, this still overlooks the fact that many Protestants, perceive the Catholic Church in a negative light. It is possible that such negative perceptions can be altered by changes in Catholic Church policy in the area of Catholic education in Northern Ireland and mixed marriages in Ireland as a whole. Until such time as the Catholic Church changes its present stance, however, one if left to speculate about the effect of such change on Catholic-Protestant relations in Ireland, especially in Northern Ireland.

APPENDIX A

Diocese

Armagh
William Conway ordained Archbishop 1963–77
                created Cardinal 1965–77
Tomas O'Fiaich ordained Archbishop 1977–
                created Cardinal 1979–

Clogher
Bishop Eugene O'Callaghan 1943–70
Bishop Patrick Mulligan 1970–79
Bishop Joseph Duffy 1979–

Derry
Bishop Neil Farren 1939–74
Bishop Edward Daly 1974–

Down and Connor
Bishop William Philbin 1962–82
Bishop Cahal B. Daly 1982–

Dromore
Bishop Eugene O'Doherty 1944–76
Bishop Francis Gerard Brooks 1976–

Kilmore
Bishop Austin Quinn 1950–72
Bishop Francis McKiernan 1972–

APPENDIX B

The New University of Ulster
Coleraine County Londonderry Northern Ireland
Telephone Coleraine 4141 Telegrams 'University Coleraine'

23rd September 1971
Most Rev. William Cardinal Conway,
'Ara Coeli',
ARMAGH.
Your Eminence,
   May I, as secretary of the Ulster Branch of the Association of Irish
Priests, draw your Eminence's attention to the following motion passed
at a meeting of the Ulster Branch on September 20th:
   "That this meeting of the Ulster Branch of the Association of Irish
   Priests request from the Cardinal that accreditation of a chaplain to
   Stormont be suspended pending the establishment of a democratic
   and representative legislature in Northern Ireland."
The meeting requested me as secretary to communicate this motion to
your Eminence.
Yours respectfully,
Terence O'Keeffe

APPENDIX C

Questionnaire

My reason for conducting such a questionnaire is quite simple: while part of my study involves discussion of the political attitudes and perceptions of the lower clergy in Northern Ireland, this is a largely unexplored area of academic research. In order to make the questionnaire as reliable as possible, I decided to contact all the priests who presently reside in Northern Ireland (i.e. the diocesan clergy as well as members of religious orders). In short, the only Catholic clerics not to be contacted were bishops, auxiliary bishops and full-time diocesan administrators. As only two of the dioceses are wholly within Northern Ireland, viz. Down and Connor and Dromore, it was necessary to distinguish between priests who live in Northern Ireland and those in the Republic of Ireland in the four cross-border dioceses of Armagh, Clogher, Derry and Kilmore. The names and addresses of priests were found in the *Irish Catholic Directory*, 1985. Although the same information pertaining to members of religious orders was contained in this directory, I wrote to the rectors of all the monasteries with a view to gaining the most up-to-date list of names. Happily, all the rectors supplied me with this information.* As a result of using two different methods in gathering the names and addresses of the two categories of priests, this made it necessary to draft two separate cover-letters.

The survey included members of religious orders as well as diocesan clergy for three main reasons. First, while many people may think of monks living a secluded life and therefore having political views which are of little academic value, it must be remembered that a number of such clerics are involved in parish work or teaching. For example, some twenty-two members of religious orders are listed in the *Irish Catholic Directory* with members of the secular clergy in the dioceses of Armagh, Clogher, Down and Connor, and Dromore.† Moreover, some monasteries are constituted as parishes, and consequently, members of such religious communities (e.g. Clonard in Belfast) would do the same parish work as members of the diocesan clergy. Second, some of the monasteries in Northern Ireland are in areas which have been badly

---

* Unfortunately, a few rectors only supplied me with this information *after* my cover-letters had been completed and photocopied.

† I made this calculation on discovering that there were seven respondents who, despite working in dioceses, identified themselves as members of religious orders. Working on the assumption, therefore, that such clerics would primarily regard themselves as members of religious orders, I decided to re-examine all the names of priests in the various dioceses to see how many of them belonged to religious orders. As each religious order has its own distinct initials, this was done quite easily.

affected by the troubles over the years, e.g. Ardoyne. Surely, it would be unsatisfactory to overlook such monasteries in a survey of this kind. Third, by including all priests resident in Northern Ireland, it becomes possible to discover whether a significant divergence exists between the political attitudes and perceptions of diocesan priests and those of religious orders.

The total sample is 628, of whom 505 are diocesan priests, while the remaining 123 are members of religious orders. In each of the two cover-letters, I outlined the objectives of my thesis and explained the purpose of the survey.* In an attempt to maximise my response rate, I used the following techniques. First, I sent each priest a self-addressed stamped envelope. Second, I numbered each of the questionnaires which enabled me to ascertain, in the most confidential way possible, which priests did not answer the questionnaire in case it became necessary to send out a follow-up questionnaire to non-respondents. As it turned out, such a follow-up questionnaire did not become necessary. Of the 628 questionnaires posted in Belfast on 25 April 1986, 232 valid responses were returned, giving an overall response rate of 36.9 per cent. Certainly, this response rate is comparable to those of earlier postal questionnaires, all of which examined various aspects of clergymen's political attitudes within the main Churches of the area, (viz. Church of Ireland, Presbyterian, Methodist, Baptist and Roman Catholic). Birrell, Greer, Roche (1979)[1] had an overall response rate of 44 per cent, with a response rate among Catholic priests of 33 per cent. Unfortunately, Birrell, Roche (1974)[2] and Birrell, Roche (1977)[3] only give their *overall* response rates, and by doing so, fail to provide a response rate per denominational group. The following passage from Birrell, Greer, Roche (1975)[4] suggests that the response rate among Catholic priests was 45 per cent, but they fail to be perfectly explicit about this . . . the response rate of 45 per cent was consistent throughout the samples drawn from the population of Northern Ireland clergy'. (p. 143) (The authors of these various articles do not make it clear as to *how many* surveys they have actually conducted.)

Table 1 (p. 198) shows how variations in the response rate of my questionnaire are most pronounced along two distinct levels:

(i) a much higher percentage of members of religious orders res- ponded to the questionnaire (58.5 per cent) than did diocesan clergy, (31.7 per cent);
(ii) there were significant variations in the overall response rates of priests within different dioceses.

The nature of the clerics' response to the questionnaire was equally

Table 1

Questionnaire sent out		Respondents	Response rate %
Armagh			
Priests	90	28	31.1
R. Orders	16	11	68.7
Total	109	39	36.8
Clogher			
Priests	42	24	57.1
R. Orders	12	6	50.0
Total	54	30	55.5
Derry			
Priests	108	36	33.3
R. Orders	5	5	100.0
Total	113	41	36.3
Down and Connor			
Priests	197	42	21.3
R. Orders	71	38	53.5
Total	268	80	29.7
Dromore			
Priests	63	29	46.0
R. Orders	19	12	63.1
Total	82	41	50.0
Kilmore			
Priests	5	1	20.0
R. Orders	0	0	0.0
Total	5	1	20.0
Overall Total, Northern Ireland			
Priests	505	160	31.7
R. Orders	123	72	58.5
Total	628	232	36.9

varied, and can be conveniently considered under the following headings: (i) a generally low non-response rate to specific questions;

(ii) the importance attached to Catholic education among priests; (iii) miscellaneous comments.

Generally speaking, non-response to specific questions was not a problem. Question 18 produced the highest rate of non-response with thirty-six priests, or 15.5 per cent of those who answered, failing to provide a valid response. The question asked priests what effect they felt they would have on their congregations if they were to advise them on how they should vote in an election. It might be speculated that many of the non-respondents found this scenario hypothetical and perhaps improbable, given the overwhelming majority of respondents (94.4 per cent) who said in the previous question that they had never given such advice to members of their congregations. By contrast, the rate of non-response for question 16, which relates to party political identification among priests, was a mere 5.2 per cent. Among other things, this figure reflects a willingness on the part of the respondents to reveal what for many people is a highly personal matter. While only 0.9 per cent said they would be likely not to vote, 94 per cent said they would be likely to vote for a specified political party if a general election were to be held in the near future. Given the low rate of non-response to this question, there is no reason to believe that there is a significant number of 'silent' Sinn Fein supporters among the clergy who are too embarrassed to admit their political sympathies.

The importance attached to Catholic education among priests was reflected by the frequency of their comments on the subject. At the end of the questionnaire, respondents were encouraged to comment on any aspect of my study. Of those priests who made comments, 52.8 per cent referred to some aspect or other of Catholic education in Northern Ireland. Catholic education, in fact, was easily the most discussed aspect of this questionnaire among respondents.

Significantly enough, 139 priests, or 60 per cent of all respondents, made no comment at all on the questionnaire. Of those clerics who did comment on my work, it is hardly surprising that their views were of a varied nature. Some of them were extremely positive in their replies, while other priests expressed reservations either about the project as a whole, or specific aspects of it.

Earlier empirical research in this area has been generally unsatisfactory. Fahy's[5] is the only survey dealing exclusively with the political attitudes of priests in Northern Ireland which has been conducted before. In the Summer/Autumn of 1968, he interviewed ten priests in a rural area of Northern Ireland. Fahy's study, however, is of limited value for three main reasons: (i) his sample of ten priests is inadequate for the purpose of establishing the political attitudes of priests throughout Northern Ireland as a whole; (ii) the focus of Fahy's study was different in that one of his two major objectives was to use the data as a means of assessing the nature and extent of the involvement of rural priests in local parish problems; (iii) as the fieldwork was carried out in the summer/autumn of 1968, some of the questions do not lend themselves to accurate comparisons with the findings of more recent surveys. For example, given the fragmentation of anti-Unionist politics at the time, Fahy's question on party political identification gives us no indication as to how these priests would be likely to vote today. Only four other studies throw any light on the political attitudes of Catholic priests in Northern Ireland, and all of these are concerned with the political attitudes and perceptions of clergymen belonging to the main religious denominations in the area, viz. Church of Ireland, Presbyterian, Methodist, Baptist and Roman Catholic. All the data for these investigations was collected in 1972/73, and while the samples were much larger than Fahy's, (20 per cent and 25 per cent of all clergymen with congregations in Northern Ireland), they were still far from being comprehensive. Moreover, two of the four studies hardly tell us anything about the political attitudes of Catholic priests in Northern Ireland. The study by Birrell and Roche (1974),[6] which is primarily concerned with the relationship that exists between theological beliefs and political attitudes, reaches the unsurprising conclusion that clergymen are divided on political issues and party preference along Protestant–Catholic lines (p. 6). Moreover, all the data contained in the article by Birrell, Greer, Roche (1979)[7] was presented in two earlier papers by Birrell, Roche (1977)[8] and to a far lesser extent in the aforementioned paper of Birrell, Roche (1974).[9]

On the positive side, it has been possible to identify three themes in at least some of those works which are useful for our purposes. First, Fahy[10] and Birrell, Greer, Roche (1975)[11] obtained some information on the views of Catholic priests towards Irish unity. Second, Birrell, Roche (1974)[12] and Fahy[13] established the party political preferences among Catholic priests in their respective samples. Third, Birrell, Roche (1977)[14] asked a number of questions on how much political influence clergymen felt they had over their respective congregations. During the course of my own analysis, it has been helpful to draw on at least some of the findings from these earlier studies.

In presenting this questionnaire* I have conformed to the well-established norms of a mail-survey such as this one.[15] The introductory set of questions, for instance, are eight background variables, most of which are standard in the social sciences. The eight variables are the following: the diocese to which the respondent belongs; his present status as a cleric; his birthplace; the occupation of his father/guardian;

his age-group; whether he has lived outside Northern Ireland as an adult; his educational background; the year of his ordination. Moreover, by placing these questions at the beginning of the questionnaire, it gradually prepares the respondent for more sensitive questions. In the formation of my questions, I scrupulously avoided ambiguities and all value-laden terms. As well as that, I organised my questions around specific themes. Given the nature of the thesis, most of the questions contained in the questionnaire concern nationalism. Questions 9–13 ask a variety of questions about Irish unity, questions 14–15 seek the priests' views on the Anglo–Irish Agreement, while question 16 identifies the party political preferences of clerics in Northern Ireland. Questions 17–19 look at different aspects of the relationship which exists between priests and their congregations with particular emphasis on whether priests perceive themselves as having the ability and the will to influence Catholics in their voting behaviour, while question 20 measures the political effect, if any, that the 1981 hunger-strikes have had on clerics in Northern Ireland. Questions 21–23 are designed to discover how members of the lower clergy perceive the response of the Catholic hierarchy to the troubles. Questions 24–26 ask respondents for their views on religiously integrated education for Northern Ireland, and as such, are the only questions which do not directly involve nationalism in some way.

* For a copy of the questionnaire, see pp. 202–206.

QUESTIONNAIRE

Please choose one answer per question unless otherwise stated.

I would like to begin by asking you some general questions about your background.

1. Could you please indicate which of the following dioceses you belong to?
   [ ] Armagh [ ] Derry   [ ] Dromore
   [ ] Clogher [ ] Down and Connor [ ] Kilmore

2. Which of the following categories best describes your present status?

   [ ] Parish priest [ ] Catholic curate [ ] Member of a
                                                religious order

3. Where were you born?

   [ ] Northern Ireland [ ] Republic of Ireland [ ] Britain

   If elsewhere, please specify:

4. What was the occupation of your father/guardian? Please be as specific as possible:

5. Could you please indicate which of the following age-groups you belong to?

   [ ] 20–29 [ ] 40–49 [ ] 60–69
   [ ] 30–39 [ ] 50–59 [ ] 70+

6. If you have lived outside Northern Ireland since your eighteenth birthday, could you please provide me with some of the details under the following headings?

   Year(s)   *Country*   *Main Reason*
                               (e.g. clerical training,
                               missionary work)

7. Which one of the following categories most accurately reflects your educational qualifications?

   [ ] Theological Diploma   [ ] Post-graduate Degree
   [ ] Theological/Primary Degree [ ] PhD/DPhil/DD

8. In what year were you ordained?

In questions 9–13, I would like to get some of your views on Irish unity.

9. Do you support the ideal of a united Ireland?

[   ] Yes   [   ] No   [   ] No opinion

10. Leaving aside your own political viewpoint, do you believe that a united Ireland will come about

    [   ] within ten years   [   ] within a century
    [   ] within twenty-five years [   ] a united Ireland is unlikely
    [   ] within fifty years   to ever come about

11. As you probably know, the New Ireland Forum Report recommended three possible models of government for the island:

a unitary state (which would have one government and parliament for the whole of Ireland);
a federal/confederal state (which would guarantee a measure of autonomy for Northern Ireland within an all-Ireland framework);
joint authority (which would involve the London and Dublin Governments having equal responsibility for all aspects of the government of Northern Ireland).

Which, if any, of these three models of government as outlined in the New Ireland Forum Report do you prefer *in principle*?

    [   ] unitary state   [   ] joint authority
    [   ] federal/confederal state [   ] none of the above

12. Leaving aside your own political viewpoint, which of the three models of government as outlined in the New Ireland Forum Report is *the most likely to be realised*?

    [   ] unitary state   [   ] federal/confederal state
    [   ] joint authority

13. In the event of a united Ireland coming about, do you feel

    [   ] that the state ought to legalise divorce for the whole of the country
    [   ] that the Irish bishops ought to liberalise their position on mixed marriages from that outlined by the Catholic Directory on Mixed Marriages (1983)
    [   ] neither change should occur   [   ] no opinion

(You may choose more than one answer for this question if you wish.)

Now I would like to ask you a couple of questions about the Anglo–Irish Agreement.

14. On balance, do you approve of the Anglo-Irish Agreement?

[ ] Yes   [ ] No   [ ] No opinion

15. If you have any reservations about the Anglo–Irish Agreement, is it because you believe that it

   [ ] is deficient in satisfying nationalist aspirations
   [ ] undermines the position of Northern Ireland as part of the United Kingdom
   [ ] will be destroyed by loyalists and/or republicans, and in the process the Northern Ireland situation will get even worse
   [ ] is unfair to Unionists as they were not consulted during the course of the negotiations
   [ ] none of the above reasons

   (*You may choose more than one answer for this question if you wish.*)

16. If a general election were to be held in the near future, which party would you be most likely to vote for?

   [ ] Alliance   [ ] Workers Party
   [ ] Official Unionist   [ ] other party – please specify:
   [ ] Sinn Fein   [ ] would not vote
   [ ] Social Democratic and
       Labour Party (SDLP)

In questions 17–19, I would like to ask you about certain aspects of the relationship which exists between priests and their congregations.

17. Have you ever given advice to your congregation in the past as to which way they should vote in an election?

   [ ] Yes   [ ] No

18. If you were to advise your congregation as to which way they should vote in an election, do you think that such an appeal would

   [ ] have a strong effect on their voting behaviour
   [ ] have a slight effect on their voting behaviour
   [ ] have no effect on their voting behaviour
   [ ] have a counter-productive effect on their voting behaviour

Now I would like to get your response to each of the following statements:

19. Priests have less political and social influence over their people nowadays as a result of the troubles

   [ ] agree   [ ] disagree   [ ] no opinion

If you gave advice to your congregation as to which way they should vote in an election, this would have a stronger impact on older members of the congregation than younger members

[ ] agree [ ] disagree [ ] no opinion

You would never advise your congregation as to which way they should vote in an election

[ ] agree [ ] disagree [ ] no opinion

20. Thinking about the hunger-strikes of 1981, would you say that they

    [ ] made you more nationalist
    [ ] made you less nationalist
    [ ] made you more disillusioned with politics
    [ ] had no real effect on your political views

In questions 21–23, I would like to ask you about the role of the hierarchy in Northern Ireland since 1968.

21. On balance, how do you feel about the response of the hierarchy to the troubles?

    [ ] Very satisfied [ ] Reasonably satisfied
    [ ] Generally unsatisfied

Now I would like to get your response to each of the following statements

22. The hierarchy has not done enough to discourage republican violence

[ ] agree [ ] disagree [ ] no opinion

The hierarchy has not done enough to criticise various forms of state violence

[ ] agree [ ] disagree [ ] no opinion

The hierarchy has not done enough to encourage reconciliation between Protestants and Catholics in Northern Ireland

[ ] agree [ ] disagree [ ] no opinion

The hierarchy ought to use more of the Church's resources to help those relatively deprived communities which tend to be most deeply affected by the troubles

[ ] agree [ ] disagree [ ] no opinion

23. If you agree with the last statement in question 22, which of these two policy options would it be preferable for the hierarchy to exercise in helping those relatively deprived communities that tend to be most deeply affected by the troubles?

[   ] A redistribution of funds from the wealthier parishes in the dioceses to the socially deprived areas for the purpose of expanding Church charities

[   ] A major redistribution of Church funds so that such money could be invested (perhaps jointly with other interested organisations) in community projects/investments which are regarded as too risky by orthodox financial institutions

Finally, I would like to ask you about your views on religiously integrated education for Northern Ireland.

24. Some people say that if Protestant and Catholic children were to be educated in the same schools, some of the problems in Northern Ireland would be reduced, whereas others disagree. Do you

    [   ] agree that integrated education would reduce some of the problems in Northern Ireland

    [   ] disagree that integrated education would reduce some of the problems in Northern Ireland

    [   ] have no opinion

25. Are you opposed *in principle* to integrated schools for Protestants and Catholics in Northern Ireland?

    [   ] Yes   [   ] No   [   ] No opinion

26. If you are not opposed in principle to integrated education, do you feel

    [   ] under the present circumstances in Northern Ireland nothing can be done to change the present schools system, except to increase contacts between children attending Catholic and Protestant schools

    [   ] the church ought to give greater encouragement to new non-denominational schools, such as Lagan College, for instance

    [   ] the Church and state ought to launch a campaign for integrated education in Northern Ireland

27. If you have any comments about this questionnaire or wish to expand on your answer to any of the questions, I should be interested to know of your views. A blank sheet is attached for this purpose. Thank you for your time and co-operation.

APPENDIX D
The New University of Ulster
Coleraine County Londonderry Northern Ireland
Telephone Coleraine 4141. Telegrams 'University Coleraine'

23rd September 1971
Most Rev. Dr. McCormack,
Mullingar,
Co. Westmeath.
My Lord,
    May I, as secretary of the Ulster Branch of the Association of Irish Priests, draw your Lordship's attention to the following motion passed at a meeting of the Ulster Branch on September 20th:
    "The meeting of the Ulster Branch of the Association of Irish Priests on 20th September 1971 referred to the teaching of 2nd Vatican Council on offences against human dignity such as arbitrary imprisonment (Church in the Modern World, par. 27). It called upon the Bishops of Ireland to issue a clear and public condemnation of internment without trial as immoral *in se*. It further requested the Irish Bishops to issue positive guidelines on legitimate means of protest against this violation of a basic human right."
The meeting requested me as secretary to communicate this motion to your Lordship as secretary to the meeting of the Irish Bishops.
Yours respectfully,
Terence O'Keeffe

Notes

Introduction (pp 1–7)

1. The most substantive empirically-based study of the Churches and the Northern Ireland problem is by Eric Gallagher, Stanley Worrall, *Christians In Ulster 1968–1980*, Oxford University Press, 1982. For our purpose, it must be noted that this book deals mainly with the Protestant Churches. John Hickey's *Religion and the Northern Ireland Problem*, Dublin: Gill and Macmillan, 1984, is a mainly theoretical work. The only Church examined in considerable detail is the Free Presbyterian Church whose moderator, Dr Paisley, is of course, best known for his political activities. The most detailed studies of Paisley as both a clergyman and politician are the following: Steven Bruce, *God Save Ulster: the religion and politics of Paisleyism*, Oxford: Clarendon Press, 1986; Patrick Marrinan, *Paisley: man of wrath*, Tralee: Anvil Books, 1973; Ed Moloney, Andy Pollak, *Paisley*, Dublin: Poolbeg, 1986.

2. The only detailed study of the Catholic Church and Northern Ireland is by Cornelius Gerard Hughes, *The Catholic Church and the Crisis in Ulster*, Unpublished PhD thesis: Pennsylvania State University, 1976. Unlike my study, this thesis adopts a mainly theoretical approach to the subject. In any case, the period of Hughes' study runs only from the late 1960s until the early 1970s.

3. Among the works which have looked at devolution for Northern Ireland in detail are the following: Paul Bew, Peter Gibbon, Henry Patterson, *The State In Northern Ireland 1921–1972 Political Forces and Social Classes*, Manchester: Manchester University Press, 1979; N Mansergh, *The Government of Northern Ireland A Study In Devolution*, London: George Allen and Unwin, 1936; D Birrell and A Murie, *Policy and Government in Northern Ireland: Lesson of Devolution*, Dublin: Gill and Macmillan, 1980; Patrick Buckland, *A History of Northern Ireland*, Dublin: Gill and Macmillan, 1981; Martin Wallace, *British Government in Northern Ireland from Devolution To Direct Rule*, Newton Abbot: David and Charles, 1982; RJ Lawrence, *The Government of Northern Ireland: Public Finance and Public Services 1921–1964*, Oxford: Clarendon Press, 1965.

4. There are many accounts of the violence that occurred during the month of August 1969. There was an official government report on violence throughout the entire year, *Violence and Civil Disturbances in Northern Ireland in 1969: Report of Tribunal of Enquiry*, (Scarman

report), 2 vols, Belfast: HMSO, April 1972, CMD566. Beyond this, one of the most objective works on the subject of the August violence is by Sunday Times Insight Team, *Ulster*, London: Andre Deutsch, 1972, pp106–142. See also, GW Target, *Unholy Smoke*, Hodder and Stoughton, 1969; M Hastings, *Ulster 1969: the fight for civil rights in Northern Ireland*, London: Gollancz, 1970, pp124–167; M Farrell, *Northern Ireland: the orange state*, London: Pluto Press, 1980, pp257–265; E McCann, *War and an Irish Town*, Harmondsworth: Penguin, 1974, pp58–62; B Devlin, *The Price of My Soul*, New York: Knopf, 1969, pp216–223. Two books have been written *exclusively* on the Derry disturbances of that month, viz. C Limpkin, *The Battle of Bogside*, Harmondsworth: Penguin, 1972; R Stetler, *The Battle of the Bogside: the politics of violence in Northern Ireland*, London: Sheed and Ward, 1970.

5. For an excellent account of the Executive's collapse see R Fisk, *The Point of No Return: the strike which broke the British in Ulster*, London: Deutsch, 1975. For views of men who served in that Executive see, P Devlin, *The Fall of the Executive*, Belfast: published privately, 1975, and B Faulkner, *Memoirs of a Statesman*, London: Weidenfeld and Nicolson, 1978, pp251–277.

6. There has been a considerable amount written about violence during the period in question. The most comprehensive work on the victims of the troubles is by Michael McKeown, *De Mortuis: a study of 2,400 fatalities arising from political disturbances in Northern Ireland between July 1969 and July 1984*, Gondregnies, Belgium: Irish Information Partnership, 1985. For a similar study of violence in an earlier period see McKeown, *The First Five Hundred*, Belfast: *Irish News*, 1972. Two good overviews are R Murray, 'Political Violence in Northern Ireland 1969–1977' in FW Boal, JNH Douglas (eds), *Integration and Division Geographical Perspectives on the Northern Ireland Problem*, London: Academic Press, 1982, pp309–331, and Barry White, 'From Conflict to Violence: the re-emergence of the IRA and the loyalist response' in J Darby (ed), *Northern Ireland The Background to the Conflict*, Belfast: Appletree, 1983, pp181–196. For an essentially republican perspective see, Kevin Kelley, *The Longest War and the IRA*, Dingle: Brandon Books, 1982, and J Bowyer Bell, *The Secret Army The IRA 1916–1979*, Dublin: Academy Press, 1979, pp373–445. For the activities of the UVF in the 1960s and 1970s see David Boulton, *The UVF: an anatomy of loyalist rebellion*, Dublin: Torc Books, 1973. For a consideration of the British perspective on violence in Northern Ireland see D Barzilay, *The British Army In Ulster*, 4 vols, Belfast: Century Services, 1973–1981, and R Clutterbuck, *Protest and the Urban Guerrilla*, London: Cassell, 1973, pp47–138. For an

assessment of British military policy in Northern Ireland see, R Faligot, *Britain's Military Strategy In Ireland The Kitson Experiment*, London: Zed, 1983.

7. See V Browne (ed), *The Magill Book of Irish Politics*, Dublin: Magill, 1981, pp52 and 275. The TDs in question were Kieran Doherty and Paddy Agnew. Mr Doherty died on hunger-strike shortly afterwards.

Chapter 1 (pp 9–65)

1. Vincent Edward Feeney, *From Reform to Resistance: A History of the Civil Rights Movement in Northern Ireland*, PhD Thesis, University of Washington, 1974, especially pp137–151. A major sub-theme of Thompson's thesis is the split within the movement, see Thompson, *The Northern Ireland Civil Rights Movement*, Belfast: MA Thesis, QUB, 1973, pp87–123.

2. For a good overview of theories on political mobilisation see, David R Cameron, 'Toward a Theory of Political Mobilisation' in *Journal of Politics*, vol36, no9, 1974, pp138–171. For an earlier analysis of mobilisation see, K Deutsch, 'Social Mobilisation and Political Development' in *American Political Science Review*, lv, September 1961, pp493–514. For an interesting discussion of political mobilisation in pre-famine Ireland see, Tom Garvin, *The Evolution of Irish Nationalist Politics*, Dublin: Gill and Macmillan, 1981, pp43–52.

3. *Belfast Telegraph*, 12 November 1968, p7, (A national opinion poll carried out for the *Belfast Telegraph*).

4. Richard Rose, *Governing Without Consensus—An Irish Perspective*, London: Faber & Faber, 1971, p383,479,491.

5. Even the Nationalist Party which was deeply damaged by the emergence of the civil rights movement, soon came to support a civil disobedience campaign. See, R Deutsch, V Magowan, *Northern Ireland 1968–1973: A Chronology of Events*. vol1, Belfast: Blackstaff, 1973, p12.

6. This is clearly reflected by the contents of the Cameron Report which examines the disturbances and the political background to this trouble in the period 1968–early 1969. See, *Disturbances in Northern Ireland Report of the Commission Appointed by the Governor of Northern Ireland*, Belfast: HMSO, cmd532, 1969.

7. There is a consensus on the importance of this day's events. This is acknowledged by, among many others, Feeney, *From Reform*, op cit, pp82–88; F. Eugene Scott, *Persuasion in the Northern Ireland Civil Rights Movement, 1968–1970*, PhD thesis, Purdue University, 1972, p85,100.

8. *Derry Journal*, 10 January 1969, p1.

9. For details see Cameron, op cit, par66,67, and Barry White, *John Hume—Statesman of the Troubles*, Belfast: Blackstaff Press, 1984, pp67–68.

10. Cameron, op cit, par123–124.

11. In a later survey, 94 per cent of Catholic priests said they had supported the civil rights campaign, see, DJD Roche, WD Birrell, JE Greer, 'A Socio-Political Opinion Profile of Clergymen in Northern Ireland', in *Social Studies*, vol4, no2, summer 1975, p149.

12. For the most sophisticated analysis of Unionism's fragmentation in the 1960s and 1970s, see, P Bew, P Gibbon, H Patterson, *The State in Northern Ireland 1921–1972: Political Forces and Social Classes*, Manchester: Manchester University Press, 1979.

13. For good analyses of how many Protestants perceived the civil rights campaign see, Sarah Nelson, *Ulster's Uncertain Defenders: Loyalists and the Northern Ireland Conflict*, Belfast: Appletree Press, 1984, pp67–75. Sarah Nelson, 'Protestant "Ideology" Considered: The Case of "Discrimination"' in Ivor Crewe (ed), *British Political Sociology Yearbook*, vol2, London: Croom Helm, 1975, pp155–187. For an unorthodox argument about NICRA see, C Hewitt, 'Catholic Grievances, Catholic Nationalism and Violence in Northern Ireland During the Civil Rights Period: a re-consideration' in *The British Journal of Sociology*, vol32(3), 1981, pp362–380.

14. For contrasting accounts of this march see the descriptions by the pro-Unionist *Dungannon News and Tyrone Courier*, 28 August 1968, p1, and the mainly Catholic *Mid-Ulster Observer*, 29 August 1968, p1.

15. Clerical activities in the Dungannon civil rights campaign were acknowledged in the letter column of the *Irish News* by the then chairman of Dungannon Civil Rights Association, Mr Aidan Corrigan. See *Irish News*, 8 October 1969, p4.

16. It has been argued, in fact, that the greatest degree of clerical involvement in the US civil rights campaigns occurred in the 1950s. See Joseph R Washington Jr, *Black Religion—The Negro and Christianity in the United States*, London: University Press of America, 1984, pp1–29, especially p18. For a brief reference to the policy of the Catholic Church in the USA towards racial discrimination see, Mary T Hanna, *Catholics and American Politics*, Cambridge, Mass: Harvard University Press, 1979, p138. For an interesting article on the relationships between religiosity and militancy among Black Americans and civil rights, see Gary T Marx, 'Religion: Opiate or inspiration of civil rights militancy among negroes?' in the *American Sociological Review*, vol32, no1, pp64–72.

17. Rose, op cit, 341, found that inter-marriage in Northern Ireland was as low as 4 per cent, thus making 'ethnicity' and religious identity synonymous to most people there. For the ethnic diversity of American Catholicism see, Harold J Abramson, *Ethnic Diversity in Catholic America*, New York: Wiley, 1973.

18. See Northern Ireland Civil Rights Association, *We Shall Overcome: The History of the Struggle for Civil Rights in Northern Ireland*, Belfast: NICRA, 1978, p11.

19. For an excellent discussion of discrimination in NI see, John Whyte, 'How Much Discrimination was there under the Unionist Regime, 1921–1969' in T Gallagher, J O'Connell (eds), *Contemporary Irish Studies*, Manchester: MUP, 1983, pp1–35.

20. M Farrell, *Northern Ireland: the Orange State*, London: Pluto Press, 1980, pp82–85.

21. For an assessment of the FEA see, C McCrudden, 'The Experience of the Legal Enforcement of the Fair Employment (Northern Ireland) Act 1976' in RJ Cormack, RD Osborne (eds), *Religion Education and Employment: Aspects of Equal Opportunity in Northern Ireland*, Belfast: Appletree, 1983, pp201–221.

22. Serious disturbances had occurred between October 1968 and January 1969, at marches or rallies in Derry, Burntollet and Newry. It ought to be pointed out that these latter events had been organised by the student-inspired People's Democracy. For various accounts of these disturbances see the following sources: *Irish News*, 7 October 1968; Bowes Egan and Vincent McCormack, *Burntollet*, London: LRS Publications, 1969; Paul Arthur, *The People's Democracy 1968–1973*, Belfast: Blackstaff, 1974, especially pp43–44.

23. For a good account of the Belfast disturbances see, Sunday Times Insight Team, *Ulster*, op cit, pp126–142.

24. For details of what became known as 'The Battle of the Bogside' see the following sources: C Limpkin, *The Battle of Bogside*, Harmondsworth: Penguin, 1972; Russell Stetler, *The Battle of Bogside*, London: Sheed and Ward, 1970; Max Hastings, *Ulster 1969—The Fight for Civil Rights in Northern Ireland*, London: Gollancz, 1970, pp132–140; Sunday Times Insight Team, *Ulster*, op cit, pp114–123; Farrell, op cit, pp259–262; McCann, op cit, pp58–63.

25. For the whole text of this communiqué and declaration see, James Callaghan, *A House Divided—The Dilemma of Northern Ireland*, London: Collins, 1973, Appendix I pp189–192.

26. For the full text of this communiqué see, Callaghan, op cit, Appendix III pp199–202.

27. Callaghan, op cit, p97.

28. There were 13 non-Unionist MPs in the Northern Ireland Parliament: 3 were independents; 2 belonged to the Northern Ireland

Labour Party; 2 were Republican Labour MPs; 6 were nationalists (but that party was rapidly becoming moribund). See, Sydney Elliott, *Northern Ireland Parliamentary Election Results 1921–1972*, Chichester: Political Reference Publications, 1973, pp70–86,95.

29. For a personal account of this see, B Devlin, *The Price of My Soul*, New York: Knopf, 1969, pp169–182.

30. Rose, op cit, p477. This was also noted in the mid-1960s by Tim Pat Coogan, *Ireland Since the Rising*, London: Pall Mall Press, 1966, p317.

31. For the report in full see, *Report of the Advisory Committee on Police in Northern Ireland*, HMSO, cmd535, October 1969.

32. R Deutsch, V Magowan, *Northern Ireland 1968–1973*, op cit, p73.

33. *Irish News*, 17 November 1969.

34. Deutsch, Magowan, op cit, p83.

35. By November 1971, the proportion of Catholics in the UDR had dropped to 8 per cent, ibid, p140.

36. For an account of army–community relations between August 1969 and April 1970 see, Desmond Hamill, *Pig in the Middle The Army in Northern Ireland*, London: Methuen, 1985, pp8–32.

37. As a result of the violence in mid-August 1969, defence committees had been formed in Belfast and Derry. The Derry barricades however, were soon seen as superfluous. See, McCann, *War and an Irish Town*, London: Pluto Press, 1980, p71.

38. *Irish News*, 18, 19 May 1970.

39. for various accounts of the IRA split see, *Ulster*, op cit, pp191–197; Farrell, op cit, pp267–271; Kevin Kelley, *The Longest War—Northern Ireland and the IRA*, Dingle: Brandon, 1982, pp124–131; J Boywer Bell, *The Secret Army—The IRA 1916–1979*, Dublin: The Academy Press, 1979, pp355–372; Sean MacStiofain, *Revolution in Ireland*, Farnborough: Saxon House, 1974, pp133–143.

40. *Irish News*, 17 April 1970. The successful candidates were Rev Ian Paisley and the Rev William Beattie.

41. The best account of the trial is by Tom MacIntyre, *Through the Bridewell Gate: a diary of the arms trial*, London: Faber & Faber, 1971. For a general background to this episode see, Kevin Boland, *We Won't Stand (Idly) By*, Dublin: Kelly Kane, 1972; Kevin Boland, *Up Dev*, Dublin: privately published, 1977, pp 31–60; Seamus Brady, *Arms and the Men: Ireland in Turmoil*, Dublin: personally published, 1971; Sean Edmonds, *The Gun, The Law, And The Irish People*, Tralee: Anvil Books, 1971, pp244–261; James Kelly, *Orders For The Captain?*, Dublin: Privately Published, 1971; James Kelly, *The Genesis of Revolution*, Dublin: Kelly Kane, 1976, pp13–19. For more objective accounts of these events see, Rose, *Governing Without*, op cit, pp165–170; a three-part account of the arms crisis by Vincent

Browne in *Magill*, 3, 8 May 1980, pp35–56; *Magill* 3, 9 June 1980, pp39–73; *Magill*, 3, 10 July 1980, pp4–6, 17–28.

42. For various accounts of the Falls curfew see, *Ulster*, op cit, pp212–221; Kelley, op cit, pp145–148; Farrell, pp273–274; J Bowyer Bell, op cit, pp376–377.

43 Sean Og O'Fearghail, *Law(?) And Orders*, Belfast: Central Citizens' Defence Committee, 1970, p13.

44. *Parliamentary debates (Hansard) House of Commons, Northern Ireland*, vol78, col2057, 24 February 1971.

45. For further details see, Ian McAllister, *The Social Democratic and Labour Party: political opposition in a divided society*, London: Macmillan 1977, pp91–95.

46. See, Irish Bishops, *Justice, Love and Peace: Pastoral Letters of the Irish Bishops 1969–1979*, Dublin: Veritas, 1979, p40.

47. For various accounts of the breakdown in the 1972 Provisional ceasefire see, Kevin Kelley, op cit, pp178–182; Farrell, op cit, p295; JB Bell, op cit, pp389–391.

48. Only days before, the IRA had formally decided to continue its military campaign. See *Irish News*, 7 April 1972.

49. An assessment by *The Guardian* of 11 April 1972, for example, described the activities of priests and peace activists in Andersonstown as 'a nucleus around which Catholics wishing to return to peace can collect, but at present, the Provisionals' grip on the ghettos is evidently still too great for peace to come about'.

50. *Irish Times*, 29 May 1972.

51. For the negotiations that led to the ceasefire see, McAllister, op cit, pp117–118; White, op cit, pp128–132; Kelley, op cit, pp178–182; JB Bell, op cit, pp389–391.

52. For various accounts of the breakdown in the ceasefire see, Kelley, op cit, pp178–182; Farrell, op cit, p295; JB Bell, op cit, pp389–391.

53. White, op cit, p131.

54. Kelley, op cit, p180. (This status was also granted to loyalists.)

55. Kelley, op cit, ch5. In fact, 1972 was easily the most violent year of the troubles. See, WD Flackes, *Northern Ireland: A Political Directory 1968–83*, London: Ariel Books, BBC, 1983, pp320–321.

56. For details of this military operation see, for instance, Kelley, op cit, pp182–186.

57. *Irish News*, 20 April 1974.

58. For details of the Northern Ireland Executive's existence and demise see, especially Robert Fisk, *The Point of No Return: The Strike that Broke the British in Ulster*, London: Andre Deutsch, 1975; Paddy Devlin, *The Fall of the NI Executive*, Belfast: personally published, 1975; B Faulkner, *Memoirs of a Statesman*, London: Weidenfeld & Nicolson, 1978, pp226–277; McAllister, op cit, pp128–146.

59. For an account of this meeting attended by one of these clergymen, see, Eric Gallagher and Stanley Worrall, *Christians in Ulster*, op cit, pp97–102.

60. Merlyn Rees, *Northern Ireland A Personal Perspective*, London: Methuen, 1985, p178.

61. For a full account of the peace people see, Ciaran McKeown, *The Passion of Peace*, Belfast: Blackstaff Press, 1984. For a shorter treatment of the subject, see Gallagher and Worrall, op cit, pp173–181.

62. For discussions of some of the SDLP's problems during this period see, the editorial comment of *Fortnight*, 30 September–13 October 1977, no154, p3; *Fortnight*, 28 October–10 November 1977, no156, p7; *Hibernia*, 4 November 1977, p5.

63. *Irish Press*, 16 January 1978, p9. (The second part of this lengthy interview was published in the *Irish Press*, 17 January 1978.)

64. Jean Blanchard, *The Church in Contemporary Ireland*, op cit, especially pp13–20.

65. Fine Gael, *Ireland—Our Future Together*, Dublin: Fine Gael, 1979.

66. White, op cit, for details, ch19, especially pp235–252.

67. *New Ireland Forum Report*, Dublin: The Stationery Office, 2 May 1984, p1, ch1,1.

68. The Irish Episcopal Conference, *Submission to the New Ireland Forum January 1984*, Dublin: Veritas Publications, 1984.

69. *Irish Episcopal Conference Delegation, Public Session New Ireland Forum*, no12, Dublin, The Stationery Office, 9 February 1984.

70. White, *John Hume*, op cit, p259.

71. *New Ireland Forum Report*, 5.10, p30. For a stimulating analysis of the Forum see, Oliver MacDonagh, 'What Was New In The New Ireland Forum' in *The Crane Bag*, 9,2, 1985, pp166–170.

72. For some of these criticisms, see the following editions of the *Irish Times*: 24 January 1985, p9; 12 March 1985, p9; 15 March 1985, pp1,7; 19 March 1985, p6.

73. *Irish Independent*, 11 June 1985, pp1,2.

74. Bishop Joseph Duffy, 'Northern Ireland—The Way Forward As I See It' in *The Furrow*, vol33, no7, July 1982, p401. (For the complete article see, pp399–406.)

75. This is inherent in Bishop Daly's position as far back as the early 1970s. If anything, it has become more explicit with the passage of time. See, CB Daly, *Violence in Ireland and Christian Conscience*, Dublin: Veritas, 1973, and his *Peace The Work of Justice—Addresses on the Northern Tragedy, 1973–1979*, Dublin: Veritas, 1979.

76. For the text of the Anglo–Irish Agreement see, *Irish Times*, 16 November 1985. For a substantive nationalist critique of the accord, see Anthony Coughlan, *Fooled Again? The Anglo–Irish Agreement and After*, Cork and Dublin: Mercier, 1986.

Chapter 2 (pp 66–89)

1. Patrick A Fahy, 'Some Political Behaviour Patterns and Attitudes of Roman Catholic Priests in a Rural Part of Northern Ireland' in *The Economic and Social Review*, vol3, no1, October 1971, pp1–24.
2. DJD Roche, WD Birrell, JE Greer, 'A Socio-Political Opinion Profile of Clergymen in Northern Ireland' in *Social Studies*, vol4, no2, summer 1975, p145.
3. WD Birrell and DJD Roche, 'Theology, Political Attitudes and Party Preference Among Clergymen in Northern Ireland' in AECW Spencer and H Tovey (eds), *Sociological Association of Ireland— Proceedings of the First and Fourth Annual Conferences*, Belfast: QUB, 1978, p4.
4. Edward Moxon-Browne, *Nation, Class and Creed in Northern Ireland*, Aldershot: Gower, 1983, p35.
5. ibid, p40.
6. Fahy, 'Some Political' in *Economic and Social Review*, op cit, pp12–13.
7. For details of this difference of interpretation between Fianna Fail leader, Charles Haughey, and other leaders of constitutional nationalist parties which centred around 5.7 and 5.10 of the *New Ireland Forum Report* see, *Irish Times*, 3 May 1984.
8. Moxon-Browne, *Nation, Class and Creed*, op cit, p21.
9. Fr Gabriel Daly was one of those priests who argued in favour of divorce. His arguments were contained in a booklet entitled *Divorce Facts, Catholic Viewpoints*. See *Irish Times*, 9 June 1986, p9.
10. *Irish Times*, 18 November 1983.
11. ibid, 17 January 1986, p6.
12. Birrell, Roche, 'Theology, Political Attitudes', op cit, p5.
13. *Fortnight*, June 1983, no195, p5.
14. *Andersonstown News*, 3 May 1975, p1.
15. *Irish News*, 25 April 1975, p1.
16. WD Birrell, DJD Roche, 'The Political Role and influence of clergymen in Northern Ireland', in AECW Spencer, H Tovey (eds), *Sociological Association of Ireland—Proceedings of the First and Fourth Annual Conferences*, Belfast: QUB, 1978, p46, table 6.
17. *New Ireland Forum Report of Proceedings Irish Episcopal Conference Delegation*, Public Session, Thursday, 9 February 1984, Dublin Castle, p4.
18. There is, for instance, an optimal statistical significance between the variables of respondents' age and year of ordination, i.e. 0.0000.

Chapter 3 (pp 90–133)

1. These figures were calculated from the data provided by K. Asmal

(chairman), *Shoot To Kill?*, Cork, Dublin: Mercier Press, 1985 pp135–150.

2. For the reasons why the priests and relatives of the victims finally decided to testify at the Widgery Inquiry see, *Irish News*, 18 February 1972, p6, and 22 February 1972, p1.

3. *Irish Times*, 21 August 1982, p16.

4. Michael McKeown, *De Mortuis A Study of 2,400 fatalities arising from political disturbances in Northern Ireland between July 1969 and July 1984*, Gondregnies, Belgium: Irish Information Partnership, 1985 p54.

5. See, *Irish News*, 19 August 1969, p1, and the editorial column of that day's edition.

6. *Irish News*, 15 November 1972.

7. *Andersonstown News*, 19 December 1981 (editorial).

8. For both statements see, *Irish News*, 13 September 1971, and 30 September 1971.

9. *Irish News*, 10 August 1971.

10. *Irish Times*, 2 November 1971, p8.

11. *Andersonstown News*, 20 October 1974, pp2, 3.

12. Merlyn Rees, *Northern Ireland A Personal Perspective*, London: Methuen, 1985, ch9.

13. *Andersonstown News*, 5 July 1975, p7. Indeed, O'Keefe feels that his relationship with Bishop Philbin had deteriorated as early as 1970, when the priest wrote an article on Christianity and socialism in *The Newman Review*, vol2, no1, summer 1970, pp8–10

14. ibid, 27 September 1975, p1.

15. *Irish News*, 22 November 1969.

16. *Mid-Ulster Observer*, 20 November 1969.

17. *Irish Times*, 26 April 1971, p1.

18. For the complete list of priests who were involved in this protest see, *Irish News*, 24 June 1971. (This was published when the same group of priests staged a follow-up protest.)

19. ibid, 27 April 1971.

20. ibid, 27 April 1971.

21. *Irish News*, 23 April 1971, p1.

22. Quoted in Andrew Boyd, *The Informers—a chilling account of the supergrasses in Northern Ireland*, Dublin: Mercier Press, 1984, p96. For a legal analysis of this system see, Lord T Gifford, *Supergrasses: the use of accomplice evidence in Northern Ireland*, London: Cobden Trust, 1984.

23. *Irish Times*, 10 September 1983, p6.

24. *Irish News*, 20 December 1984, p1.

25. For a brief description of the Black case see, Boyd, op cit, pp 47–51.
26. *Irish Times*, 16 June 1984.
27. ibid, 11 June 1984.

Chapter 4 (pp 134–162)
1. For details of the Dungiven disturbances see Scarman, op cit, ch8, pp40–77. The Sunday Times Insight Team, *Ulster*, London: Deutsch, 1972, p98; *Belfast Telegraph*, 13 August 1969, p8.
2. For peace-keeping activities of priests in Ardoyne see, Scarman, op cit, pp26–27, and *Belfast Telegraph*, 16 July 1969, p9.
3. Scarman, op cit, 12.17–12.18, p81.
4. ibid, 26.39–26.40, p217.
5. For more detailed accounts of the violence in Clonard see, Scarman, op cit, pp195–209, and *Ulster*, op cit, pp140–141.
6. This was the interpretation given to me by two sources who preferred to remain anonymous. Interviewed in Belfast on 17 February and 3 September 1987.
7. In an interview in Belfast, 3 September 1987.
8. Kevin Kelley, *The Longest War Northern Ireland and the IRA*, Dingle: Brandon, 1982, p146.
9. See JD Douglas (ed), *The New International Dictionary of the Christian Church*, Exeter: The Paternoster Press, 1978, 2nd ed, p1029, and FL Cross, EA Livingstone, *The Oxford Dictionary of the Christian Church*, Oxford: Oxford University Press, 1983, 3rd ed, p1459.
10. For a biography of Constantine see, for instance, Hermann Doerries, (trans by Roland H Bainton), *Constantine The Great*, London: Harper & Row, 1972.
11. *Irish Times*, 2, 3 January 1984, p5.
12. *Justice, Love and Peace Pastoral Letters of the Irish Bishops 1969–1979*, Dublin: Veritas Publications, 1979, p40.
13. JH Whyte, 'Revolution and Religion' in FX Martin (ed), *Leaders and Men of the Easter Rising: Dublin 1916*, Dublin: Browne & Nolan, 1966, p223.
14. Frank Burton, *The Politics of Legitimacy—Struggles in a Belfast community*, London: Routledge & Kegan Paul, 1978, p94.
15. *Andersonstown News*, 3 August 1974.
16. Such a policy was not formulated until the time of the hunger-strikes. See, *The Catholic Church in Ireland Information and Documentation*, Dublin: Catholic Press and Information Office of Ireland, 1981, p43.
17. Such cases are referred to by *Andersonstown News*, 26 January 1980, p1.

18. This was revealed to me in an interview with Bishop Edward Daly in Derry, 3 March 1988. While naturally reluctant to speak on behalf of his colleagues, Dr Daly believed that none of the Northern bishops would see excommunication of the IRA as having any meaning in the context of the Northern Ireland troubles.
19. Bishop Edward Daly made it clear to me that no such historical considerations have affected his judgment on this issue.
20. This is observed in an objective account of the Civil War. See, Calton Younger, *Ireland's Civil War*, Glasgow: Collins/Fontana, 1979, 3rd ed, p483.
21. Garret FitzGerald, 'The Priest In Irish Politics' in *Doctrine and Life*, vol22, no3, March 1972, p140–142.
22. It ought to be noted that, in general, more priests living outside Northern Ireland have identified themselves with republicans than those in that region. Though politically active as a curate in Co. Down in the early 1970s, it was after he had spent several years in New York that Fr Vincent Forde was later charged with bank robbery in the Republic of Ireland. Fr Forde absconded on bail during his trial in 1980. See, *Hibernia*, 10 April 1980, p13. Although this source claims that Fr Forde was still a practising priest at the time of his trial, his clerical status is unclear. Certainly, his name is not listed in the *Irish Catholic Directory* of 1980. An English priest, Fr Fell has served a prison sentence in Great Britain for IRA activities (see, *Irish News*, 2 November 1973, p3, and *Irish Times*, 10 July 1982, for further details). Similarly, a US based priest, Fr Patrick Moloney, was among a group charged with illegal possession of arms in Limerick in 1982, (see, *Irish Times*, 21 June 1982, p1). It was claimed in *An Phoblacht* of June 1973, p7, that one Fr Bartholomew Burns of Co. Kerry was sought by the authorities in Scotland for questioning about alleged arms offences in that country. Finally, Fr Hugh Burke of New York, described as a 'representative' of Noraid, addressed a crowd in Northern Ireland during the course of which he read a statement from that organisation's leader, Martin Galvin, in which unending support for the IRA was promised (see, *Irish Times*, 14 August 1984, p1).
23. *Andersonstown News*, 27 September 1975, p1.
24. See the following books: David Beresford, *Ten Men Dead The Story of the 1981 Hunger-Strike*, London: Grafton Books, 1987, p429; Liam Clarke, *Broadening The Battlefield—The H-Blocks and the Rise of Sinn Fein*, Dublin: Gill & Macmillan, 1987, pp201–204; Tom Collins, *The Irish Hunger-Strike*, Dublin: White Island Book Company, 1986, pp603–604.
25. Viz Beresford, *Ten Men*, op cit, especially pp87,164,169,227; Clarke,

Broadening The, op cit, especially pp73–75,138; Collins, *The Irish,* op cit, especially 402–403,472; Coogan, *On The Blanket,* op cit, especially p3; John M Feehan, *Bobby Sands and the Tragedy of Northern Ireland,* Dublin, Cork: Mercier Press, 1983, especially pp98,120; Bobby Sands, *One Day In My Life,* Dublin & Cork: Mercier, 1982, especially pp62,67,101.

26. See, Beresford, *Ten Men,* p406, and Collins, op cit, especially pp273–274,472,482–484.

27. See, Edward Daly, 'In Place of Terrorism' in *The Furrow,* vol26, no10, October 1975, p590.

28. No consensus exists with regard to whether there is any relationship between people's levels of religiosity and their political outlook in Northern Ireland. Thus, for instance, Terence G Carroll, *Political Activists,* op cit, pp358–359, found in his fieldwork that more devout Catholics were less than half as likely to adopt an anti-regime position than those whose religious beliefs were weak. By contrast, Ian McAllister, 'The Devil, Miracles and the Afterlife: the political sociology of religion in Northern Ireland' in the *British Journal of Sociology,* vol33, 1982, p342, concluded that religious commitment among Catholics was unrelated to their political attitudes.

29. Darby, *Intimidation and the Control,* op cit, pp155–156.

30. This tendency has been recognised among republican activists *outside* prison too. Burton, *The Politics of,* op cit, p23, found in his fieldwork in Belfast's Ardoyne area that IRA men frequently turned to religion in periods of crisis.

31. *Irish News,* 6 May 1972.

32. For O'Fiaich's lengthy statement see, Beresford, op cit, pp183–185.

33. Collins, op cit, pp333–336.

34. Collins, ibid, pp352–355, for details.

35. For a full account of his efforts, see, Clarke, op cit, pp177–200.

36. For accounts of these events see, Beresford, op cit, pp343–346, and *Magill,* August 1981, pp58–59.

37. See, Beresford, op cit, pp275–276. This is corroborated by Collins' account, pp344–345.

38. Beresford, op cit, pp39–43 and 292–300 for details.

39. *Irish Times,* 5 May 1983, p6.

40. Statement of the Irish Episcopal Conference, *Conscience and Morality A Doctrinal Statement,* Dublin: Irish Messenger Publications, 1980, p32.

41. *An Phoblacht,* February 1971, p1.

42. *Republican News,* 5 May 1973; 2 June 1973; 29 September 1973.

43. ibid, 2 November 1974, p6.

44. *An Phoblacht,* March 1972, p5.

45. For some examples see, ibid, 3 October 1981, p16; 26 November 1981, p12.

Chapter 5 (pp 163–187)

1. For a few such examples see, statements by Bishop Philbin in the *Irish Times*, 3 March 1969 and the *Irish Press*, 16 February 1975. Probably the most lengthy *apologia* of this kind by the late Cardinal Conway is his pamphlet entitled *Catholic Schools*, Dublin: Catholic Communications Institute, 1970.

2. The existence of widespread clerical influence in the Republic of Ireland is acknowledged in a comparative study by an American priest. See, Bruce Francis Biever, *Religion, Culture and Values A Cross-Cultural Analysis of Motivational Factors in Native Irish and American Irish Catholicism*, New York: Arno Press, 1976, passim, especially pp280–522. Studies of Irish institutions have referred to clerical influence in the Republic. See, for instance: RK Carty, *Party and Parish Pump Electoral Politics in Ireland*, Waterloo, Ontario: Wilfrid Laurier University Press, 1981, especially pp142–143; Basil Chubb, *The Government and Politics of Ireland*, London: Oxford University Press, 1970, especially pp53–54, 100–104.

3. Edward Moxon-Browne, *Nation, Class and Creed in Northern Ireland*, Aldershot: Gower, 1983, pp37–38. For references to this fear in a recent analysis of Unionist ideology see, Jennifer Todd, 'Two Traditions In Unionist Political Culture' in *Irish Political Studies*, vol2, 1987, especially pp7,19.

4. This fear was probably best articulated by Terence O'Neill, a few days after he had resigned as Prime Minister of Northern Ireland. He said: 'The basic fear of Protestants in Northern Ireland is that they will be outbred by Roman Catholics'. See, Ken Heskin, *Northern Ireland: a psychological analysis*, Dublin: Gill and Macmillan, 1980, p105. For a more recent reference to the religious demography of Northern Ireland see, Liam Kennedy, *Two Ulsters: a case for repartition*, Belfast: QUB, 1986, pp28–29.

5. The best-known advocate of this position, as Professor Ryan points out, is Bishop Newman of Limerick. For an elaboration of the latter's ideas in this area see, Jeremiah Newman, *Ireland Must Choose*, Dublin: Four Courts Press, 1983.

6. For the full statement by the hierarchy on the 1983 amendment see, *Irish Times*, 23 August 1983, p5. For the full hierarchical statement on the proposed constitutional amendment on divorce see, ibid, 12 June 1986. For the bishops' pastoral on divorce see, *Marriage, the Family and Divorce*, Dublin: Veritas, 1986. It ought to be noted that in Northern Ireland, the Catholic bishops have attempted tᵣ

influence laws on marital breakdown too. In 1978, for instance, the Northern bishops vigorously (but unsuccessfully) opposed the introduction of a more liberal divorce regime in their region. For their full statement on the subject see, *The Furrow*, vol29, no8, August 1978, pp527–528.

7. With regard to the divorce referendum, for instance, Brian Girvin, 'The Divorce Referendum in the Republic—June 1986', *Irish Political Studies*, vol2, 1987, p97, has pointed out: 'It has been argued that there is a close correlation between those who identified with the Church as the main source of influence on their subsequent voting patterns in the Referendum. Moreover, the poll findings show that those sectors of Irish society most clearly identified with the Church were those who, between April and June, changed their opinion.'

8. *New Ireland Forum No. 12*, especially pp2,11,36.

9. For brief references to this, see, for instance, N McNeilly, 'Integration in Education: Past, Present, Future' in *Belfast Natural History and Philosophical Society Proceedings and Reports*, vol9, 1976–1977, pp58–60.

10. By the 1840s, the Irish Catholic bishops were deeply divided over the national school system. For details of these divisions see, Donal A Kerr, *Peel, Priests and Politics—Sir Robert Peel's Administration and the Roman Catholic Church in Ireland, 1841–1846*, Oxford: Clarendon Press, 1982, pp59–64.

11. For the most comprehensive historical background to the schools system in Northern Ireland, see Donald H Akenson, *Education and Enmity—The Control of Schooling in Northern Ireland 1920–1950*, Newton Abbot: David & Charles, 1973. For other useful references to the historical background of the schools system in Northern Ireland see, Norman Atkinson, *Irish Education—a history of educational institutions*, Dublin: Allen Figgis, 1969, pp177–193, and Dominic Murray, *Worlds Apart—Segregated Schools in Northern Ireland*, Belfast: Appletree Press, 1985, pp14–30. For a specifically Catholic view of education in Northern Ireland see, D Kennedy, 'Catholic Education in Northern Ireland 1921–1970' in *Aspects of Catholic Education—Papers read at a Conference organised by the Guild of Catholic Teachers Diocese of Down and Connor*, Belfast: St Joseph's College of Education, 1971, pp30–46. For a brief description of the educational *status quo* in Northern Ireland see, HM Knox 'Religious Segregation in the Schools of Northern Ireland' in *British Journal of Educational Studies*, volxxi, no3, October 1973, pp307–312.

12. Such advocates of integrated education include the following sources: Elizabeth Benton, 'Integrated Education' in *Scope*, no29, November 1979, pp12–14; *Disturbances in Northern Ireland—Report of*

the Commission appointed by the Governor of Northern Ireland, Belfast: HMSO, cmd532 1969, par10, p14; John Magee, *Northern Ireland: Crisis and Conflict*, London: Routledge & Kegan Paul, 1974, p9; Rona M Fields, *Northern Ireland: Society Under Siege*, New Brunswick, New Jersey: Transaction Books, 1980, p225; William Moles, 'Integrated Education' in *Community Forum*, 2,1, 1972, pp16–17; Kevin Boyle, Tom Hadden, *Ireland A Positive Proposal*, Harmondsworth: Penguin, 1985, p56. Similarly unsubstantiated cases for the continuation of the Catholic school system include: John McCann, 'Northern Schools and Integration' in *Christus Rex*, vol23, no3, 1969, pp162–177; T O'Raifeartaigh, 'Integrated Education Not the Answer?' in *Proceedings of the Educational Studies Association of Ireland Conference*, Galway: Galway University Press, 1979, ppix–xv; M Dallat 'Integrated Education', in *Community Forum* 2,1, 1972, pp18–19.

13. This was admitted by early studies such as John Darby, *Conflict in Northern Ireland: The Development of a Polarised Community*, Dublin: Gill & Macmillan, 1976, p138; John Darby, 'Divisiveness in Education' in *The Northern Teacher*, winter 1973, p10; John F Fulton, 'Some Reflections on Catholic Schools in Northern Ireland' in *Studies*, vollviii, no232, winter 1969, pp341–356, treated the matter by saying that more research was needed. The most recent major study of children in Northern Ireland by Ed Cairns, *Caught in Crossfire—Children and the Northern Ireland Conflict*, Belfast: Appletree Press, 1987, p142, reviewed the controversy over education there. He wrote: 'For the moment however the verdict in the case against the [segregated] schools must remain one of "not proven".'

14. Donald H Akenson, *Education and Enmity*, op cit, pp269–270, and D Murray, *Worlds Apart*, op cit, p123. Murray largely reiterates these arguments in 'Educational Segregation: "Rite" or Wrong?' in P Clancy (*et al*), *Ireland A Sociological Profile*, Dublin: Institute of Public Administration, 1986, especially pp253–254.

15. IF Turner and J Davies, 'Religious Attitudes in an Integrated Primary School: A Northern Ireland Case-Study', in *British Journal of Religious Education*, vol5, no1, autumn 1982, pp31–32. Liz McWhirter adopts a similar view in 'Contact and Conflict: The Question of Integrated Education', in *The Irish Journal of Psychology*, vol6, no1, autumn 1983, p23, when she writes: 'although much more research is obviously needed, the available evidence would suggest that the attitudes to religion held by children attending religiously mixed schools are highly favourable'.

16. The conflicting nature of these interpretations is underlined by referring to a few works which have addressed this theme. Thus, A Lijphart, 'Review Article: The Northern Ireland Problem: Cases

Theories and Solutions' in *British Journal of Political Science*, vol5, no1, 1975, pp83–106, identifies ten different views of the conflict. In his own opinion, p96, Lijphart believes that 'Northern Ireland can be understood best as a plural society, our understanding being complemented by images of the country as a colony, a fragment society and a majority dictatorship'. For his part, JH Whyte, 'Interpretations of the Northern Ireland Problem: an appraisal', in *Economic and Social Review*, vol9, no4, July 1978, pp257–282, puts considerable emphasis on the 'double-minority' model, p276, but also lists three Marxist interpretations, six 'internal conflict theories' as well as the traditional nationalist and Unionist viewpoints. He admits that none of these approaches can provide a complete explanation to the problem, p278. Hunter in 'An Analysis of the Conflict in Northern Ireland' in D Rae (ed), *Political Co-operation in Divided Societies: a series of papers relevant to the conflict in Northern Ireland*, Dublin: Gill & Macmillan, 1982, pp9–59, categorises various theories into four broad groups. He admits that no one group of theories provides a totally satisfactory explanation to the Northern Ireland conflict, p14.

It is hardly surprising then, to note that academics are pessimistic as to the finding of a solution *per se* to the Northern Ireland problem. To cite just a few, Richard Rose, *Northern Ireland: a time of choice*, London: Macmillan, 1976, p139, believes that there is no solution to the problem. Marxist scholars Bew, Gibbon and Patterson in their 'Some Aspects of Nationalism and Socialism in Ireland: 1968–1978' in A Morgan, B Purdie (eds), *Ireland Divided Nation Divided Class*, London: Ink Links, 1980, p169, believe that there is no solution at the level of constitutional arrangements but only different frameworks within which the problems of Northern Ireland will continue to be expressed. Finally, Boal and Douglas, 'The Northern Ireland Problem' in (eds), FW Boal, JNH Douglas, *Integration and Division—Geographical Perspectives on the Northern Ireland Problem*, London: Academic Press, 1982, p355, astutely point out that in Northern Ireland desired solutions tend to define the problem.

17. For work by Salters in this general area see, 'Integrated Education in Northern Ireland: Some Assumptions to be Examined' in *Proceedings Education Conference*, Galway: UCG, 1976, pp14–18.

18. For the original sources of these quotations from Russell see, 'The Sources of Conflict' in *The Northern Teacher*, vol11, no3, winter 1974/75, pp3–11. For similar arguments see J Russell, 'Socialisation into Conflict' in *Social Studies*, vol4,2, summer 1975, pp109–123, and J Russell, 'Replication of Instability: Political Socialisation in Northern Ireland' in *British Journal of Political Science*, vol7, 1977, pp115–

125. It is interesting to note that in more recent years, Russell appears to have changed his position somewhat. See, J Russell, 'The Extent and Possible Consequences of Inter-Communal Group Friendships in Northern Ireland: Secondary Analysis of Four Surveys' in *Proceedings Education Conference 1980*, pp164–175, especially p173.

19. In Austria, the federal government, an education commission, the Lander and district bodies all play a part in the administration of education there. See Steiner, *Politics in Austria*, Boston: Little Brown, 1972, pp100–101. In Switzerland, each of the 26 cantons has its own 'ecclesiastical' law. See, 'The Catholic Church in Switzerland', in *Pro Mundi Vita*, 1982/84, op cit, p9.

20. In Belgium, attendance at Catholic educational institutions has remained fairly constant between the late 1950s and 1980–1981. See *Pro Mundi Vita*, July 1982, table 8, p15. This is equally true of Holland. See JA Van Kermenade, 'Roman Catholics and their Schools' in *Sociologia Neerlandica*, vol7, no1, 1971, pp15–27, especially p15. For details of political realignment in Belgium see, John Fitzmaurice, *The Politics of Belgium—Crisis and Compromise in a Plural Society*, London: Hurst, 1983; Keith Hill, 'Belgium: Political Change in a Segmented Society' in Richard Rose (ed), *Electoral Behaviour—A Comparative Handbook*, London: Collier Macmillan, 1974, pp29–107; Martin O Heisler, 'Institutionalising Societal Changes in a Cooptive Polity: the growing importance of the output side in Belgium' in Martin O Heisler (ed), *Politics in Europe: Structures and Processes in Some Postindustrial Democracies*, New York: McKay, 1974, pp178–220. For changes in Dutch political alignment see, Jacques Thomassen, 'Party Identification as a cross-national concept: Its meaning in the Netherlands' in Budge, Crewe, Farlie (eds), *Party Identification*, op cit, pp63–79, especially p78; Arend Lijphart, 'Continuity and Change In Voting Behaviour' in R Rose (ed), *Electoral Behaviour—A Comparative Handbook*, op cit, pp227–268; Galen A Irwin, 'The Netherlands' in Peter H Merkl (ed), *Western European Party Systems—Trends and Prospects*, New York: The Free Press, 1980, pp161–184.

21. Irish Episcopal Conference, *Directory on Mixed Marriages*, Dublin: Veritas, 1983, 11.4, pp24–25. For a brief historical overview on mixed marriage see, Bernard Haring, *Marriage in the Modern World*, Dublin: The Mercier Press, 1965, pp200–206.

22. For a brief consideration of this neglected theme see, TP Cunningham, 'Mixed Marriages in Ireland Before Ne Temere Decree' in *The Irish Ecclesiastical Record*, vol101, no1, January 1964, pp53–56.

23. For an interesting analysis of change between the *Codex Iuris Canonici*, 1918, (which rested on the *Ne Temere Decree*) and *Motu*

Proprio Matrimonia Mixta, 1970, see, Alasdair Heron, *Two Churches One Love—Interchurch Marriage between Protestants and Roman Catholics*, Dublin: APCK, 1977, pp38–62.

24. For an analysis of the decline in the Protestant population in the South see, Brendan M Walsh, *Religion and Demographic Behaviour in Ireland*, Dublin: The Economic and Social Research Institute, Paper No.55, 1970. For two studies of the Protestant minority community in independent Ireland see: Kurt Bowen, *Protestants in a Catholic State: Ireland's Privileged Minority*, Dublin: Gill & Macmillan, 1983; Jack White, *Minority Report The Protestant Community in the Irish Republic*, Dublin: Gill & Macmillan, 1975.

25. See, 'An Apostolic Letter Issued "Motu Proprio" Determining Norms For Mixed Marriages' in *One In Christ*, volvii, nos2–3, 1971, p212.

26. See, 'Matrimonia Mixta: Some Episcopal Directories' in *One In Christ*, volvii, nos2–3, 1971, p230. For a full copy of the German bishops' statement (in French) see 'Directives Des Eveques Allemands' in *La Documentation Catholique*, vollxvii, no1574, 15 November 1970, pp1033–1040.

27. *One in Christ*, op cit, p231. For a copy of the Swiss document, see 'Directives Des Eveques Suisses' in *La Documentation Catholique*, vollxvii, no1574, 15 November 1970, pp1031–1033. The radical difference between the Swiss and Irish interpretations of *Motu Proprio* is underlined by the comparative analysis of Declan Deane SJ, on this subject. See, Declan Deane 'Mixed Marriage: Irish and Swiss Bishops' statements compared' in *The Furrow*, vol25, no10, October 1974, pp544–548.

28. Fr Patrick Devine, 'Joint Pastoral Care of Interchurch Marriages' in *The Furrow*, vol33, no6, June 1982, p358. This inter-church approach was advocated by the Irish Theological Association in its submission to the New Ireland Forum. For this document in full see, 'The New Ireland Forum Submission by the Executive of the Irish Theological Association' in *Doctrine and Life*, vol34, no2, February 1984, pp85–88.

29. For instances of this see, the comments of Bishop Cahal Daly in his *Peace The Work of Justice Addresses on the Northern Tragedy 1973–1979*, Dublin: Veritas Publications, 1979, p33, and those of Bishop Cassidy of Clonfert in *New Ireland Forum No. 12*, op cit, p49.

30. To cite just a few works that address themselves to some extent to this influence in the US Church see, the following: Patrick K Egan, *The Influence of the Irish on the Catholic Church in America in the Nineteenth Century*, Dublin: National University of Ireland, 1968; Thomas T McAvoy, 'The Irish Clergyman' in Patrick J Corish (ed),

A History of Irish Catholicism—The United States of America, Dublin: Gill & Macmillan, 1970, volvi, no2, pp1–44; Thomas N Brown, 'The Irish Layman' in PJ Corish (ed), *A History of Irish Catholicism—The United States of America*, Dublin: Gill & Macmillan, 1970, volvi, no2, pp45–97; James Hennessy SJ, *American Catholics—A History of the Roman Catholic Community in the United States*, New York: Oxford University Press, 1981. For a few accounts of Irish influence on the Catholic Church in Britain, see: PJ Corish (ed), *A History of Irish Catholicism—Irish Catholicism in Great Britain*, Dublin: Gill and Son, 1968, volvi, no1; Edward Norman, *The English Catholic Church in the Nineteenth Century*, Oxford: Clarendon Press, 1984 passim; Edward Norman, *Roman Catholicism in England from the Elizabethan Settlement to the Second Vatican Council*, Oxford: Oxford University Press, 1985 passim. For the Irish influence in other English-speaking Churches see: Arthur P Monahan, 'Canada' in PJ Corish (ed), *A History of Irish Catholicism*, Dublin: Gill & Macmillan, 1971, volvi, no3; JJ McGovern and Patrick J O'Farrell, 'Australia' in PJ Corish (ed), *A History of Irish Catholicism*, Dublin: Gill & Macmillan, 1971, volvi, no6; Eileen Duggan, 'New Zealand' in PJ Corish (ed), *A History of Irish Catholicism*, Dublin: Gill & Macmillan, 1971, volvi, no7.

Conclusion (pp 188–193)

1. See, Ian McAllister, *The Northern Ireland Social Democratic and Labour Party: political opposition in a divided society*, London: Macmillan, 1977, p63. Claims that two emissaries from Cardinal Conway had a secret meeting with John Hume to discuss the establishment of the Party were vigorously denied at the time. See, *Fortnight*, 25 September 1970, p14. I wrote to the author of this article, Barry White, in the hope that he could throw some light on these events. He replied that he had been unable to prove any clerical links with the SDLP.
Source: letter from Barry White, 17 March 1987

2. Fr Des Wilson has argued, in fact, that the Church's position *vis-à-vis* Sinn Fein has had the effect, to some extent, of flinging the SDLP 'into the arms of the clergy'. See, Des Wilson, *An End To Silence*, Cork, Dublin: The Mercier Press, 1985, p67. In an interview in Belfast on 25 March 1987, however, Fr Wilson provided no specific instance of overt clerical support being given to the SDLP in elections.

3. For examples of this, see: Bishop Cahal B Daly, *Peace The Work of Justice Addresses on the Northern Tragedy 1973–1979*, Dublin: Veritas, 1979, pp103–107; *New Ireland Forum No. 12: Public Session Thursday, 9*

February 1984, Dublin Castle Report of Proceedings Irish Episcopal Conference Delegation, Dublin: The Stationery Office, pp6–7.

Appendix D (p 207)

1. WD Birrell, JE Greer, DJD Roche, 'The Political Role and Influence of the Clergy in Northern Ireland' in *The Sociological Review*, August 1979, pp491–512.

2. WD Birrell, DJD Roche, 'Theology, Political Attitudes and Party Preference Among Clergymen in Northern Ireland — Proceedings of the first annual conference of the Sociological Association of Ireland, 19–21 April 1974, in AECW Spencer and H Tovey (eds), *Sociological Association of Ireland — Proceedings of the First and Fourth Annual Conferences,* Belfast: QUB, 1978, pp2–7.

3. WD Birrell, DJD Roche, 'The Political Role and Influence of Clergymen in Northern Ireland' SAI, 1977, in Spencer, Tovey (eds), op cit, pp44–48.

4. WD Birrell, JE Greer, DJD Roche, 'A Socio-Political Opinion Profile of Clergymen in Northern Ireland' in *Social Studies*, vol4, no2, summer 1975, pp143–151.

5. Patrick A Fahy, 'Some Political Behaviour Patterns and Attitudes of Roman Catholic Priests in a Rural Part of Northern Ireland' in *Economic and Social Review*, vol3, no1, October 1971, pp1–24.

6. Birrell, Roche, 1974, op cit.

7. Birrell, Greer, Roche, 1979, op cit.

8. Birrell, Roche, 1977, op cit.

9. Birrell, Roche, 1974, op cit.

10. Fahy, op cit.

11. Birrell, Greer, Roche, 1975, op cit.

12. Birrell, Roche, 1974, op cit.

13. Fahy, op cit.

14. Birrell, Roche, 1977, op cit.

15. For more details of mail surveys see, Paul L Erdos, *Professional Mail Surveys*, New York: McGraw-Hill, 1970. For a consideration of questionnaires generally see, Isidor Chein, Harold M Proshansky (eds), *Research Methods in Social Relations*, London: Methuen, 1969, pp235–278.

Bibliography

This bibliography is presented under the following headings:
- (i) books and pamphlets
- (ii) articles
- (iii) list of journals and magazines
- (iv) list of newspapers
- (v) theses
- (vi) interviews
- (vii) official publications

Books and Pamphlets

Abramson, Harold J., *Ethnic Diversity in Catholic America*, New York: Wiley, 1973.

Akenson, Donald H., *Education and Enmity—The Control of Schooling in Northern Ireland 1920–1950*, Newton Abbot: David & Charles, 1973.

Akenson, Donald H., *The Irish Education Experiment—The National System of Education in the Nineteenth Century*, London: Routledge & Kegan Paul, 1970.

Alford, Robert A., *Party and Society: The Anglo–American Democracies*, Chicago: Rand McNally, 1963.

Arthur, Paul, *Government and Politics of Northern Ireland*, London: Longman, 1980.

Arthur, Paul, *The People's Democracy 1968–1973*, Belfast: Blackstaff Press, 1974.

Ascherson, Neal, *The Polish August: The Self-Limiting Revolution*, Harmondsworth: Penguin, 1981.

Ash, Timothy Garton, *The Polish Revolution 1980–1982*, London: Jonathan Cape, 1983.

Asmal, Kader, (Chairman), *Shoot To Kill? International Lawyers' Inquiry into the Lethal Use of Firearms by the Security Forces in Northern Ireland*, Cork and Dublin: Mercier Press, 1985.

Assmann, H., *A Practical Theology of Liberation*, London: Search Press, 1975.

Atkinson, Norman, *Irish Education—a history of educational institutions*, Dublin: Allen Figgis, 1969.

Bakvis, Herman, *Catholic Power In The Netherlands*, Montreal: McGill—Queen's University Press, 1981.

Barkley, John M., *St Enoch's Congregation 1972—An account of*

Presbyterianism in Belfast through the life of a congregation, Belfast: St Enoch's Church, 1972.

Barritt, Denis P. and Charles F. Carter, *The Northern Ireland Problem: a study in group relations*, London: Oxford University Press, 1972, 2nd edition.

Barzilay, D., *The British Army In Ulster*, 4 vols, Belfast: Century Services, 1973–1981.

Bell, Geoffrey, *The Protestants of Ulster*, London: Pluto Press, 1976.

Bell J. Bowyer, *The Secret Army — The IRA 1916–1979*, Dublin: The Academy Press, 1979.

Beresford, David, *Ten Men Dead The Story of the 1981 Hunger Strike*, London: Grafton Books, 1987.

Bew, P. Gibbon, P., Patterson, H., *The State in Northern Ireland 1921–1972: Political Forces and Social Classes*, Manchester: Manchester University Press, 1979.

Biever, Bruce Francis, *Religion, Culture and Values A Cross Cultural Analysis of Motivational Factors in Native Irish and American Irish Catholicism*, New York: Arno Press, 1976.

Bingham Powell, G. Jr, *Social Fragmentation and Political Hostility: An Austrian Case-Study*, Stanford: Stanford University Press, 1970.

Birrell, D., Murie, A., *Policy and Government in Northern Ireland: Lessons of Devolution*, Dublin: Gill & Macmillan, 1980.

Blake, R., *A History of Rhodesia*, London: Eyre Methuen, 1973.

Blanchard, Jean, *The Church in Contemporary Ireland*, Dublin: Clonmore & Reynolds, 1963.

Blanshard, Paul, *The Irish and Catholic Power — An American Interpretation*, Boston: The Beacon Press, 1953.

Bluhm, William T., *Building an Austrian Nation — The Political Integration of a Western State*, New Haven: Yale University Press, 1973.

Boland, Kevin, *Up Dev*, Dublin: privately published, 1977.

Boland, Kevin, *We Won't Stand (Idly) By*, Dublin: Kelly Kane, 1972.

Boulton, David, *The UVF: an anatomy of loyalist rebellion*, Dublin: Torc Books, 1973.

Bowen, Desmond, *Paul Cardinal Cullen and the Shaping of Modern Irish Catholicism*, Dublin: Gill & Macmillan, 1983.

Bowen, Kurt, *Protestants in a Catholic State: Ireland's Privileged Minority*, Dublin: Gill & Macmillan, 1983.

Bowman, John, *De Valera and the Ulster Question 1917–1973*, Oxford: Clarendon Press, 1982.

Boyd, Andrew, *The Informers — a chilling account of the supergrasses in Northern Ireland*, Dublin: Mercier Press, 1984.

Boyle, Kevin and Hadden, Tom, *Ireland A Positive Proposal*, Harmondsworth: Penguin, 1985.

Brady, Seamus, *Arms and the Men: Ireland in Turmoil*, Dublin: personally published, 1971.

Browne, V., (ed), *The Magill Book of Irish Politics*, Dublin: Magill, 1981.

Bruce, Steven, *God Save Ulster: the religion and politics of Paisleyism*, Oxford: Clarendon Press, 1986.

Buckland, Patrick, *A History of Northern Ireland*, Dublin: Gill & Macmillan, 1981.

Buckland, Patrick, *James Craig, Lord Craigavon*, Dublin: Gill & Macmillan, 1980.

Buckland, Patrick, *The Factory of Grievances: Devolved Government in Northern Ireland 1921-1939*, Dublin: Gill & Macmillan, 1979.

Burton, Frank, *The Politics of Legitimacy—struggles in a Belfast Community*, London: Routledge & Kegan Paul, 1978.

Cairns, Ed., *Caught In Crossfire—Children and the Northern Ireland Conflict*, Belfast: Appletree Press, 1987.

Callaghan, James, *A House Divided—The Dilemma of Northern Ireland*, London: Collins, 1973.

Campbell, T.J., *Fifty Years of Ulster, 1890-1940*, Belfast: Irish News, 1941.

Carty, R.K., *Party and Parish Pump Electoral Politics in Ireland*, Waterloo, Ontario: Wilfrid Laurier University Press, 1981.

Chein, Isidor, Phoshansky, Harold M., (eds), *Research Methods in Social Relations*, London: Methuen, 1969.

Chubb, Basil, *The Government and Politics of Ireland*, London: Oxford University Press, 1970.

Clark, Robert P., *The Basques: The Franco Years and Beyond*, Nevada: University of Nevada Press, 1979.

Clarke, Desmond M., *Church and State Essays in Political Philosphy*, Cork: Cork University Press, 1984.

Clarke, Liam, *Broadening The Battlefield—The H-Blocks and the Rise of Sinn Fein*, Dublin: Gill & Macmillan, 1987.

Clutterbuck, R., *Protest and the Urban Guerrilla*, London: Cassell, 1973.

Coleman, John A., *The Evolution of Dutch Catholicism*, London: University of California Press, 1978.

Collins, Tom, *The Irish Hunger Strike*, Dublin: White Island Book Company, 1986.

Conway, Cardinal William, *Catholic Schools*, Dublin: Catholic Communications Institute, 1970.

Coogan, Tim Pat, *Ireland Since The Rising*, London: Pall Mall Press, 1966.

Coogan, Tim Pat, *On The Blanket*, Dublin: Ward River Press, 1980.

Cooney, John, *The Crozier and the Dail—Church and State in Ireland 1922-1986*, Dublin & Cork: Mercier Press, 1986.

Corish, Patrick J., (ed), *A History of Irish Catholicism*, vol6, no1, Dublin:

Gill & Son, 1968, and vol6, nos2,3,6,7, Dublin: Gill & Macmillan, 1970 and 1971.

Coughlan, Anthony, *Fooled Again? The Anglo–Irish Agreement and After*, Dublin and Cork: The Mercier Press, 1986.

Craig, F.W.S., *British Parliamentary Election Results 1918–1949*, Glasgow: Political Reference Publications, 1969.

Cross, F.L. and Livingstone, E.A., *The Oxford Dictionary of the Christian Church*, Oxford: Oxford University Press, 1983, 3rd edition.

Curtis, Liz, *Ireland The Propaganda War*, London: Pluto, 1984.

Daly, Bishop Cahal B., *Peace The Work of Justice Addresses on the Northern Tragedy 1973–1979*, Dublin: Veritas, 1979.

Daly, Bishop Cahal B., *Violence in Ireland and Christian Conscience*, Dublin: Veritas, 1973.

Daly, Bishop Cahal B. and Worrall, A.S., *Ballymascanlon: an Irish venture in inter-church dialogue*, Dublin: Veritas, 1978.

Darby, John, *Conflict in Northern Ireland: The Development of a Polarised Community*, Dublin: Gill & Macmillan, 1976.

Darby, John, *Intimidation and the Control of Conflict in Northern Ireland*, Dublin: Gill & Macmillan, 1986.

De Paor, Liam, *Divided Ulster*, Harmondsworth: Penguin, 1974.

Dash, S., *Justice Denied: A Challenge to Lord Widgery's Report on Bloody Sunday*, London: National Council for Civil Liberties, 1972.

Deutsch, R. and Magowan, V., *Northern Ireland 1968–1973: A Chronology of Events*, Belfast: Blackstaff Press, 1973, vol1.

Devlin, B., *The Price Of My Soul*, New York: Knopf, 1969.

Devlin, Paddy, *The Fall of the NI Executive*, Belfast: personally published, 1975.

Dillon, M. and Lehane, D., *Political Murder In Northern Ireland*, London: Penguin Books, 1973.

Doerries, Hermann, *Constantine The Great*, London: Harper & Row, 1972.

Douglas, J.D., (ed), *The New International Dictionary Of The Christian Church*, Exeter: The Paternoster Press, 1978, 2nd edition.

Dziewanowski, M.K., *The Communist Party of Poland—An outline of History*, Cambridge, Mass: Harvard University Press, 1976.

Eberstein, W.G., *Church and State in Franco's Spain*, Princeton: Princeton University Press, 1960.

Edmonds, Sean, *The Gun, The Law, And The Irish People*, Tralee: Anvil Books, 1971.

Edwards, Owen Dudley, *The Sins Of Our Fathers Roots of Conflict In Northern Ireland*, Dublin: Gill & Macmillan, 1970.

Egan, Patrick K., *The Influence of the Irish on the Catholic Church in America in the Nineteenth Century*, Dublin: National University of Ireland, 1968.

Elliott, Sydney, *Northern Ireland Parliamentary Election Results 1921–1972*, Chichester: Political Reference Publications, 1973.

Elliott, Sydney, *Northern Ireland: the first election to the European Parliament*, Belfast: QUB, 1980.

Elliott, Sydney and Wilford, Richard A., *The 1982 Northern Ireland Assembly Elections*, Glasgow: Centre for the Study of Public Policy, University of Strathclyde, 1983.

Erdos, Paul L., *Professional Mail Surveys*, New York: McGraw-Hill, 1970.

Ervine, St John, *Craigavon Ulsterman*, London: George Allen & Unwin, 1949.

Faligot, R., *Britain's Military Strategy In Ireland The Kitson Experiment*, London: Zed, 1983.

Farrell, Michael, *Arming the Protestants The Formation of the Ulster Special Constabulary and the Royal Ulster Constabulary 1920–1922*, Dingle: Brandon Books, 1983.

Farrell, Michael, *Northern Ireland: the orange state*, London: Pluto Press, 1980, 2nd edition.

Faul, Fr Denis, *The stripping naked of the women prisoners in Armagh Gaol, November 1982–January 1984: the shame of James Prior and Nicholas Scott*, Dungannon: personally published, 1984.

Faul, Fr Denis, *The stripping naked of the women prisoners in Armagh prison*, Dungannon: personally published, 1983.

Faulkner, Brian, *Memoirs of a Statesman*, London: Weidenfeld & Nicholson, 1978.

Feehan, John M., *Bobby Sands and the Tragedy of Northern Ireland*, Dublin and Cork: Mercier Press, 1983.

Fennell, Desmond, *The Changing Face of Catholic Ireland*, London: Geoffrey Chapman, 1968.

Fennell, Desmond, *The Northern Catholic An Inquiry*, Dublin: Mount Salus Press, 1958.

Fianna Fail Policy on Northern Ireland, Dublin: Fianna Fail, 1975.

Fields, Rona M., *Northern Ireland: Society Under Siege*, New Brunswick, New Jersey: Transaction Books, 1980.

Fine Gael, *Ireland—Our Future Together*, Dublin: Fine Gael, 1979.

Fisk, Robert, *The Point of No Return: The Strike that Broke the British in Ulster*, London: Andre Deutsch, 1975.

FitzGerald, Garret, *Towards a New Ireland*, London: Knight, 1972.

Fitzmaurice, John, *The Politics of Belgium—Crisis and Compromise in a Plural Society*, London: Hurst, 1983.

Flackes, W.D., *Northern Ireland: A Political Directory 1968–83*, London: Ariel Books, BBC, 1983, 2nd edition.

Fogarty, Michael, Ryan, Liam and Lee, Joseph, (eds), *Irish Values and Attitudes The Irish Report of the European Value Systems*, Dublin: Dominican Publications, 1984.

Forester, Margery, *Michael Collins—The Lost Leader*, London: Sidgwick & Jackson, 1971.

Fraser, Morris, *Children in Conflict*, London: Secker & Warburg, 1973.

Gallagher, Eric and Worrall, Stanley, *Christians in Ulster 1968–1980*, Oxford: Oxford University Press, 1982.

Galligher, John F. and De Gregory, Jerry L., *Violence in Northern Ireland: Understanding Protestant Perspectives*, Dublin: Gill & Macmillan, 1985.

Garvin, Tom, *The Evolution of Irish Nationalist Politics*, Dublin: Gill & Macmillan, 1981.

Gibellini, R., (ed), *Frontiers of Theology in Latin America*, London: SCM Press, 1979.

Gifford, Lord T., *Supergrasses: the use of accomplice evidence in Northern Ireland*, London: Cobden Trust, 1984.

Goddijn, Walter, *The Deferred Revolution—A Social Experiment in Church Innovation in Holland 1960–1970*, Amsterdam: Elsevier, 1975.

Gutierrez, G., *A Theology of Liberation*, London: SCM Press, 1975.

Hamill, Desmond, *Pig in the Middle The Army in Northern Ireland*, London: Methuen, 1985.

Hand, Geoffrey J. (introduced by), *Irish Boundary Commission 1925: Report*, Shannon: Irish University Press, 1969.

Hanna, Mary T., *Catholics and American Politics*, Cambridge, Mass: Harvard University Press, 1979.

Hanson, Eric O., *The Catholic Church in World Politics*, Princeton: Princeton University Press, 1987.

Harbinson, J.F., *The Ulster Unionist Party, 1882–1973—its development and organisation*, Belfast: Blackstaff Press, 1973.

Harding, Stephen, Phillips, David, Fogarty, Michael, (eds), *Contrasting Values in Western Europe: Unity, Diversity and Change*, Basingstoke: The Macmillan Press, 1986.

Haring, Bernard, *Marriage in the Modern World*, Dublin: The Mercier Press, 1965.

Hastings, M., *Ulster 1969: the fight for civil rights in Northern Ireland*, London: Gollancz, 1970.

Hennessy, James SJ, *American Catholics—A History of the Roman Catholic Community in the United States*, New York: Oxford University Press, 1981.

Heron, Alasdair, *Two Churches One Love—Interchurch Marriage between Protestants and Roman Catholics*, Dublin: APCK, 1977.

Heskin, Ken, *Northern Ireland: a psychological analysis*, Dublin: Gill & Macmillan, 1980.

Hezlitt, Sir A., *The 'B' Specials: A History of the Ulster Special Constabulary*, London: Stacey, 1972.

Hickey, John, *Religion and the Northern Ireland Problem*, Dublin: Gill & Macmillan, 1984.

Hull, R.H., *The Irish Triangle: Conflict in Northern Ireland*, Princeton: Princeton University Press, 1978.

Inglis, Brian, *West Briton*, London: Faber & Faber, 1962.

Inglis, Tom, *Moral Monopoly – The Catholic Church in Modern Irish Society*, Dublin: Gill & Macmillan, 1987.

Irish Bishops, *Marriage, The Family and Divorce*, Dublin: Veritas, 1986.

Irish Bishops, *Justice, Love and Peace Pastoral Letters of the Irish Bishops 1969–1979*, Dublin: Veritas, 1979.

Irish Council of Churches/Roman Catholic Church Joint Groups, *Violence In Ireland: a report to the churches*, Dublin: Veritas, 1976.

Irish Episcopal Conference, *Conscience and Morality A Doctrinal Statement*, Dublin: Irish Messenger Publications, 1980.

Irish Episcopal Conference, *Directory On Ecumenism*, Dublin: Veritas, 1976.

Irish Episcopal Conference, *Directory on Mixed Marriages*, Dublin: Veritas, 1983.

Kapungee, Leonard T., *Rhodesia: the struggle for freedom*, Maryknoll: Orbis, 1974.

Keenan, Desmond, *The Catholic Church In Nineteenth-Century Ireland A Sociological Study*, Dublin: Gill & Macmillan, 1983.

Kelley, Kevin, *The Longest War – Northern Ireland and the IRA*, Dingle: Brandon, 1982.

Kelly, James, *Orders For The Captain?*, Dublin: privately published, 1971.

Kelly, James, *The Genesis of Revolution*, Dublin: Kelly Kane, 1976.

Kennedy, Anthony, *The Road to Hillsborough The Shaping of the Anglo–Irish Agreement*, Oxford: Pergamon Press, 1986.

Kennedy, Liam, *Two Ulsters: a case for repartition*, Belfast: QUB, 1986.

Keogh, Dermot, *The Nation, The Bishops and Irish Politics 1919–1939*, Cambridge: Cambridge University Press, 1986.

Kerr, Donal A., *Peel, Priests and Politics – Sir Robert Peel's Administration and the Roman Catholic Church in Ireland 1841–1846*, Oxford: Clarendon Press, 1982.

Kerr, Henry J., *Switzerland: Social Cleavages and Partisan Conflict*, London: Sage Contemporary Political Sociology Series, no06–002, vol1, 1974.

Kirby, Peadar, *Is Irish Catholicism Dying?*, Dublin, Cork: The Mercier Press, 1984.

Larkin, Emmet, *The Consolidation of the Roman Catholic Church in Ireland 1860–1870*, Dublin: Gill & Macmillan, 1987.

Larkin, Emmet, *The Historical Dimensions of Irish Catholicism*, New York: Arno Press, 1976.

Lawrence, R.J., *The Government of Northern Ireland: public finance and public services 1921–1964*, Oxford: Clarendon Press, 1965.

Lee, Alfred McClung, *Terrorism In Northern Ireland*, New York: General Hall, 1983.

Letemandia, Francisco, *Les Basques Un Peuple Contre Les Etats*, Paris: Editions Du Seuil, 1977.

Lewy, Gwenter, *Religion and Revolution*, New York: Oxford University Press, 1974.

Lijphart, A., *Democracy In Plural Societies A Comparative Exploration*, London: Yale University Press, 1977.

Lijphart, A., *The Politics of Accommodation: Pluralism and Democracy in the Netherlands*, Los Angeles: University of California Press, 1975.

Limpkin, C., *The Battle of Bogside*, Harmondsworth: Penguin, 1972.

Linden, Ian, *The Catholic Church and the Struggle for Zimbabwe*, London: Longman, 1980.

Lipset, Seymour Martin, *Political Man: The Social Bases of Politics*, Garden City, New York: Doubleday, 1960.

Longford, Lord and McHardy, Anne, *Ulster*, London: Weidenfeld & Nicolson, 1981.

MacArdle, Dorothy, *The Irish Republic*, Dublin: The Irish Press, 1951, 4th edition.

MacGreil, Michael, *Prejudice and Tolerance in Ireland—Based on a survey of intergroup attitudes of Dublin adults and other sources*, Dublin: College of Industrial Relations, 1977.

MacIntyre, Tom, *Through the Bridewell Gate: a diary of the arms trial*, London: Faber & Faber, 1971.

MacStiofain, Sean, *Revolution in Ireland*, Farnborough: Saxon House, 1974.

MacSuibhne, Peadar, *Paul Cullen and his Contemporaries with their Letters from 1820–1902*, Naas: Leinster Leader 1961–1977, 5 vols.

Magee, John, *Northern Ireland: Crisis and Conflict*, London: Routledge & Kegan Paul, 1974.

Mansergh, Nicholas, *Survey of British Commonwealth Affairs Problems of Wartime Co-operation and Post-War Change 1939–1952*, London: Oxford University Press, 1958.

Mansergh, Nicholas, *The Government of Northern Ireland A Study In Devolution*, London: George Allen & Unwin, 1936.

Marrinan, Patrick, *Paisley: man of wrath*, Tralee: Anvil Books, 1973.

Martin, David, *A General Theory of Secularization*, Oxford: Basil Blackwell, 1978.

Maxley, Kees, *From Rhodesia to Zimbabwe*, London: Fabian Society, 1972.

Mayo, Patricia Elton, *The Roots of Identity: Three National Movements In Contemporary European Politics*, London: Lane, 1975.

McAllister, Ian, *The Northern Ireland Social Democratic and Labour Party: political opposition in a divided society*, London: Macmillan, 1977.

McCann, Eamonn, *War and an Irish Town*, Harmondsworth: Penguin, 1974, and its second edition published by Pluto Press in 1980.

McClean, Raymond, *The Road To Bloody Sunday*, Dublin: Ward River Press, 1983.

McDonagh, Enda, *Demands of Simple Justice A Study of the Church, Politics and Violence with Special Reference to Zimbabwe*, Dublin: Gill & Macmillan, 1980.

McGuffin, John, *Internment*, Tralee: Anvil, 1973.

McGuffin, John, *The Guineapigs*, Harmondsworth: Penguin, 1974.

McKeown, Ciaran, *The Passion of Peace*, Belfast: Blackstaff Press, 1984.

McKeown, Ciaran, *The Price of Peace*, Belfast: personally published, 1976.

McKeown, Michael, *De Mortuis A Study of 2,400 fatalities arising from political disturbances in Northern Ireland between July 1969 and July 1984*, Gondregnies, Belgium: Irish Information Partnership, 1985.

McKeown, Michael, *The First Five Hundred: three Irelands or one: two essays on aspects of the Northern Ireland problem*, Belfast: Irish News, 1972.

McRae K., (ed), *Consociational Democracy*, Toronto: McClelland & Stewart, 1974.

Medhurst, Kenneth, *The Basques*, London: Minority Rights Group, report no9. 1972.

Medvedev, Igor, *et al*, *Who Pushed Poland to the Brink?*, Moscow: Novosti Press, 1982.

Mescal, John, *Religion in the Irish System of Education*, Dublin: Clonmore & Reynolds, 1957.

Miller, David W., *Church State and Nation in Ireland 1898–1921*, Dublin: Gill & Macmillan, 1973.

Moloney, Ed and Pollak, Andy, *Paisley*, Dublin: Poolbeg, 1986.

Moxon-Browne, Edward, *Nation, Class and Creed in Northern Ireland*, Aldershot: Gower, 1983.

Murray, Dominic, *Worlds Apart—Segregated Schools in Northern Ireland*, Belfast: Appletree Press, 1985.

Myant, Martin, *Poland: A Crisis for Socialism*, London: Lawrence & Wishart, 1982.

Nelson, Sarah, *Ulster's uncertain Defenders: Loyalists and the Northern Ireland Conflict*, Belfast: Appletree Press, 1984.

New Catholic Encyclopedia, New York: McGraw-Hill, 1967, volv.

Newman, Bishop Jeremiah, *Ireland Must Choose*, Dublin: Four Courts Press, 1983.

Norman, Edward, *Roman Catholicism in England from the Elizabethan Settlement to the Second Vatican Council*, Oxford: Oxford University Press, 1985.

Norman, Edward, *The English Catholic Church in the nineteenth Century*, Oxford: Clarendon Press, 1984.

Northern Ireland Civil Rights Association, *We Shall Overcome: The*

History of the Struggle for Civil Rights in Northern Ireland, Belfast: NICRA, 1978.

O'Brien, Conor Cruise, *States of Ireland*, St Albans: Panther, 1974.

O'Carroll, Michael, *Poland and John Paul II*, Dublin: Veritas, 1979.

O'Donnell, E.E., *Northern Irish Stereotypes*, Dublin: College of Industrial Relations, 1977.

O'Fearghail, Sean Og, *Law (?) And Orders*, Belfast: Central Citizens' Defence Committee, 1970.

O'Halloran, Clare, *Partition and the Limits of Irish Nationalism An Ideology Under Stress*, Dublin: Gill & Macmillan, 1987.

O'Malley, Padraig, *The Uncivil Wars*, Belfast: Blackstaff Press, 1983.

O'Neill, Terence, *The Autobiography of Terence O'Neill*, London: Rupert Hart-Davis, 1972.

O'Riordain, John J., *Irish Catholics: Tradition and Transition*, Dublin: Veritas, 1980.

Payne, Stanley G., *Basque Nationalism*, Reno: University of Nevada Press, 1975.

Peel, J.P.G. and Ranger, T.O., *Past and Present in Zimbabwe*, Manchester: Manchester University Press, 1983.

Philbin, Bishop William, *Ireland's Problem*, Manchester: Irish Association, 1974.

Philbin, Bishop William, *Lenten Pastoral, 1970*, Belfast: P. Quinn & Co, 1970.

Raina, Peter, *Independent Social Movements in Poland*, London: London School of Economics and Political Science, 1981.

Raina, Peter, *Political Opposition In Poland 1954–1977*, London: Poets' and Printers' Press, 1978.

Ranger, Terence, *Peasant Consciousness and Guerrilla War in Zimbabwe A Comparative Study*, London: James Currey, 1985.

Rees, Merlyn, *Northern Ireland A Personal Perspective*, London: Methuen, 1985.

Rose, Richard, *Governing Without Consensus: an Irish Perspective*, London: Faber & Faber, 1971.

Rose, Richard, *Northern Ireland: a time of choice*, London: Macmillan, 1976.

Ruane, Kevin, *The Polish Challenge*, London: BBC, 1972.

Rumpf, E., Hepburn, A.C., *Nationalism and Socialism in Twentieth-Century Ireland*, Liverpool: Liverpool University Press, 1977.

Russell, James L., *Some Aspects of the Civic Education of Secondary Schoolboys in Northern Ireland*, Belfast: Northern Ireland Community Relations Commission, 1972.

Sands, Bobby, *One Day In My Life*, Dublin & Cork: The Mercier Press, 1982.

Sequndo, J.L., *The Liberation of Theology*, Dublin: Gill & Macmillan, 1977.
Sheehy, Michael, *Is Ireland Dying? Culture and the Church in Modern Ireland*, London: Hollis & Carter, 1968.
Spencer, A.E.C.W., *Ballymurphy—A Tale of Two Surveys*, Belfast: QUB, 1973.
St John's & Corpus Christi Parish Council Steering Committee, *Open the Window, Let in the Light*, Belfast: privately published, 1975.
Steiner, Jurg, *Amicable Agreement Versus Majority Rule—Conflict Resolution in Switzerland*, Chapel Hill: The University of North Carolina Press, 1974.
Steiner, Kurt, *Politics In Austria*, Boston: Little Brown, 1972.
Stetler, Russell, *The Battle of Bogside*, London: Sheed and Ward, 1970.
Stewart, A.T.Q., *The Narrow Ground: aspects of Ulster 1609–1969*, London: Faber & Faber, 1977.
Submission to the New Ireland Forum from the Irish Episcopal Conference, Dublin: Veritas Publications, 1984.
Target, G.W., *Unholy Smoke*, Hodder & Stoughton, 1969.
Taylor, Peter, *Beating The Terrorists? Interrogation at Armagh, Gough and Castlereagh*, Harmondsworth: Penguin, 1980.
Taylor, Rex, *Michael Collins*, London: Hutchinson, 1958.
The Catholic Church in Ireland Information and Documentation, Dublin: Catholic Press and Information Office of Ireland, 1981.
The Sunday Times Insight Team, *Ulster*, London: Andre Deutsch, 1972.
Thomas, Hugh, *The Spanish Civil War*, London: Eyre & Spottiswoode, 1961.
Vambe, Lawrence, *From Rhodesia to Zimbabwe*, London: Heinemann, 1976.
Van Der Plas Suer, Michael, *Those Dutch Catholics*, London: Geoffrey Chapman, 1967.
Van Voris, W.H., *Violence in Ulster*, Massachusetts: The University of Massachusetts Press, 1975.
Wallace, Martin, *British Government In Northern Ireland From Devolution To Direct Rule*, Newton Abbot: David & Charles, 1982.
Wallace, Martin, *Drums and Guns Revolution in Ulster*, London: Geoffrey Chapman, 1970.
Wallace, Martin, *Northern Ireland 50 Years of Self-Government*, Newton Abbot: David & Charles, 1971.
Washington, Joseph R. Jr, *Black Religion—The Negro and Christianity in the United States*, London: University Press of America, 1984.
White, Barry, *John Hume—Statesman of the Troubles*, Belfast: Blackstaff Press, 1984.
Whyte, J.H., *Church And State In Modern Ireland 1923–1979*, Dublin: Gill & Macmillan, 1980, 2nd edition.

Wilson, Fr Desmond, *An End To Silence*, Dublin, Cork: The Mercier Press, 1985.
Winchester, S., *In Holy Terror Reporting the Ulster Troubles*, London: Faber & Faber, 1974.
Younger, Calton, *Ireland's Civil War*, Glasgow: Collins/Fontana, 1979, 3rd edition.

Articles
Barry, B., 'Political Accommodation and Consociational Democracy' in *British Journal of Political Science*, vol5, 1975, pp477–505.
Benton, Elizabeth, 'Integrated Education' in *Scope*, no29, November 1979, p12–14.
Berman, D., Lalor, S. and Torode, B., 'The Theology of the IRA' in *Studies*, vollxxii, no286, summer 1983, pp137–144.
Bew, Paul, Gibbon, Peter and Patterson, Henry, 'Some Aspects of Nationalism and Socialism in Ireland: 1968–1978' in A. Morgan, B. Purdie, *Ireland Divided Nation Divided Class*, London: Ink Links, 1980, pp152–171.
Billiet, Jaak, 'Secularization and Compartmentalization in the Belgian Educational System—an analysis of the problems relevant to the revision of the school pact, in *Social Compass*, volxx, 1973/74, pp569–91.
Birrell, D., 'Local Government Councillors in Northern Ireland and the Republic of Ireland: their social background, motivation and role' in T. Gallagher, J. O'Connell (eds), *Contemporary Irish Studies*, Manchester: Manchester University Press, 1983, pp95–109.
Birrell, D., 'The Stormont–Westminster Relationship' in *Parliamentary Affairs*, vol2, no4, 1973, pp471–91.
Birrell, W.D., Greer, J.E., Roche, D.J.D., 'A Socio-Political Opinion Profile of Clergymen in Northern Ireland' in *Social Studies*, vol4, no2, summer 1975, pp143–151.
Birrell, W.D., Greer, J.E., Roche, D.J.D., 'The Political Role and Influence of the Clergy in Northern Ireland' in *The Sociological Review*, August 1979, pp491–512.
Birrell, W.D. and Roche, D.J.D., 'Theology, Political Attitudes and Party Preference Among Clergymen in Northern Ireland' in A.E.C.W. Spencer and H. Tovey (eds), *Sociological Association of Ireland—Proceedings of the First and Fourth Annual Conferences*, Belfast: QUB, 1978, p2–7.
Birrell, W.D. and Roche, D.J.D., 'The political role and influence of clergymen in Northern Ireland' in A.E.C.W. Spencer, H. Tovey (eds), *Sociological Association of Ireland—Proceedings of the First and*

Fourth Annual Conferences, Belfast: QUB, 1978, pp44–48.

Blease, M., 'Maladjusted Schoolchildren In A Belfast Centre' in J. Harbison (ed), *Children of The Troubles—Children In Northern Ireland*, Belfast: Stranmillis College, 1983, pp21–32.

Brady, Fr John SJ, 'Pluralism and Northern Ireland' in *Studies*, vollxvii, nos265–266, spring/summer 1978, pp88–99.

Brady, Fr John SJ, 'The Meaning and Relevance of Pluralism in Northern Ireland' in *Studies*, vollxviii, no271, Autumn 1979, pp147–156.

Brown, Thomas N., 'The Irish Layman' in P.J. Corish (ed), *A History of Irish Catholicism—The United States of America*, Dublin: Gill & Macmillan, 1970, volvi, no2, pp45–97.

Browne, V., 'Arms Crisis 1970' in *Magill*, May 1980, pp33–56; June 1980, pp39–73; July 1980, pp17–25.

Breslin, Ann, Weafer, John, *Religious Beliefs, Practice and Moral Attitudes A Comparison of Two Irish Surveys 1974–1984*, report no21 Maynooth: Council for Research and Development, 1984.

Buckley, Fr Pat, 'Where is the Courage in the Catholic Church?' in *Fortnight*, no207, September 1984, pp7–8,11.

Budge, Ian and Farlie, Denis, 'A Comparative Analysis of Factors Correlated With Turnout and Voting Choice' in Ian Budge, Ivor Crewe, Denis Farlie (eds), *Party Identification and Beyond—Representations of Voting and Party Competition*, London: Wiley, 1976, pp103–126.

Cameron, David R., 'Toward a Theory of Political Mobilisation' in *Journal of Politics*, vol36, no9, 1974, pp138–171.

Chrypinski, Vincent, 'Church and State in Gierek's Poland' in M.D. Simon, R.K. Kanet (eds), *Background to Crisis: Policy and Politics in Gierek's Poland*, Colorado: Westview Press, 1981, pp239–268.

Crutchley, J., 'Joyriding Problem—West Belfast' in *Constabulary Gazette*, volxlix, no5, May 1982, p9.

Cunningham, T.P., 'Mixed Marriages in Ireland Before Ne Temere Decree' in *The Irish Ecclesiastical Record*, vol101, no1, January 1964, pp53–56.

Daalder, Hans, 'The Consociational Democracy Theme' in *World Politics*, 26, 1974, pp604–621.

Daalder, Hans, 'On Building Consociational Nations: the case of the Netherlands and Switzerland' in *International Social Science Journal*, vol23, no3, 1971, pp355–370.

Dallat, M., 'Integrated Education', in *Community Forum*, 2,1, 1972, pp18–19.

Daly, Bishop Cahal B., 'A Vision of Ecumenism in Ireland' in *Eire–Ireland*, vol17, no1, spring 1982, pp7–30.

Daly, Bishop Cahal B., 'Ecumenism in Ireland Now: Problems and

Hopes' in *Irish Theological Quarterly*, vol45, no1, 1978, pp3–27.

Daly, Bishop Edward, 'In Place of Terrorism' in *Furrow*, vol26, no10, October 1975, pp587–599.

Daly, G., Falconer, A., 'To Be One' in A. Falconer, E. McDonagh, S. MacReamoinn (eds), *Freedom To Hope: a festschrift for Austin Flannery OP*, Dublin: The Columba Press, 1985, pp27–38.

Darby, John, 'Divisiveness in Education' in *The Northern Teacher*, Winter 1973, pp3–12.

Deane, Fr Declan SJ, 'Northern Ireland and Ecumenism' in *Doctrine and Life*, vol34, no4, April 1984, pp190–196.

De Bhaldraithe, Eoin, 'The Ecumenical Marriage' in *Furrow*, vol32, no10, October 1981, pp639–648.

De Burca, Fr Brian, 'The Northern Ireland Conflict and the Christian Churches' in *Doctrine and Life*, vol23, no9, September 1973, pp463–475.

Deutsch, K., 'Social Mobilisation and Political Development' in *American Political Science Review*, lv, September 1961, pp493–514.

Devine, Fr Patrick, 'Joint Pastoral Care of Interchurch Marriages' in *Furrow*, vol33, no6, June 1982, pp358–369.

Douglas, J.N.H.D. and Boal, Frederick W., 'The Northern Ireland Problem' in F.W. Boal, J. Neville, H. Douglas (eds), *Integration and Division Geographical Perspectives on the Northern Ireland Problem*, London: Academic Press, 1982, pp1–18.

Duffy, Bishop Joseph, 'Northern Ireland—The Way Forward As I See It', in *Furrow*, vol33, no7, July 1982, pp399–406.

Duffy, Paul, 'Positions and Trends in Australia' in Michael Hurley (ed), *Beyond Tolerance—The Challenge of Mixed Marriage—A record of the International Consultation held in Dublin, 1974*, London: Geoffrey Chapman, 1975, pp145–156.

Duggan, Eileen, 'New Zealand' in P.J. Corish (ed), *A History of Irish Catholicism*, Dublin: Gill & Macmillan, 1971, volvi, no7.

Egan, Bowes and McCormack, Vincent, *Burntollet*, London: LRS Publications, 1969.

Fahy, Patrick A., 'Some Political Behaviour Patterns and Attitudes of Roman Catholic Priests in a Rural Part of Northern Ireland' in *The Economic and Social Review*, vol3, no1, October 1971, pp1–24.

Feeney, Vincent Edward, 'The Civil Rights Movement in Northern Ireland' in *Eire–Ireland*, vol9, no2, 1974, pp30–40.

Feeney, Vincent Edward, 'Westminster and the Early Civil Rights Struggle in Ireland, in *Eire–Ireland*, volII, no4, 1976, pp3–13.

FitzGerald, Garret, 'The Priest in Irish Politics' in *Doctrine and Life*, vol22, no3, March 1972, pp135–142.

Fitzpatrick, Barre, 'The Role of the Churches In Northern Ireland

Interview with Brian Smeaton and Des Wilson' in *Crane Bag*, vol4, no2, 1980, pp79–84.

Frognier, Andre Paul, 'Party Preference, Spaces and Voting Change in Belgium, in Dan Budge, Ivor Crewe, Denis Farlie (eds), *Party Identification and Beyond—Representations of Voting and Party Competition*, London: Wiley, 1976, pp189–202.

Fulton, John F., 'Some Reflections on Catholic Schools in Northern Ireland' in *Studies*, vollviii, no232, winter 1969, pp341–356.

Gallagher, Fr Michael Paul, 'Atheism Irish Style' in *Furrow*, vol25, no4, April 1974, pp183–192.

Girvin, Brian, 'Social Change and Moral Politics: the Irish constitutional referendum 1983' in *Political Studies*, vol34, no1, 1986, pp61–81.

Girvin, Brian, 'The Divorce Referendum in the Republic June 1986' in *Irish Political Studies*, vol2, 1987, pp93–99.

Heisler, Martin O., 'Institutionalising Societal Changes in a Cooptive Polity: the growing importance of the output side in Belgium' in Martin O. Heisler (ed), *Politics in Europe: Structures and Processes in Some Postindustrial Democracies*, New York: McKay, 1974, pp178–220.

Hewitt, C., 'Catholic Grievances, Catholic Nationalism and Violence in Northern Ireland During the Civil Rights Period: A Reconsideration' in *British Journal of Sociology*, 32,3, 1981, pp362–380.

Hickey, J., 'Religion in a Divided Society' in P. Clancy *et al*, *Ireland: A Sociological Profile*, Dublin: Institute of Public Administration, 1986, pp265–81.

Hill, Keith, 'Belgium: Political Change in a Segmented Society' in Richard Rose (ed), *Electoral Behaviour—A Comparative Handbook*, London: Collier Macmillan, 1974, pp29–107.

Hoffman, Joseph, 'Positions and Trends in France' in Michael Hurley (ed), *Beyond Tolerance—The challenge of mixed marriage—a record of the International Consultation held in Dublin, 1974*, London: Geoffrey Chapman, 1975, pp120–126.

Hunter, J., 'An Analysis of the Conflict in Northern Ireland' in Rae (ed), *Political Co-operation in Divided Societies: a series of papers relevant to the conflict in Northern Ireland*, Dublin: Gill & Macmillan, 1982, pp9–59.

Hurley, Michael SJ, 'Ecumenism, Ecumenical Theology and Ecumenics' in *Irish Theological Quarterly*, vol45, no2, 1978, pp132–139.

Hurley, Michael SJ, 'Peace-Making in Lent' in *Doctrine and Life*, vol34, no3, March 1984, pp132–136.

Hurley, Michael SJ, 'Reconciliation in Northern Ireland: the Contribution of Ecumenism' in *Studies*, vollxxiii, no292, winter 1984, pp300–308.

Hurley, Michael SJ, 'Two Decades of Ecumenism 1963–1983' in *Doctrine and Life*, September 1983, pp399–414.

Inglehart, Ronald and Dusan, Sidjanski, 'The Left, The Right, The Establishment and the Swiss Electorate' in Ian Budge, Ivor Crewe, Denis Farlie (eds), *Party Identification and Beyond—Representations of Voting and Party Competition*, London: Wiley, 1976, pp225–242.

Irwin, Galen A., 'The Netherlands' in Peter H. Merkl (ed), *Western European Party Systems—Trends and Prospects*, New York: The Free Press, 1980, pp161–184.

Jeffrey, Frederick, 'Anglican–Methodist Relations' in Michael Hurley SJ (ed), *Irish Anglicanism 1869–1969—Essays on the role of Anglicanism in Irish Life presented to the Church of Ireland on the occasion of the centenary of its Disestablishment by a group of Methodist, Presbyterian, Quaker and Roman Catholic scholars*, Dublin: Allen Figgis, 1970, pp79–92.

Kane, T.J., 'Civil Rights in Northern Ireland' in *Review of Politics*, 33,1, 1971, pp54–77.

Kealy, Fr Sean P., 'A Plea for an Irish Theology' in *Doctrine and Life*, vol27, no1, January 1977, pp26–29.

Keane, Thomas B., 'Attitudes To The Religious Integration In Schools In A Sample Of Secondary School Children In The Newry and South Down Area' in *Proceedings Third Annual Education Conference of the Educational Studies Association of Ireland*, Belfast: QUB, 1978, pp21–25.

Kennedy, David, 'Catholic Education in Northern Ireland 1921–1970' in *Aspects of Catholic Education—Papers read at a Conference organised by the Guild of Catholic Teachers Diocese of Down and Connor*, Belfast: St Joseph's College of Education, 1971, pp30–46.

Kennedy, David, 'Catholics in Northern Ireland 1926–1939' in F. McManus (ed), *The Years of the Great Test*, Dublin, Cork: Mercier Press, 1967, pp138–149.

Kennedy, David, 'Ulster During the War and After' in Kevin B. Nowlan and J. Desmond Williams (eds), *Ireland In The War Years And After*, Dublin: Gill & Macmillan, 1969, pp52–66.

Kennedy, David, 'Whither Northern Nationalism, in *Christus Rex*, volxiii, no4, October 1959, pp269–283.

Kirby, Peadar M., 'The Irish Church: the shifting sands' in *Doctrine and Life*, vol28, no10, October 1977, pp28–37.

Knox, H.M., 'Religious Segregation in the Schools of Northern Ireland' in *British Journal of Educational Studies*, volxxi, no3, October 1973, pp307–312.

Kruijt, J.P., 'The Netherlands: the influence of denominationalism on social life and organisational patterns' in K. McRae (ed), *Consociational Democracy*, Toronto: McClelland & Stewart, 1974, pp128–136.

Lancelot, Alain, 'Comparative Political Behaviour' in *European Journal of Political Research*, vol3, 1975, 413–424.

Lennon, Fr Brian SJ, 'Interchurch Marriages: Torn between divided Churches, in *Furrow*, vol31, no5, May 1980, pp309–321.

Leon, Donald E., 'Politics of Civil Rights in Northern Ireland; some views and observations' in *Cithera*, 10,1, 1970, pp1–12.

Lijphart, A., *Class Voting and Religious Voting in the European Democracies: a preliminary report*, Glasgow: University of Strathclyde, occasional paper no8, 1971.

Lijphart, A., 'Consociational Democracy' in *World Politics*, 21, 1969, pp207–225.

Lijphart, A., 'Continuity and Change in Voting Behaviour' in Richard Rose (ed), *Electoral Behaviour—A Comparative Handbook*, London: Collier Macmillan, 1974, pp227–268.

Lijphart, A., 'Religious v Linguistic v Class Voting: the crucial experiment of comparing Belgium, Canada, South Africa and Switzerland' in *American Political Science Review*, vol73, no2, 1979, pp442–458.

Lijphart, A., 'Review Article: The Northern Ireland Problem: Cases Theories and Solutions' in *British Journal of Political Science*, vol5, no1, 1975, pp83–106.

Lockhart, William H. and Elliott, Ruth, 'Changes in the attitudes of young offenders in an integrated assessment centre' in Jeremy and Joan Harbison, *A Society Under Stress: Children and Young People in Northern Ireland*, Somerset: Open Books, 1980, pp100–112.

Lorwin, Val R., 'Belgium: conflict and compromise' in K. McRae (ed), *Consociational Democracy*, Toronto: McClelland & Stewart, 1974, pp179–206.

Lorwin, Val R., 'Segmented Pluralism: ideological cleavages and political cohesion in the smaller European democracies' in *Comparative Politics*, 3,2, 1971, pp141–175.

MacDonagh, Oliver, 'What Was New In The New Ireland Forum' in *The Crane Bag*, 9,2, 1985, pp166–170.

Marx, Gary T., 'Religion: Opiate or inspiration of civil rights militancy among negroes?' in *American Sociological Review*, vol32, no1, pp64–72.

McAllister, Ian, 'Political Opposition in Northern Ireland: The National Democratic Party 1965–1970' in *Economic and Social Review*, vol6, no3, April 1975, pp353–366.

McAllister, Ian, 'Political Parties: traditional and modern' in J. Darby (ed), *Northern Ireland: the background to the conflict*, Belfast: Appletree Press, 1983, pp61–78.

McAllister, Ian, 'Religious Commitment and Social Attitudes in Ireland' in *Review of Religious Research*, 25,1, September 1983, pp1–13.

McAllister, Ian, 'Territorial differentiation and party development in Northern Ireland' in T. Gallagher, J. O'Connell (eds), *Contemporary Irish Studies*, Manchester: Manchester University Press, 1983, pp37–63.

McAllister, Ian, 'The Devil, miracles and the afterlife: the political sociology of religion in Northern Ireland' in *British Journal of Sociology*, vol33, no3, 1982, pp330–347.

McAvoy, Thomas T., 'The Irish Clergyman' in Patrick J. Corish (ed), *A History of Irish Catholicism—The United States of America*, Dublin: Gill & Macmillan, 1970, volvi, no2, pp1–44.

McCann, John, 'Northern Schools and Integration' in *Christus Rex*, vol23, no3, 1969, pp162–177.

McCrudden, C., 'The Experience of the Legal Enforcement of the Fair Employment (Northern Ireland) Act 1976' in R.J. Cormack, R.D. Osborne (eds), *Religion Education and Employment: Aspects of Equal Opportunity in Northern Ireland*, Belfast: Appletree, 1983, pp201–221.

McDonagh, Enda, 'An Irish Theology of Liberation?' in Dermot A. Lane (ed), *Liberation Theology—An Irish Dialogue*, Dublin: Gill & Macmillan, 1977, pp87–102.

McDonagh, Enda, 'Modes of Violence' in *The Irish Theological Quarterly*, volxli, no3, July 1974, pp183–204.

McEvoy, A.J., 'A Northern Analysis' in *Furrow*, vol23, no10, 1972, pp607–610.

McGovern, J.J. and O'Farrell, Patrick J., 'Australia' in P.J. Corish (ed), *A History of Irish Catholicism*, Dublin: Gill & Macmillan, 1971, volvi, no6.

McNeilly, N., 'Integration in Education: Past, Present, Future' in *Belfast Natural History and Philosophical Society Proceedings and Reports*, vol9, 1976–1977, pp58–60.

McWhirter, Liz, 'Contact and Conflict: The Question of Integrated Education' in *Irish Journal of Psychology*, vol6, no1, autumn 1983, pp13–27.

Miller, Robert, 'Opinions on School, Desegregation in Northern Ireland' in A.E.C.W. Spencer, H. Tovey (eds), *Sociological Association of Ireland—Proceedings of the First and Fourth Conferences*, Belfast: QUB, 1978, pp50–55.

Moles, William, 'Integrated Education' in *Community Forum*, 2,1, 1972, pp16–17.

Monahan, Arthur P., 'Canada' in P.J. Corish (ed), *A History of Irish Catholicism*, Dublin: Gill & Macmillan, 1971, volvi, no3, pp1–32.

Murray, Dominic, 'Educational Segregation: "Rite" or Wrong?' in P. Clancy *et al*, *Ireland A Sociological Profile*, Dublin: Institute of Public Administration, 1986, pp244–264.

Murray, R., 'Political Violence in Northern Ireland 1969–1977' in F.W. Boal, J.N.H. Douglas, *Integration and Division Geographical Perspectives on the Northern Ireland Problem*, London: Academic Press, pp309–331.

Nelson, Sarah, 'Protestant "Ideology" Considered: The Case of "Discrimination"' in Ivor Crewe (ed), *British Political Sociology Yearbook*, vol2, London: Croom Helm, 1975, pp155–187.

Newe, G.B., 'The Catholic in the Northern Ireland Community' in *Christus Rex*, volxviii, no1, 1964, pp22–36.

Nic Ghiolla Phadraig, Maire, 'Roman Catholics in England, Wales and Ireland: surveys compared' in *Doctrine and Life*, vol31, no10, December 1981, pp612–621.

Nordlinger, E.A., *Conflict Regulation in Divided Societies*, Cambridge: Harvard University Press, 1972 — occasional papers in International Affairs, no29.

O'Donoghue, Fr N.D., 'A Plea for Celtic Theology' in *Doctrine and Life*, vol27, no1, January 1977, pp29–31.

O'Keefe, Terry, 'Christianity — Left or Right?' in *The Newman Review*, vol2, no1, Summer 1970, pp8–10.

O'Leary, Fr Paul, 'An Irish Theology' in *Doctrine and Life*, vol27, no2, February 1977, pp97–100.

O'Neill, Thomas P., 'Political Life: 1870–1921' in Michael Hurley, SJ (ed), *Irish Anglicanism 1869–1969 — Essays on the role of Anglicanism in Irish Life presented to the Church of Ireland on the occasion of the centenary of its Disestablishment by a group of Methodist, Presbyterian, Quaker and Roman Catholic Scholars*, Dublin: Allen Figgis, 1970, pp101–109.

O'Raifeartaigh, T., 'Integrated Education Not The Answer?' in *Proceedings of the Educational Studies Association of Ireland Conference*, Galway: Galway University Press, 1979, ppix–xv.

Osborne, R.D., 'The Northern Ireland Parliamentary Electoral System: the 1929 reapportionment' in *Irish Geography*, vol12, 1979, pp42–56.

Osborne, R.D., 'Voting Behaviour in Northern Ireland 1921–1977' in F.W. Boal, J.N.H. Douglas (eds), *Integration and Division — Geographical Perspectives on the Northern Ireland Problem*, London: Academic Press, 1982, pp137–166.

Pro Mundi Vita, 'The Irish Conflict and the Christian Conscience' in *Furrow*, vol24, no9, September 1973, pp554–580.

Purdie, Bob, 'The Friends of Ireland British Labour and Irish Nationalism 1945–49' in T. Gallagher, J. O'Connell (eds), *Contemporary Irish Studies*, Manchester: Manchester University Press, 1983, pp81–94.

Report from the Research and Development Unit, 'Religious Practice In Ireland' in *Intercom*, vol6, no9, 1975, pp2–6.

Research and Development Commission, *Students and Religion, 1976*, Maynooth: Research and Development Commission, 1978.

Robinson, Alan, 'Education and Sectarian Conflict in Northern Ireland' in *The New Era*, vol52, no1, January 1971, pp384–388.

Roche, D.J.D., Birrell, W.D., Greer, J.E., 'A Socio-Political Opinion Profile of Clergymen in Northern Ireland' in *Social Studies*, vol4, no2, summer 1975, pp143–151.

Rose, Richard, Urwin, Derek W., 'Social Cohesion Political Parties and

Strains in Regimes' in *Comparative Political Studies*, vol2, 1969, pp7–67.

Russell, J., 'Integrated Schooling—A Research Note' in *Secondary Teacher*, autumn 1977, p11.

Russell, J., 'Replication of Instability: Political Socialisation in Northern Ireland' in *British Journal of Political Science*, vol7, 1977, p115–125.

Russell, J., 'Socialisation into Conflict' in *Social Studies*, vol4, no2, summer 1975, pp109–123.

Russell, J., 'The Extent and Possible Consequences of Inter-Communal Group Friendships in Northern Ireland: Secondary Analysis of Four Surveys' in *Proceedings Education Conference 1980*, pp164–175.

Russell, J., 'The Sources of Conflict' in *The Northern Teacher*, vol11, no3, winter 1974/75, pp3–11.

Ryan, Liam, 'Church and Politics: The Last Twenty-Five Years' in *Furrow*, vol30, no1, January 1979, p3–18.

Ryan, Liam, 'Faith Under Survey' in *Furrow*, vol34, no1, January 1983, pp3–15.

Salters, J., 'Integrated Education In Northern Ireland: Some Assumptions To Be Examined' in *Proceedings Education Conference*, Galway: UCG, 1976, pp14–18.

Sayers, John E., 'The Political Parties and the Social Background' in Thomas Wilson (ed), *Ulster Under Home Rule A Study of the Political and Economic Problems of Northern Ireland*, London: Oxford University Press, 1955, pp55–78.

Thomassen, Jacques, 'Party Identification as a cross-national concept: Its meaning in the Netherlands' in Ian Budge, Ivor Crewe, Denis Farlie, *Party Identification and Beyond—Representations of Voting and Party Competition*, London: Wiley, 1976, pp63–79.

Todd, J., 'Two Traditions In Unionist Political Culture' in *Irish Political Studies*, vol2, 1987, pp1–26.

Turner, I.F. and Davies, J., 'Religious Attitudes in an Integrated Primary School: A Northern Ireland Case Study' in *British Journal of Religious Education*, vol5, no1, Autumn 1982, pp28–32.

Van Kermenade, J.A., 'Roman Catholics and the Schools' in *Sociologia Neerlandica*, vol7, no1, 1971, pp15–27.

Walsh, Brendan M., *Religion and Demographic Behaviour in Ireland*, Dublin: The Economic and Social Research Institute Paper, no55, 1970.

Weafer, John, Breslin, Ann, *Irish Catholic Clergy and Religious 1970–1981*, Maynooth: Council for Research and Development, 1983.

White, B., 'From Conflict to Violence: the re-emergence of the IRA and the loyalist response' in J. Darby (ed), *Northern Ireland The Background to the Conflict*, Belfast: Appletree Press, 1983, pp181–196.

Whyte, John, 'How Much Discrimination was there under the Unionist

Regime, 1921–1969' in T. Gallagher, J. O'Connell (eds), *Contemporary Irish Studies*, Manchester: Manchester University Press, 1983, pp1–35.

Whyte, John, 'Interpretations of the Northern Ireland Problem: an appraisal' in *Economic and Social Review*, vol9, no4, July 1978, pp257–282.

Whyte, John, 'Recent Developments in Church–State Relations' in *Seirbhis Phoibli Journal of the Department of the Public Service*, vol6, no3, 1985, pp4–10.

Whyte, John, 'Revolution and Religion' in F.X. Martin (ed), *Leaders and Men of the Easter Rising: Dublin 1916*, Dublin: Browne & Nolan, 1966, pp215–226.

Wilson, Fr Des, 'Ireland—in need of Conversion?' in *The Month*, September 1975, pp240–243.

Wilson, Fr Des, 'Is Belfast a Pagan City?' in *The Cross*, vol63, no11, March 1973, pp8–10.

Wilson, Fr Des, 'Northern Ireland' in John Cumming, Paul Burns (eds), *The Church Now—An Inquiry into the present state of the Catholic Church in Britain and Ireland*, Dublin: Gill & Macmillan, 1980, pp47–54.

Wilson, Fr Des, 'Northern Ireland: A Christian Conscience in the Making' in *Doctrine and Life*, vol22, no2, February 1972, pp91–98.

Wilson, Fr Des, 'Our Kind of Leadership' in *Aquarius*, no4, 1971, pp113–116.

Wilson, Fr Des, 'The Church and Politics' in *Doctrine and Life*, vol25, no4, April 1975, pp276–280.

Wilson, Fr Des, 'The Church of the Future in Ireland, in *The Cross*, vol64, no7, November 1973, pp6–8.

Wilson, Fr Des, 'The Northern Ireland Situation' in *The Newman Review*, vol1, no2, October 1969, pp7–8.

List of Journals and Magazines

American Political Science Review; American Sociological Review; Aquarius; Belfast Natural History and Philosophical Society Proceedings and Reports; British Journal of Educational Studies; British Journal of Political Science; British Journal of Sociology; Christus Rex; Cithera; Community Forum; Comparative Politics; Crane Bag; Cross; Doctrine and Life; Economic and Social Review; Eire–Ireland; Fortnight; Furrow; Holy Cross; Intercom; International Social Science Journal; Irish Ecclesiastical Record; Irish Geography; Irish Theological Quarterly; Irish Political Studies; Journal of Politics; La Documentation Catholique; Magill; Month; New Era; Newman Review; Northern Teacher; One In Christ; Parliamentary Affairs; Political Studies; Pro Mundi Vita; Review of Politics; Review of Religious Research; Scope; Social

Compass; Social Studies; Sociological Review; Sociologia Neerlandica; Studies; World Politics.

List of Newspapers

Andersonstown News; An Phoblacht; Armagh Observer; Belfast Telegraph; Derry Journal; Dungannon News and Tyrone Courier; Fermanagh Herald; Guardian; Hibernia; Irish Catholic; Irish Independent; Irish News; Irish Press; Irish Times; Londonderry Sentinel; Mid-Ulster Observer; Newry Telegraph; Newsletter; Republican News; Sunday World; United Irishman.

Theses

Carroll, Terence G., *Political Activists in Disaffected Communities: Dissidence, Disobedience and Rebellion in Northern Ireland*, PhD thesis, Carleton University, 1975.

Douglas, Malcolm Jr, *Conflict Regulation vs Mobilization: The Dilemma of Northern Ireland*, PhD thesis, Columbia University, 1976.

Dutter, L.E., *Electoral Competition in Plural Societies: the case of Northern Ireland*, New York: unpublished PhD thesis, The University of Rochester, 1974.

Feeney, Vincent Edward, *From Reform to Resistence: A History of the Civil Rights Movement in Northern Ireland*, Unpublished PhD thesis, University of Washington, 1974.

Grant, Henry Joseph, *A Study of the Perspectives of Moderate Opinion Leaders in the Northern Ireland Social Conflict*, PhD thesis, United States International University, 1976.

Hughes, Cornelius Gerard, *The Catholic Church and the Crisis in Ulster*, PhD thesis, Pennsylvania State University, 1976.

Kennedy, David, *Northern Attitudes to the Independent Irish State*, PhD thesis, Department of Political Science, Trinity College Dublin, 1984.

Martin, J., *The Anti-Partition League*, Belfast: MA thesis, QUB, 1984.

Morgan, Michael, *The Civil Rights Movement: A Re-Interpretation*, Belfast: MSS thesis, QUB, 1984.

Scott, F. Eugene, *Persuasion in the Northern Ireland Civil Rights Movement, 1964–1970*, PhD thesis, Purdue University, 1972.

Thompson, J., *The Northern Ireland Civil Rights Movement*, Belfast: MA thesis, QUB, 1973.

Interviews

Asmal, Kadar; Daly, Bishop Edward; Devlin, Paddy; Flannery, Fr Austin; MacGiolla, Tomas TD; O'Keefe, Terry; two sources who wish to remain anonymous; Wilson, Fr Des.

Official Publications
Disturbances in Northern Ireland—Report of the Commission appointed by the Governor of Northern Ireland, Belfast: HMSO, cmd532, 1969.
House of Commons Northern Ireland Parliamentary Debates (Hansard).
House of Commons Parliamentary Debates (Hansard).
New Ireland Forum No 12: Public Session, Thursday, 9 February 1984, Dublin Castle: Report of Proceedings, Dublin: Stationery Office, 1984.
New Ireland Forum Report May 1984, Dublin: Stationery Office.
Northern Ireland Constitutional Proposals, London: HMSO, 1973.
Report of the Advisory Committee on Police in Northern Ireland, Belfast: HMSO, cmd535, October 1969.
Report of the allegations against the security forces of Physical Brutality 1971, London: HMSO, cmd4823, 1971.
Report to the Tribunal appointed to inquire into the events on Sunday, 30th January, 1972, which led to loss of life in connection with the procession in Londonderry on that day, by the Rt Hon Lord Widgery OBE, TD, HMSO, London, HC220, 1972.
Scarman Report, *Violence and Civil Disturbances in Northern Ireland in 1969 Report of Tribunal of Inquiry*, Belfast: HMSO, cmd566, April 1972, vol1.
The Government of Northern Ireland: proposals for further discussion, London: HMSO, July 1980.

Index

Panorama, 42
Park, Fr Gerald, 129
Paul VI, Pope, 52
peace movements, 42–6, 48, 50–52
  peace people, 52–4
People Together, 51
Philbin, Dr William, Bishop of Down
  and Connor, 27, 95, 109, 117,
  143
  attack on socialism, 137
  calls for peace, 41
  and CCDCs, 32–3
  and census protest, 124, 129
  on military harassment, 105
  Northern Ireland Executive, 49
  on republicans, 138, 159, 161
  on security policy, 92
Phoblacht, An, 159, 161–2
plastic bullets, 97, 101–3
Porter, Mr, 14, 121
power-sharing, 54–7
Presbyterians, 12
priests, 10, 11, 42; *see also*
  questionnaire
  accused of violence, 135–6
  attitude to IRA, 142–4, 161–2
  on Bloody Sunday, 99–100
  call for end to violence, 42–5
  call for justice inquiry, 126–7
  census forms protest, 123–6,
  128–30
  civil rights participation, 14–16,
  18–21
  and education system, 170–71
  on harassment, 95, 104–5
  and hierarchy's responses, 90–91,
  106
  influence of, 31–6, 164–9, 188–9
  on internment, 114–16
  peace-keeping role, 14–15, 134–7
  political profile of, 66–89
    attitude to hierarchy, 77, 81–5,
    87, 89
    class background, 68
    place of birth, 71, 80, 89
    status in church, 73–5, 83–5,
    87–9
    voting advice, 77–80
    voting habits, 75–6

year of ordination, 67–8, 73–5,
  78, 83–5, 89
political protest, 189–91
republican sympathies, 144–5,
  161–2
and state violence, 105–7
on treatment of internees, 118–19
view of Anglo–Irish Agreement, 65
Prior, James, 130, 133
prisoners, 47, 91; *see also*
  hunger-strikes
  Compton Report, 119–21
  dirty protest, 148–9
  religious observance, 146–7
  torture allegations, 112, 115, 117–
  21, 129, 190
Protestants, 36–7
  attitude to Catholic Church, 163–4,
  164–5, 191–3
  Catholic hierarchy and rights of,
  168–9
  and civil rights campaign, 11
  and *Ne Temere* decree, 180–81
  and segregated education, 170
  survey of, 10
  views of Northern Ireland conflict,
  174, 181
Provisional IRA, 3–4, 7, 36, 38, 43,
  44, 47, 97–8, 99
  burials, 143–4
  and Catholic Church, 33–4, 137,
  191
  and CCDC, 33–4, 136
  ceasefire, 42, 46
  criticised by priests, 142–4
  and Daly peace plan, 50
  Feakle talks, 51–2
  and hierarchy, 113, 120, 138, 140
  no Church sanctions on, 143–4
  policy of, 46–8
  and Sinn Fein, 7, 145, 155–8
  treatment of Catholic Church in
  literature, 145, 159–62
  truce, 51–2

questionnaire, 1, 66–89, 170
  on Anglo–Irish Agreement, 65
  hierarchy and security policy,
  90–91

Ulster Defence Regiment (UDR),
30–31, 95, 97
Ulster Freedom Fighters (UFF), 110
Ulster Workers' Council, 5, 142
Unionists, 2–3, 4, 48, 55
and Anglo–Irish Agreement, 6, 75
and Bloody Sunday, 99–100
and Catholic Church, 26, 164, 181
criticism of bishops' statement, 62
criticism of O'Fiaich, 57
criticism of SDLP, 155
election results, 36
and local government, 21
and Northern Ireland Executive, 49
and state violence, 109
united Ireland
in questionnaire, 66–8
United Irishman, 123
United States, 177

United Ulster Unionist Council, 5

Van Voris, W. H., 18
Vatican II, 117, 181
violence, statistics of, 7

White, B., 7
White, Barry, 60
White Paper on Northern Ireland,
48–9
Whitelaw, William, 42
Whyte, J. H., 141–2, 164, 166
Widgery Report, 100–101, 101n
Williams, Betty, 54n
Wilson, Fr Des, 123, 144–5, 148
Wilson, Harold, 52
Workers' Party, 76
Worrall, Stanley, 114